Vol.3

Birds of Marsh and Shore

The Orbis Encyclopedia of Birds of
Britain and Europe

Volume Three

Birds of Marsh and Shore

Edited by John Gooders

ORBIS PUBLISHING
London

© 1979 Orbis Publishing Ltd., London
© 1971 Rizzoli Editore, Milan
Printed in Great Britain by Jarrold & Sons Ltd., Norwich
ISBN 0 85613 370 1

Frontispiece: Black-winged Stilt (Eric Hosking)

Contents

Editor's Preface

The way in which birds are arranged in bird books is a continual source of puzzlement to many. Confusion arises not only because authors can do what they want between their own covers, providing only that they can find someone prepared to publish it, but also because even when authors agree about how birds should be arranged they then disagree about the actual order. The ordering of birds in a single list is totally artificial in any case, but all too often authors who should know better set themselves up as expert systematists when they are nothing of the sort. It is the job of systematists to sort the birds out and put them into some kind of order, thereby expressing the relationships between them. In this encyclopedia we have followed the general line of starting with the most primitive and ending with the most advanced species. We thus have the same order (more or less) as most modern field guides and the vast majority of modern text books. To the beginner this 'systematic' order, as it is called, can be utterly confusing, but it does have one immediate advantage – birds of a feather are placed together. This not only makes for continuity and ease of comparison, but as similar birds tend to live in the same way and in much the same places we can divide up the birds into more or less distinct groups based on the areas in which they occur. Thus the present volume is both a complete account of the birds that inhabit marsh and shore, and also an equally comprehensive account of the great order Charadriiformes. But it also forms part of a larger work that encompasses all the birds of Europe, no matter to which family or order they belong, or where they are to be found.

Strangely, just as to put birds into a simple list is artificial because it hides the more complex (and therefore more interesting) relationships between them, putting birds into strict habitat groups is also artificial. Birds do have preferred habitats it is true and sometimes they will go to extreme lengths to find them. One of my favourite habitat stories concerns a Stone Curlew, a bird that inhabits sandy wastelands in southern and eastern England. In its efforts to find a suitable stop-over on migration it ended up in a children's sand-pit in a Kilburn recreation ground. But not all birds are as determined as this individual and the works of bird migration are full of stories of birds in strange places. Woodpeckers have been seen climbing steadily up the masts of ships, and on completely tree-less islands where they still managed to eke out a living. Bitterns have pointed their bills motionless at the sky in the middle of green fields where their reed-like camouflage simply makes them look silly, as well as in the streets of London apparently waiting at a bus stop. But I digress. Most birds stick to where they belong, but not all

birds dealt with in this volume actually live on marshes or shorelines. The Buff-breasted Sandpiper prefers golf-courses and airstrips. The Woodcock prefers woodlands. The Dotterel is a mountain bird that likes ploughed fields. Nevertheless when we talk about waders, gulls, terns, skuas and auks we are talking about the birds of marsh and shore, even if some of them actually prefer to live elsewhere.

Unfortunately marsh and shore are habitats that are fast disappearing. Marshes and estuaries are increasingly being regarded as wastelands by modern businesses and governments – areas where they can plan development without causing undue upset to local industry and residents. So they plan airports at places like the Maplin Sands at Foulness, barrages for fresh water in the Wash, and for agricultural land in the Ribble Estuary. Each of these areas is unique, each rich in birds, each a part of our national heritage. The destruction of any one of these sites would be a disaster – all three would do unimaginable harm. When it comes to non-estuarine shorelines it is difficult to imagine how they could be destroyed, yet here too developers cast their eyes. The promenade, a typically British institution, has become popular all around the world, making large stretches of natural shoreline unsuitable for the birds which lived there before. The general increase in leisure-time and the greater mobility enjoyed by people nowadays has led to larger numbers heading towards the seaside for weekends and holidays. Beaches are thronged in summer to the detriment (and decline) of Little Terns, Ringed Plovers, Oystercatchers and others. Barrages, pipelines, docks, airports and holiday developments all take their toll on the birds of marsh and shore.

Every bird that has ever occurred in Europe can be found in the pages of these five volumes, which together make up the most comprehensive work yet published on the birds of this continent. They are packed full of information and illustrated throughout with colour photographs showing the birds as they are seen in life. Additionally, each species is illustrated by a specially commissioned painting that shows the main points of identification, and many birds are grouped together in special in-flight diagrams to facilitate comparison. So while each of the five volumes is discrete and self-contained, each also marries with the other four to form a truly great work of reference. They tell me that there are over 800,000 words in this encyclopedia, but having read all of them at least three times I don't believe it! Reading a book some fifteen times longer than the average novel three times over is more than can I bear thinking about. Yet I cannot remember being bored.

John Gooders

Introduction

If an ornithologist was asked to name the greatest bird spectacle on Earth he would almost certainly name a marsh, or a particular length of shoreline. He might choose an African marsh like Lake Nakuru or an American sanctuary like Utah's Bear River Refuge. Personally I have always favoured the marshy reserve at Bharatpur in India, a wonderland if ever there was one. Alternatively our ornithologist might choose the marvellous bird islands of the Peruvian coast; the magnificent cliffs of Alaska's Pribiloff Islands; or the fastnesses of St. Kilda in Scotland's Hebrides. The point is that, although individual choice may vary, the category of landscape chosen will probably be standard – marshes and shorelines.

The reasons for such a choice are not difficult to find. Birds occur in marshes and along shorelines in immense numbers. One of the candidates for the title 'The World's Most Numerous Bird' is a coastline species – the Little Auk. But more than simple numbers it is the concentration of birds that is so spectacular. There might be more House Sparrows or Wilson's Petrels than Little Auks in the world, but these species do not pack together on the screes of some remote Arctic island. Nor do they form flocks that may number a million as they fly high overhead. However, many of these birds are not really numerous at all – it is the spectacle of their gathering together which takes our breath away.

For a start there are the waders – they are called 'shorebirds' in North America. Out over the lonely mud flats they feed, scattered here and there, feeding in their different ways and finding mostly different food in the ooze. The Curlew's long decurved bill enables it to reach worms deep in the mud. The Avocet sweeps its bill from side to side fastening on any edible items that come its way. Dunlin probe away busily, sometimes looking almost like little clockwork toys, feeding on the creatures that remain near the surface of the mud; stints pick food items delicately from the surface itself. As the tide turns these scattered birds are forced by the rising water into tighter packed groups until eventually they give up feeding and fly away to a safe roosting place to sit out high water and wait for the tide to recede. These high-tide roosts are terribly important to the birds. As many as a hundred thousand waders may squeeze onto a single rocky islet or safe sand-bar – a superb spectacle but one that we should be careful not to disturb.

(Below) Grey-rumped Sandpiper *Tringa brevipes*

As the water begins to recede exposing the muddy shoreline once again, the birds gradually move out. Not all at once, but in small trips, a dozen or so at a time. Soon they are all scattered again over the mud, but a single shot or a thoughtless watcher can send them all towering into the air. Packed wingtip to wingtip they turn this way and that in unison, thousands of birds reacting together in the air at over 60 kilometres per hour. The spectacle is worth seeing, worth those long cold hours out on the sea-wall, worth travelling for, and certainly worth conserving.

Gulls too gather on shorelines, but they are such catholic birds that there are few places they are not found today. It is quite amazing, but a hundred years ago a bird-watcher would have been thrilled to see a gull inland. Now we take this everyday sight for granted. Gulls are everywhere, and more and more they are becoming a real pest. They have flourished as a group by their adaptability, and particularly in their ability to exploit new food sources. They learned to scavenge around fishing boats, then they found rubbish tips. They found out about sewage, and then discovered safe roosting places on our drinking water reservoirs. They found they were not disturbed on the grassy areas between airport runways, despite the extremely noisy contraptions that passed by every few minutes. And they discovered that bird reserves were great places for safe nesting. This remarkable series of discoveries has brought gulls into sharp conflict with many diverse groups of people. The health authorities worry about contamination of our water supplies. Farmers worry about the spread of disease. Airport authorities worry about aircraft-bird collisions and the disasters that have and doubtless will occur. The Royal Air Force is worried about the million pounds it spends each year extracting gulls from the jet engines of its aeroplanes. And conservationists are worried by the depredations that gulls make on other rarer species that they are trying to protect. Yet, despite this tale of gloom, we must not lose sight of the fact that gulls are superbly attractive birds, even if they are a nuisance. Certainly many happy days have been spent watching the Kittiwakes as their cries echo around the seabird cliffs where they breed.

These northern cliffs are really exquisite places. A good seabird colony like that at Marwick Head in the Orkney Islands, which is a reserve of the Royal Society for the Protection of Birds, is a constant source of interest in summer. For hour after hour one can sit and watch the cliffs virtually moving before one's eyes. All is motion, all action. Long lines of Guillemots, dense packs of Puffins, stiff-winged Fulmars, Black Guillemots on the lower jumble of rocks and Kittiwakes constantly calling. Anyone who cares for birds would be enthralled, anyone who had not previously been interested would almost certainly be persuaded to share in the fascination that such a sight produces in a seasoned bird-watcher. For me the seabird cliffs of Scotland are among the most impressive bird spectacles in the world.

The reasons for the concentration of cliff-nesting seabirds are not hard to find. The birds spend their lives at sea and are completely at home among the waves. They find all of their food at sea and indeed are so well adapted to a seaborne existence that they really do not cope with land at all well. The auks, the Guillemots, Razorbills and Puffins look comical on land because their feet are set well back on their bodies to act as rudders. They also look funny in the air because their wings are a compromise between what they need to fly and what is best for underwater flippering. In fact cliff-nesting seabirds only come to land to breed, or when they are ill. As they need to feed at sea they choose only those cliffs that are within easy flying distance of good fishing grounds. There they pack together because they only need a territory large enough to accommodate themselves and their egg. In general there is no shortage of nesting sites. It is the supply of food within easy reach that limits these colonies.

No introduction to our marsh and shore birds would be complete without mention of the disaster that befalls thousands of seabirds every year. I can still remember my first encounter with a washed-up Guillemot. It sat on an east coast beach, upright but tottering, its breast covered with brown oil. As I approached it scurried toward the sea. I cut it off as it reached the tide, got a sharp bite for my trouble and took it off to where I was staying. It was warmed, force fed, and died in a cardboard box overnight. Perhaps it would have been less cruel to have killed it on the spot?

At one time tankers used the sea indiscriminately as a dumping ground for the washings from their tanks. Today they 'load-on-top', or at least most of them do. Ships sailing under a flag of convenience do more or less what they like. Major accidents are inevitable and it is also quite inevitable that from time to time large numbers of seabirds are going to be killed. It is sad, but a fact of life. We must do what we can to prevent accidents and also learn to clean up the mess in the least harmful biological way, but we will not stop accidents altogether. Perhaps the auks, who are the main sufferers, can cope with an occasional disaster? What is sure is that they are beginning to decline quite seriously as a result of more widespread pollution.

The world of *Birds of Marsh and Shore* is dramatic and attractive, and in this book every species that has ever occurred in Europe is fully described and illustrated. But it is a world full of threats. Man has so changed the planet he inhabits that he has changed the lives of the creatures that live alongside him. We have threatened the very existence of vast populations of auks at the same time as we have turned gulls into an international pest. We have drained marshes and estuaries, dispossessing thousands of waders, and driven them into fewer and fewer wintering and migration stop-over marshes. So far the destruction is not total. It may not be too late to look at our surroundings and see what we can do to put things right. It does seem strange that the greatest of all bird spectacles is also among the most threatened.

Birds of Marsh and Shore

FAMILY HAEMATOPODIDAE: Oystercatchers

O.-S. Pettingill/Photo Researchers

(Above) New Zealand Black Oystercatcher *Haematopus unicolor.* (Below right) American Oystercatcher *H. palliatus* and Lava Gull *Larus fulginosus* in the background on the Galapagos Islands. (Right) A group of Oystercatchers *H. ostralegus.* (Preceding page) Black-tailed Godwit *Limosa limosa*

Oystercatchers are medium-sized coastal birds. They share a distinctive appearance and have been grouped together into the family Haematopodidae: there are four to seven species in the family depending upon the classification followed. Oystercatchers have a long and powerful bill which is laterally compressed. The bill is brilliant orange in colour and the plumage a mixture of black and white or all-black. The red-pinkish legs are long and robust: they have only three toes which are slightly webbed. The tail is short and the wings are long and pointed. The body appears rather plump and the sexes are similar.

Oystercatchers are good walkers and fast runners: if necessary they can also swim reasonably well. They fly with rapid shallow wingbeats. Oystercatchers frequent the sea coast and are gregarious birds, sometimes gathering in flocks several thousand strong. Their courtship, particularly that of the Oystercatcher *Haematopus ostralegus* which occurs in Europe, has been the subject of study. The courtship rituals includes a

G. Holton/Photo Researchers

L. Norstrom

S. & D. McCutcheon

(Right) Black Oystercatchers
H. bachmani and (below)
world distribution of the
Haematopodidae family

variety of group ceremonies and there is a curious 'piping ceremony' which appears to assist in pair formation. The nest consists of a scrape in the ground: seashells, stones, bone and other objects are included in its construction. Two to four eggs are laid (average of three in the European species) which are cream coloured with bold brown or black spots. Both sexes incubate the eggs for approximately twenty-four to twenty-seven days. Both sexes also care for the young.

The Oystercatcher nests on most European sea coasts and also the coasts of inland waters, stretching from arctic Europe to the Caspian. It may be present in the Canary Islands but could already be extinct there. The Oystercatcher is also found on the coasts of southern Africa and Australasia.

Two oystercatchers are present in North America: one, the Black Oystercatcher *H. bachmani*, has entirely dark plumage and is similar to the Sooty Oystercatcher *H. fuliginosus* of the Australian coast. Two more species are found in South America: the Blackish Oystercatcher *H. ater* and the Magellanic Oystercatcher *H. leucopodus* which has black and white plumage.

The diet of oystercatchers consists mainly of molluscs and also crustaceans, insects and worms. They show a special preference for bivalve molluscs such as the oyster—hence their common English name. The bill of oystercatchers is particularly well adapted for a diet of molluscs as it is stout and flattened. The muscle is then severed and the animal extracted intact from its protective shell. The Oystercatcher has a 'chisel' on the tip of the bill which is used to chip through the hard shell of molluscs. The Oystercatcher is prone to a curious foot problem: weeds become twisted around their legs and restrict the circulation, thus causing the loss of a toe or sometimes of an entire foot.

Oystercatcher
Haematopus ostralegus

HABITAT Found on seashores, near estuaries, on grassy islands and inland along rivers.

IDENTIFICATION Length: 43 cm. A large bird, unmistakable with its conspicuous black and white plumage, long orange bill and long pink legs. Head, breast, wings and back are black, with a broad white band along the wing; rump and underparts white; tail white, with a wide black band at the end. In winter plumage the throat is white.

A very noisy and gregarious bird. Flies straight, with regular wingbeats, sometimes attaining considerable heights. Also moves well on land, occasionally breaking into a run. Swims well and will dive if injured. Feeds mainly on mussels, which it opens with great skill: a sharp blow with the bill obliquely against the hinge of the shell makes it open just wide enough for the bird to introduce the tip of its tightly-closed bill, after which it can severe the retaining muscle and open the shell.

Groups of Oystercatchers, from two or three up to ten, take part in a 'piping' ceremony. It consists of walking back and forth with the bill bent towards the ground, uttering plaintive cries. See also page 144.

CALL A strident 'kleep' or 'lir-eep', and an alarm call: 'pick-pick-pick'. Its song is a long whispering trill.

REPRODUCTION Mid-April to May. Nests on or near the seashore or on the banks of a river. Nest consists of a hollow in the ground lined with small stones and shells. Eggs: three, pale buff with black blotches and spots. Both sexes incubate the eggs for twenty-four to twenty-seven days. The young fledge in about five weeks.

FOOD Molluscs, crustaceans, insects and other invertebrates.

DISTRIBUTION AND MOVEMENTS Northern European coasts, Atlantic coast of the Iberian peninsula and coastal areas of France, Italy, Yugoslavia, Albania, Greece and Turkey. Also southern USSR and Asia. Both sedentary and migratory: northern populations winter south to the Mediterranean area, the Red Sea, Ceylon and southeast Asia. In Britain it breeds on all coasts and has spread inland along rivers to penetrate the whole of Scotland and northwestern England. Winter gatherings several thousand strong occur at some localities: these include British and Irish residents as well as birds from Iceland and north-west Europe.

French: HUÎTRIER-PIE
Italian: BECCACCIA DI MARE
Spanish: OSTRERO
German: AUSTERNFISCHER

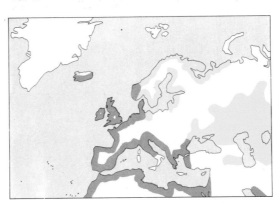

(Left) Wintering areas (magenta) and areas where the Oystercatcher may be seen all year round (orange)

ORDER Charadriiformes
FAMILY **CHARADRIIDAE:**

G. Hansson

6

Plovers, Dotterels and Lapwings

Some ornithologists allocate most species of the order Charadriiformes—which includes the sand-pipers, woodcock and snipe as well as plovers—to the single family Charadriidae. However the more common classification and the one followed here places the plovers, lapwings and dotterels in the Charadriidae while the sandpipers, snipe and woodcock are placed in the Scolopacidae family. The sixty-two species of the Charadriidae family are currently included in far fewer genera than they were in earlier classification systems, and for convenience the family is divided into three main groups: the lapwings, plovers and dotterels.

Species of the family are generally rather stocky and are small to medium-sized waders. The neck is short and thick and the bill is usually straight, fairly sturdy and of a regular length: members of this family do not present as many differing adaptations as those of the Scolopacidae. They generally live on open or sparsely vegetated ground. Most species live close to fresh or salt water although some species, such as the Caspian Plover *Charadrius asiaticus* frequent grassy plains. The wings are long and usually pointed and the tail short or medium in length. The length of the legs varies between species and they may have three or four toes (four-toed species have rudimentary hind toes). They are adept runners and fliers, and when feeding run a short distance then stop, sometimes bobbing the head.

Coloration of the plumage includes various combinations of brown, olive-green, grey, black and white, often with large bold markings. Despite its apparently striking appearance, this plumage

(Left) Lapwing *Vanellus vanellus*. (Above left) Golden Plover *Pluvialis apricaria* and (top left) Ringed Plover *Charadrius hiaticula*. (Facing page) Dotterel *Eudromias morinellus*

7

J. L. Roberts/Aquila

J. S. Wightman/Ardea

usually serves as highly effective camouflage because of the way it breaks up the bird's outline against a background of sandy or shingly ground. White bands on the nape, dark bands or patches on the breast and dark bands at or near the tip of the tail are also field marks which are common to many species.

Some species of the family Charadriidae have two periods of peak activity, one during the day and the other at night. Such peaks are usually related to movements of the tide, although hunting pressure may be a factor in some areas. They usually nest in isolation although it is possible to come across several nests of the same species fairly close together. The nest consists of a simple depression in the ground or sand. Two to five eggs

(Above right) Kentish Plover *C. alexandrinus* and (below) world distribution of the Charadriidae family

(four on average) are laid. Incubation is generally carried out by both parents, but the males are not always involved with the rearing of their offspring. Many species feign injury when confronted by a predator during the nesting season. They move away from their nests, giving the impression of having a broken wing or some other injury in order to induce predators to pursue them and thus distracting attention from the eggs or fledglings.

Although the various lapwings of the genus *Vanellus* may appear to differ from one another, they are a distinct genus which shares common characteristics. The tail is always white at the base and usually edged with black towards the tip. The primaries are black and there is almost invariably a broad white streak on the wings. Some species of the genera often have wattles and crests which are not found in other members of the family. Lapwings often have long legs—such as the Red-wattled Plover *Vanellus indicus*. Lapwings appear to originate from Africa and many of the species are still present there. There are no birds of the genus *Vanellus* in North America except the few Common Lapwings *V. vanellus* which are driven to the North American coasts from Europe when on migration. However there are three species present in South America which are believed to descend from African species which crossed the Atlantic. Until recently there were no birds of the

genus in New Zealand but during the past thirty years an Australian sub-species of the Masked Plover *V. miles* has successfully invaded New Zealand. The Common Lapwing is the most distinctive and common of the lapwings and is the only species of the genus which breeds in much of Europe.

There are three species of the genus *Pluvialis*. They differ from other plovers in that they do not have a white band on the nape and their upper parts are speckled instead of being uniform. The Golden Plover *P. apricaria* from northern Europe and northwest Asia is similar in appearance to the Lesser Golden Plover *P. dominica* which nests in arctic North America and Asia. The migration of the latter species is extraordinary: they spend the winter as far away as Australia and South America. The Alaskan population travels thousands of kilometres over the sea to Hawaii for the winter. The Grey Plover *P. squatarola*, which is distributed in the northern Holarctic region, migrates to Chile, southern Africa and Australia in the winter.

Species of the genus *Charadrius* are known as plovers or true plovers (although often the whole family is also referred to as plovers). They are small to medium-sized waders. Plumage of the upper parts is brown, grey or a mixture of white and sandy coloration. Some species, such as the Ringed Plover *Charadrius hiaticula* which is one of the

commonest northern European shore birds, have striking black and white markings on the head and neck. In common with other members of the family more species are present in the Old World than the New World.

The third main group of the Charadriidae consists of the dotterels. The Dotterel *Eudromias morinellus* is present in northern Europe where it breeds in mountainous areas of Scotland, Fenno-Scandinavia and eastern Europe. The Dotterel is also present in the Netherlands. It winters in northern Africa. Another species of this genus, the Tawny-throated Dotterel *E. ruficollis* lives in South America.

(Below left) Wattled Plover *Vanellus senegallus.* (Above) A group of Turnstone *Arenaria interpres:* as its name implies, this species turns over small stones and weeds in search of food. (Overleaf, pages 10 and 11) Golden Plover *P. apricaria* on the nest

R. M. Bloomfield/Ardea

French: GRAND GAVELOT
Italian: CORRIERE GROSSO
Spanish: CHORLITEJO GRANDE
German: SANDREGENPFEIFER

Ringed Plover
Charadrius hiaticula

HABITAT Sandy and muddy shores, steppes and open tundra. In winter frequents shorelines and estuaries.

IDENTIFICATION Length: 19 cm. A fast-running plover marked with a distinctive black breast band and facial mask. Upper parts of the Ringed Plover are a sandy-brown colour broken at the nape by the black and white chest pattern. Crown also sandy-brown. Band across the front of the crown is separated from the bill by a white area, and a brown eyestripe runs from the base of the bill through the eye to the nape. The eye ring is yellow. Underparts white marked only with the black breast band. Legs are orange as is the basal half of the black-tipped bill. In winter the bold 'rings' are replaced by somewhat indistinct brown smudges and the legs become dirty yellow. The bill is generally dark, and the dark tail is bordered with white. In flight the wings show a broad bar which serves as the main distinguishing mark between it and the similar Little Ringed Plover. See also page 108.

CALL A melodious 'too-lee' or 'coo-eep'.

REPRODUCTION April to July depending upon the latitude. Lays four eggs in a simple scrape in the ground on a beach or among the stones of tundra. Like other shorebirds they are camouflaged in pale olive grey speckled and blotched with brown and black. Incubation, by both sexes, takes twenty-four or twenty-five days with

remarkably frequent change-overs among the pair. The young leave the nest as soon as they hatch and are cared for by both parents until they fly.

FOOD Molluscs, crustaceans, insects and some vegetable matter.

DISTRIBUTION AND MOVEMENTS Breeds throughout the northern Palearctic region as far as the Bering Straits. Also found in Iceland and enters the Nearctic region in Greenland and Baffin Island. In Britain breeds on most coasts. Most populations migrate southwards and westwards to milder parts of Europe, the Mediterranean, Africa and Asia.

SUB-SPECIES *C.h. hiaticula* is present in Europe and *C.h. tundrae* is found in the Arctic.

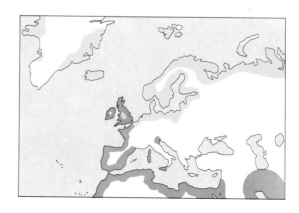

(Above) Adult Ringed Plover (foreground) and immature. (Right) Breeding areas (yellow), wintering areas (magenta) and areas where the Ringed Plover may be seen all year round (orange)

Little Ringed Plover
Charadrius dubius

HABITAT Rivers, lakes and gravel pits. Winters by lakes and lagoons.

IDENTIFICATION Length: 15 cm. Very similar to the Ringed Plover but smaller and more compact. Lacks the wing bar of the Ringed Plover. Has a distinctive call, flesh-coloured legs and a white margin separating the black crown band from the brown cap. Also favours a different habitat than the Ringed Plover: fresh water rather than shorelines although both species occur alongside one another at some inland sites.

Upper parts are grey-brown and less warm in coloration than the Ringed Plover. Facial and breast band and markings are black and similar to that of the Ringed Plover: the yellow eye ring is, however, more prominent. Underparts are white. In winter the bold pattern fades and it is more difficult to distinguish from the Ringed Plover. See also page 108.

CALL A shrill 'pee-ooo . . . pip-pip'. Also emits a reedy note which resembles that of the Little Tern.

REPRODUCTION April to June. Lays four well camouflaged grey-brown eggs speckled or blotched with dark brown. Eggs are laid in a simple depression among sand or gravel. Incubation, which is carried out by both male and female, lasts for twenty-four or twenty-five days. The chicks leave the nest as soon as they are dry: they are tended by both parents. In the north usually only a single brood is raised but in southern Europe two broods are regular.

FOOD Insects and larvae but also small molluscs and worms.

DISTRIBUTION AND MOVEMENTS Huge range which covers most of the Palearctic region except for the extreme north. In general breeds further south than the Ringed Plover. Also breeds southwards through India, Malaysia, Vietnam, the Philippines and as far as New Guinea. In Britain it first nested at Tring in Hertfordshire in 1938 and has since spread throughout much of England. In Britain it generally prefers working gravel pits to all other habitats.

SUB-SPECIES Sub-species are present in New Guinea, the Philippines, India and the Far East.

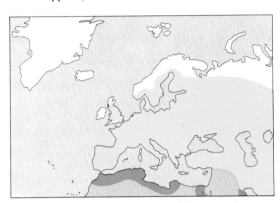

French: PETIT GRAVELOT
Italian: CORRIERE PICCOLO
Spanish: CHORLITEJO CHICO
German: FLUSSREGENPFEIFER

(Below) Adult Little Ringed Plover (foreground) and immature. (Left) Breeding areas (yellow), areas where the Little Ringed Plover may be seen all year round (orange) and on passage (pink)

French: GRAVELOT À COLLIER
INTERROMPU
Italian: FRATINO
Spanish: CHORLITEJO PATINEGRO
German: SEEREGENPFEIFER

Kentish Plover
Charadrius alexandrius

HABITAT Sandy and muddy shorelines, salt pans, coastal lagoons, lakes and sandy wastes.

IDENTIFICATION Length: 16 cm. A slim, light 'ringed plover', easily distinguished from both Ringed and Little Ringed Plovers by the incomplete breast band. Even in winter plumage the other two retain a more pronounced band on the chest. However the Kentish Plover is more difficult to separate from the so-called sand plovers of the south and east. Upper parts are brown and underparts white. The breast band is no more than two black markings at the sides of the breast. There is a bold black eyestripe and the forehead is white. Male is generally more boldly marked than the female and has a chestnut crown in summer. In winter male and female are similar: plumage generally a washed out version of summer plumage. The black eyes are a useful aid to identification as is the bold white wing bar and white outer tail feathers. See also page 108.

CALL A clear 'wit' or 'wee-it' and a rolling 'priip'.

REPRODUCTION Early May. The nest is a scrape among shingle or dried mud or on sand. The eggs are frequently buried in the ground. A few dead grasses may be added as lining when available. Four eggs are laid: grey-buff in colour marked with black streaks and spots. Incubation is carried out by both sexes for twenty-four days. The chicks, which leave the nest soon after hatching, are tended by both parents. It is likely that there are two broods per year.

FOOD Predominantly insects and larvae. Also crustaceans.

DISTRIBUTION AND MOVEMENTS Remarkable world-wide distribution. Found on the west coast of the United States and high up in the Rocky Mountains. Also present in the West Indies, western coasts of South America and on all temperate and tropical coasts of the Old World from France to Australia. In Britain its name stems from its former breeding in Kent but it has not bred there for many years. Is a rare passage visitor to Norfolk and very irregularly on the east and south coasts from Yorkshire to the Isles of Scilly. Northern European populations migrate to the Mediterranean and Africa.

SUB-SPECIES Apart from the nominate sub-species which breeds in Europe, six other sub-species inhabit different parts of the world.

(Above) Adult Kentish Plover
and immature. (Below)
Breeding areas (yellow),
areas where the Kentish Plover
may be seen all year round
(orange) and on passage
(pink)

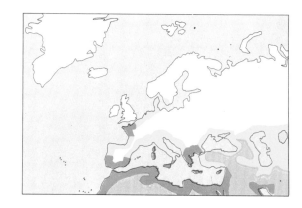

Greater Sand Plover
Charadrius leschenaultii

HABITAT Sand and gravel banks of rivers and lakes, extensive stony barren flats in steppe and semi-desert country. Is often found a considerable distance from water.

IDENTIFICATION Length: 22 cm. In summer the male is grey-brown marked with a chestnut breast band. Chestnut coloration extends up the sides of the neck to form a border along the upper edge of the black eyestripe and crown band. Bill is strong and heavy in comparison with some other members of the Charadriidae. Underparts white with some chestnut mottling on the flanks. In flight a white wing bar shows on the secondaries. In winter the chestnut coloration and facial pattern is lost and the male resembles the female—a nondescript grey-brown bird with speckling forming a band on the breast. In this plumage it closely resembles the Lesser Sand Plover, however the Lesser Sand Plover is smaller, lacks a wing bar and has a smaller bill. See also page 108.

CALL A clear whistle which may be repeated twice.

REPRODUCTION The nest is a hollow in the ground lined with a few grasses. The three, occasionally four eggs, are laid at the beginning of May and are buff-brown marked with black blotches and speckles. Both parents remain with the nestlings but fly off when disturbed, relying on the chicks' natural camouflage to protect them.

FOOD Little data available. Specimens captured in the USSR had been feeding on beetles and ants.

DISTRIBUTION AND MOVEMENTS Breeds in a belt from the vicinity of the eastern edge of the Black Sea through the Caspian region to central Asia. May well breed in central Anatolia. Winters from the east coast of Africa, India, the Far East to Australia. Accidental in Europe in Greece, Germany and Sweden.

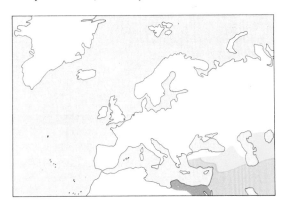

French: GRAVELOT DE LESCHENAULT
Italian: PIVIERE DI LESCHENAULT
Spanish: CHORLITEJO DE LESCHENAULT
German: WÜSTENREGENPFEIFER

(Below) Female Greater Sand Plover (foreground) and male. (Left) Breeding areas (yellow), wintering areas (magenta) and areas where the Greater Sand Plover may be seen on passage (pink)

S. C. Brown/Aquila

(Above) Little Ringed Plover *C. dubius* approaching the nest: four well camouflaged eggs may be seen in the centre foreground. (Right) Ringed Plover *C. hiaticula* on the nest

W. S. Patson/Aquila

Eric Hosking

Eric Hosking

(Above) Oystercatchers
H. ostralegus: like other
waders they gather in large
flocks on the seashore.
Oystercatchers may be easily
identified by their pink legs
and orange bill. (Left)
Oystercatcher returning to its
nest among the seashore
rocks. Its eggs are well
camouflaged from the eyes of
hungry predators

17

French: PLUVIER ASIATIQUE
Italian: CORRIERE ASIATICO
Spanish: CHORLITEJO ASIATICO
German: KASPISCHER
REGENPFEIFER

Caspian Plover
Charadrius asiaticus

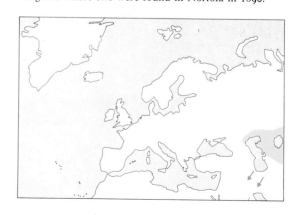

(Above right) Adult Caspian Plover and (right) immature. (Below right) Breeding areas (yellow) of the Caspian Plover

HABITAT Arid steppes and semi-desert or desert country. Winters on coasts, marshes and on open sandy wastes.

IDENTIFICATION Length: 20 cm. A well-marked plover: in summer plumage has brown chestnut band across the breast bordered below with black. A dark stripe extends back from the eye. Remainder of upper parts sandy-buff although primaries are a prominent black. In flight a pale wing bar crosses the all-buff secondaries and the contrast between the light inner-wing and dark outer wing is diagnostic. In winter closely resembles other sand plovers although the flight pattern remains a useful feature. See also page 108.

CALL A low double whistling 'queet' which is emitted in flight.

REPRODUCTION Early May to June. Nest is situated on open ground and consists of a small hollow lined with a few twigs or grasses with perhaps the addition of horse dung. The three eggs are clay-coloured with numerous cinnamon markings, particularly at the ends. Incubation is apparently carried out by both male and female.

FOOD Little data is available on the food of the Caspian Plover. Apparently feeds on insects in summer.

DISTRIBUTION AND MOVEMENTS Breeds in central Siberia from the Caspian eastwards with a separate population extending westwards from the Kamchatka Peninsula. The western population moves southwards to winter in the Persian Gulf and in eastern and southern Africa. Eastern population moves to Malaya, Borneo, Java, the Philippines and Australia. It is an accidental visitor to Bulgaria, Italy, Heligoland and England where two were found in Norfolk in 1890.

Killdeer Plover
Charadrius vociferus

French: GRAVELOT A DOUBLE COLLIER
Italian: CORRIERE AMERICANO
Spanish: CHORLITEJO CULIRROJO
German: KEILSCHWANZREGEN-PFEIFER

(Above) Adult Killdeer (foreground) and immature

HABITAT It nests on meadows, sometimes close to lakes or pools, among crops or on ploughed fields. Winters on marshes and coasts.

IDENTIFICATION Length: 26 cm. It bears a slight resemblance to the Ringed Plover, though it is larger and has two black pectoral bands instead of one. Dark brown crown and back. White forehead edged with black; white patch between the eyes and blackish band on the sides of the head. The white coloration of its throat continues round its neck to form a sort of collar; wing-bar white. In flight its reddish, wedge-shaped tail and golden-reddish rump distinguish it from other species of plover. It is very noisy and excitable. Rapid flight. In behaviour similar to the Ringed Plover. See also page 108.

CALL During nuptial flight emits a repeated 'keel-dee-ee' and a mournful 'dee-ee-ee'.

REPRODUCTION From March to July, depending on the locality. The nest is a depression in the ground which is lined with grasses. It lays four pale, dull yellow eggs with black streaks and speckles. Incubation is probably carried out by both parents for twenty-four to twenty-nine days. The young birds leave the nest as soon as their downy plumage has dried.

FOOD Mainly insects in summer, but a more varied diet in winter.

DISTRIBUTION AND MOVEMENTS North America. It winters in North, Central and South America. Occasionally wanders to Europe mainly in autumn and winter.

SUB-SPECIES Sub-species are present in South America.

French: PLUVIER GUIGNARD
Italian: PIVIERE TORTOLINO
Spanish: CHORLITO CARAMBOLO
German: MORNELLREGENPFEIFER

Dotterel
Eudromias morinellus

HABITAT In arctic regions it nests on tundra and on barren hillsides; it also frequents high, stony ground. On migration, lingers on meadows, coasts and marshland.

IDENTIFICATION Length: 21 cm. Rather like a small Golden Plover, but with darker plumage and a broad white band over each eye which meet at the nape to form a distinctive 'V'. It also differs in having a brown breast crossed by a white band, and orange-chestnut coloured underparts. Blackish-brown crown and upper parts; white cheeks and throat; black belly and white border to tail. Winter plumage is paler and with less sharply contrasting coloration. Juvenile plumage is like the adult's winter plumage. Yellow legs. Flight is fast and powerful, with rapid wingbeats. It moves nimbly on the ground and runs, pausing to capture its prey. Small groups of between four and twelve birds gather together on migration. In winter, however, the flocks are large.

During courtship, the female selects a male from the flock, emitting call notes and performing various displays. The two birds then set off in search of a suitable nesting site, each scraping small depressions in the ground. Once the right place has been located, the female stops at the top of the the depression, turns her back on the male and with her tail held almost vertically, calls to attract his attention. Both birds then continue scraping together. See also page 108.

CALL A trilling 'tee-tee-ree-tee-tee-ree'.

REPRODUCTION Late May to early June. The nest is a scrape in the ground. It is either unlined or roughly lined with moss and lichen. The Dotterel lays three eggs. Incubation is carried out almost solely by the male for twenty-one to twenty-five days. The young birds remain in the nest for twenty-four hours and are cared for almost exclusively by the male.

FOOD Mainly insects.

DISTRIBUTION AND MOVEMENTS Northern Europe, the mountainous regions of central Europe and Asia. It winters in North Africa and western Asia. In Britain it is confined to the highest of Scottish mountain plateaus, but occurs in East Anglia on passage.

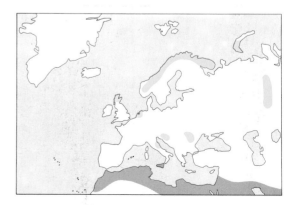

(Above) Adult Dotterel (foreground) and adult in winter plumage. (Right) Breeding areas (yellow) and wintering areas (magenta) of the Dotterel

(Above left) Kittlitz's Plover
C. pecuarius and (above)
Kentish Plover *C. alexandrinus.*
Unlike many other plovers,
Kittlitz's and Kentish Plovers have
only incomplete breast bands.
(Left) Grey Plover
P. squatarola in winter
plumage

French: PLUVIER DORÉ
Italian: PIVIERE DORATO
Spanish: CHORLITO DORADO
COMÚN
German: GOLDREGENPFEIFER

Golden Plover
Pluvialis apricaria

HABITAT Heath and moorland, both low-lying and in the hills, and tundra. Winters in fields, on sea coasts or near estuaries.

IDENTIFICATION Length: 28 cm. A typical plover, with a rounded head, slender, medium-length bill and characteristic dark upper parts flecked with golden-yellow all year round. It lacks wing-bars and the under-parts of its wings are completely white; distinguished from the Lapwing by its pointed wings. Tail and rump are dark and its face and throat black. The black of its breast and belly is interrupted by white and yellow markings. The black coloration disappears during the winter and its underparts turn whitish with blackish and yellow bars. Its flight is rapid and it runs easily over the ground. It winters in flocks which are often quite large. See also page 110.

CALL A 'tloo-ee' and an alarm note: 'tloo-ee-ee'. During the nuptial flight emits a varied trill consisting of several repeated phrases: 'too-ree . . . too-ree-pew'.

REPRODUCTION April to May. Its nest is made of grasses and lichens and is situated on the ground among heather. It normally lays four eggs, buff or green tinged spotted with brown. Incubation is carried out by both sexes for about twenty-seven days, but the female takes the larger share. The young are cared for by both parents.

FOOD Insects, caterpillars, molluscs: also plants.

DISTRIBUTION AND MOVEMENTS Northern Europe and northern Asia east to the Taimyr Peninsula. It winters in the Mediterranean region and in south-west Asia. In Britain is a fairly numerous resident breeder. Also winters on many coasts of England (and inland) and occurs as a passage visitor.

SUB-SPECIES *P.a. oreophilos:* Great Britain, Ireland, the Netherlands, northwest Germany, Denmark, southern Sweden and Norway and the northern USSR. *P.a. apricaria:* Iceland, the Faeroes, Scandinavia, Finland and the northern USSR.

(Left) Juvenile Golden Plover (top), Golden Plover of the southern race *P.a. oreophilos* in summer plumage (centre) and the northern race *P.a. apricaria* in summer plumage (below). (Below) Breeding areas (yellow), wintering areas (magenta), areas where the bird may be seen all year round (orange) and on passage (pink)

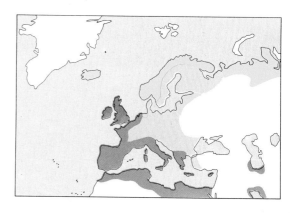

Lesser Golden Plover
Pluvialis dominica

French: PLUVIER DORÉ ASIATIQUE
Italian: PIVIERE DORATO
ASIATICO E AMERICANO
Spanish: CHORLITO DORADO CHICO
German: SIBIRISCHER
GOLDREGENPFEIFER

HABITAT During the nesting season lives in barren Arctic zones. At other times of year frequents meadows with sparse grass; steppes and sandy regions.

IDENTIFICATION Length: 24 cm. In summer plumage resembles the Golden Plover with an attractive black and white pattern; can only be distinguished from the Golden Plover by its axillaries and underwings which are smoke-grey rather than whitish. In winter similar to the Golden Plover but the feathers of its upper parts are no longer dappled with yellow but only have yellow tips. In habits and behaviour similar to the Golden Plover. See also page 110.

CALL A 'quee-ee-eek' and a melodious 'wee'. Emits various other notes on the nesting site.

REPRODUCTION June to July. The nest consists of a depression in the ground or among moss. The Lesser Golden Plover normally lays four eggs which vary in colour from pink to pale dull yellow. Incubation is carried out by both parents.

FOOD Insects, molluscs, shellfish and worms; also plants.

DISTRIBUTION AND MOVEMENTS North America and northern Siberia. It winters in South America, southeast Asia and Australia. It is accidental in Britain, Ireland, Norway, the Netherlands, Italy and Spain. In Britain is a scarce visitor: but has been reported almost annually in recent years, all sighted in the autumn. Birds from western north America migrate 10,000 kilometres over the open Pacific to Hawaii.

SUB-SPECIES *P.d. dominica*: North America. *P.d. fulva* (more brilliantly coloured plumage): northern Siberia.

(Above) Summer plumage of the Lesser Golden Plover (left), juvenile plumage (centre) and winter plumage (right)

French: PLUVIER ARGENTÉ
Italian: PIVIERESSA
Spanish: CHORLITO GRIS
German: KIEBITZREGENPFEIFER

Grey Plover
Pluvialis squatarola

(Above) Summer plumage of
the Grey Plover (foreground)
and winter plumage. (Right)
Breeding areas (yellow) and
wintering areas (magenta)

HABITAT Nests on tundra; lives on sea coasts and estuaries at other times.

IDENTIFICATION Length: 28 cm. In summer and winter plumage very like the Golden Plover although larger and more heavily built and its bill is more powerful. May also be distinguished by black axillaries. In winter, its upper parts become an almost uniform grey-brown colour. However the juveniles of the two species can be confused. At any age can be identified in flight by their black axillaries and whitish tail and rump.

They gather in small groups and sometimes associate with other shorebirds. They occasionally swim for short distances. In general the Grey Plover is more likely to be found on open shores rather than the meadows and fields which are frequented by the Golden Plover. See also page 110.

CALL Emits a 'too-ee'.

REPRODUCTION Late June to early July. The nest consists of a small, circular depression dug in the moss and lined with moss and lichen. The Grey Plover lays four cream or greyish speckled eggs. Incubation is carried out by both sexes for twenty-three days. The young are cared for by both parents.

FOOD Worms, molluscs and insects; also plants.

DISTRIBUTION AND MOVEMENTS Northern Holarctic: breeds on arctic tundra of Eurasia and North America. It winters in northern Europe and western Asia and sometimes on the coasts and estuaries of southern Europe: sometimes winters as far south as Brazil and South Africa. In Britain winters on the coasts of nearly all the maritime counties. Is also a passage visitor to coastal areas.

White-tailed Plover
Vanellus leucurus

HABITAT Lagoons and salt-water marshes. Also margins of fresh water lakes.

IDENTIFICATION Length: 27 cm. Slightly smaller than the Sociable Plover *V. gregarius* but with longer yellow legs. White coloration of rump is particularly noticeable in flight. Adults in nuptial plumage; ash-brown upper parts washed with bronze-pink coloration. Off-white forehead, cheeks and supercilium. Pinkish-brown breast. Black primaries, white secondaries with black tips and tertiaries the same colour as the back. Wing coverts with a white band at the end and a black band just above the base: white underwing: this striking black and white wing pattern, which is most visible in flight is a distinguishing feature. Clear yellow legs, cinnamon-red iris and black bill. Both sexes are alike and winter and summer plumage is similar.

CALL Call is similar to the Lapwing's *V. vanellus*—a loud double 'pee-wit' although less high-pitched.

REPRODUCTION Little information is available about the nesting habits of this species. It starts laying its eggs in late April in a hollow in the ground which is lined with vegetation. The clutch usually consists of four pale ochre or sometimes slightly olive-green eggs with dark markings and speckles which often merge into each other.

FOOD Insects and their larvae, especially grasshoppers.

DISTRIBUTION AND MOVEMENTS During the nesting season its distribution area includes the region from the Caspian Sea south to the Persian Gulf and northwards. It winters in Egypt, eastern Sudan, southern Iran and northern India. It is accidental in Siberia, southern France, Malta, northern Africa, Britain and Austria.

(Left) Summer or nuptial plumage of the White-tailed Plover (foreground) and juvenile plumage

French: PLUVIER À QUEUE BLANCHE
Italian: PAVONCELLA CODABIANCA
Spanish: CHORLITO COLIBLANCO
German: WEISSSCHWANZSTEPPEN-KIEBITZ

Eric Hosking

(Above) Common Lapwing
Vanellus vanellus taking off.
In display-flight the wings are
flapped erratically––the
derivation of the English name
of this species. (Right) Red-
wattled Plover *Vanellus indicus:*
the black and white head
pattern and bright red wattle
make it easily distinguishable.
(Facing page) Lapwing and
Golden Plover *P. apricaria* on
migration: the Golden Plover
are on the ground, their
plumage blending well with
the field

E. H. Rao/Photo Researchers

French: VANNEAU HUPPÉ
Italian: PAVONCELLA
Spanish: AVEFRÍA
German: KIEBITZ

Lapwing
Vanellus vanellus

HABITAT Open fields, pastures, water meadows, marshes, lakes and moorland bogs. Also coastal flats and estuaries on migration and in winter.

IDENTIFICATION Length: 32 cm. One of the most distinctive of all shorebirds. At a distance it is a large black and white bird of rather dumpy appearance, marked with a black breast band. When seen close to, there is an iridescent green gloss to the upper parts, distinctive face pattern and a fine crest rising from the crown. Legs are pinkish in summer. Immatures and adults in winter plumage have a less pronounced crest, smaller breast band and greyish-yellow legs.

In flight the large rounded wings are boldly patterned black and white below: white tail has a broad subterminal black band. Orange under-tail coverts are often difficult to see in the field. Flight is buoyant and the wingbeats are erratic, giving this species a distinctive character in the air. Display makes the most of the bird's black and white patterns. In particular a territorial and nuptial flight consists of circling over the ground and diving in an almost out of control tumble. Though gregarious for most of the year, Lapwings pair off early in the season and then move away from the marshes into a variety of different countryside. At this time they may occupy dry arable fields some distance from the nearest water. See also page 110.

CALL A distinctive 'pee-wit' from which one of its English vernacular names (Peewit) is derived.

REPRODUCTION In Britain most eggs are laid in early April, but elsewhere they are generally later. Normally four olive-brown spotted eggs are laid in a simple hollow in the ground which is well lined with grasses. Sometimes a substantial nest is built. Incubation, which is shared by the male and female although the female takes a larger part, lasts from twenty-four to twenty-seven days. The chicks leave the nest as soon as they are dry. They are cared for by both parents although again the female plays the larger part. In defence of their nest and brood Lapwings will circle above an intruder, dive-bombing from time to time. They will also attract attention away from the nest by feigning injury on the ground.

FOOD Insects, molluscs, worms and some vegetable matter.

DISTRIBUTION AND MOVEMENTS The whole of the southern Palearctic region from Britain to the Pacific. In Europe absent only from northern Scandinavia, the high regions of the Alps, most of Italy, Iberia and southern Greece. Breeds throughout Britain. Populations from the northern and central parts of Europe migrate southwards and westwards. Being a surface feeder the Lapwing is particularly vulnerable to hard weather and undertakes considerable local movements to escape frost.

(Right) Breeding areas (yellow), wintering areas (magenta), areas where the Lapwing may be seen all year round (orange) and on passage (pink)

Spur-winged Plover
Vanellus spinosus

HABITAT Rivers, lakes, irrigated fields and other fresh water areas. In colonising Europe, birds have occupied saline estuary areas but always with fresh water nearby.

IDENTIFICATION Length: 28 cm. A boldly patterned bird with distinctive black and white face and underparts. Upper parts light buff-brown. Legs long, much longer than the Lapwing's, and gait is delicate and purposeful. Crown black to below the eye: eye is dark and often difficult to see. Cheeks and side of the face white, extending down in a shallow 'V' on either side of the chest. Black chin stripe extends down to meet the black of the breast. Belly and under-tail coverts white. In flight the black and white pattern is accentuated by the white under-wing coverts contrasting with the black flight feathers. See also page 110.

CALL A high 'zi-zeet-zeet'.

REPRODUCTION Depending on location, breeding begins from March to June. The four eggs are laid in a simple scrape on sand or shingle by a river. The eggs are greyish-yellow in colour and are boldly blotched and spotted with brown and black. The role of the sexes in incubation requires confirmation, but the female may incubate for all of the twenty-two to twenty-four days required. The chicks leave the nest as soon as they are dry.

FOOD Insects, worms and crustaceans, also frogs and tadpoles: is said to attack stranded fish.

DISTRIBUTION AND MOVEMENTS From eastern Europe, where it was first found nesting in 1960 in northern Greece, through the Middle East to Egypt, East Africa, India and Vietnam. Generally resident although some seasonal nomadic movements occur.

(Below) Breeding areas (yellow), wintering areas (magenta) and areas where the Spur-winged Plover may be seen all year round (orange).

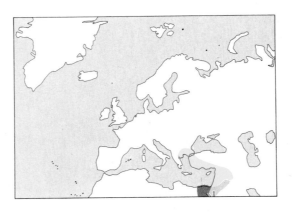

French: VANNEAU ÉPERONNÉ
Italian: PAVONCELLA ARMATA
Spanish: AVEFRÍA ESPOLADA
German: SPORNKIEBITZ

(Overleaf, page 30) Turnstone *Arenaria interpres* and (page 31) Dotterel *Eudromias morinellus* on the nest

29

French: PLUVIER SOCIABLE
Italian: PAVONCELLA GREGARIA, OR CHETTUSIA
Spanish: CHORLITO SOCIAL
German: STEPPENKIEBITZ

Sociable Plover
Vanellus gregarius

HABITAT Breeds on steppes and winters on open, grassy or sandy terrain, in uncultivated regions. Also found on freshwater margins.

IDENTIFICATION Length: 30 cm. Distinguished from the Lapwing by the absence of a crest and by its greyish back; its wings are less wide and rounded and its legs are longer. Crown black; its white supercilia meet at the nape to form a characteristic 'V' shape. General coloration grey-brown. In flight, its white secondaries and its white tail with a black band just above the tip are conspicuous features. Like other species of the genus *Vanellus* wingtips are black.

In summer plumage, it has dark rufous cheeks and lower throat, pinkish-grey breast and back and a black belly shading into dark chestnut coloration (in marked contrast to the white undertail which is visible in flight). In winter plumage, its crown and supercilia are less noticeable and there are a few dark streaks on its breast. Juvenile plumage is similar to the adult's winter plumage: underparts are chestnut-coloured with black streaks on the throat and breast. Their legs are blackish. Generally gregarious in behaviour. See also page 110.

CALL A short, sharp whistle and a harsh 'aytk-aytk-aytk'.

REPRODUCTION Late April to early May. Nest is a depression lined with dry grass. The Sociable Plover usually lays four greyish or stone-coloured eggs tinged with black. Incubation is carried out by both sexes for about three weeks. The young are cared for by both parents. Like other species of the genus *Vanellus* it is fairly noisy in the breeding season.

FOOD Mainly insects.

DISTRIBUTION AND MOVEMENTS Central southern USSR. It is a migrant and winters in southern Pakistan and northwest India. It has been recorded as accidental in Britain and Ireland, Belgium, Germany and Spain.

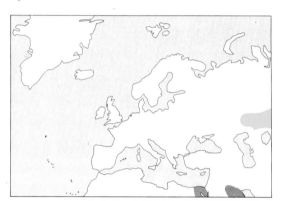

(Below) Adult Sociable Plover (foreground) and juvenile. (Right) Breeding areas (yellow) and wintering areas (magenta) of the Sociable Plover

Turnstone
Arenaria interpres

HABITAT Usually nests on rocky, open country near the sea, on islands not far from the coast and on islets in rivers. Winters on rocky or weedy coasts; however the Turnstone is also found on sandy and muddy shores with scattered pebbles and shells.

IDENTIFICATION Length: 23 cm. A sturdy shorebird, somewhat larger than the Ringed Plover. Instantly recognisable in summer plumage by its distinctive tortoiseshell upper parts, orange legs and black bill. The dark upper parts and pectoral band are in sharp contrast with its white underparts: its plumage serves as a camouflage when it is among stones. In winter its plumage turns a dull brown-grey with a white throat though the tortoiseshell pattern remains. Juvenile plumage is like adults' winter plumage.

The Turnstone lives in small groups. It moves about incessantly among the rocks and on the sand when searching for food, sometimes turning over pebbles and shells with its powerful bill. During the nesting season, it defends its territory courageously. The male pursues the female during courtship, both in flight and on the ground. See also page 116.

CALL A clear, staccato 'kititit' and a grunting 'tuk-u-tuk'.

REPRODUCTION Mid-May in northern Europe. Early June in arctic regions. The nest consists of a depression in the ground lined with grass, leaves and lichen. The Turnstone normally lays four greyish-green eggs, covered with irregular brown speckles and streaks of different shades. Incubation is carried out by both

sexes although predominantly by the female. The young are cared for by both parents, although the male may do the greater share.

FOOD Insects, molluscs and occasionally the remains of fish and other shoreline carrion.

DISTRIBUTION AND MOVEMENTS The coasts of northern Europe, northern Siberia, North America and Greenland. It winters on the shores of the Baltic and southwest Europe, on Atlantic islands and on the coasts of Africa. It sometimes spends the summer in its winter haunts or in places it passes through. In Britain winters on most coasts, is a passage visitor and is occasionally found inland.

SUB-SPECIES A sub-species is present in North and South America.

French: TOURNEPIERRE À COLLIER
Italian: VOLTAPIETRE
Spanish: VUELVEPIEDRAS
German: STEINWÄLZER

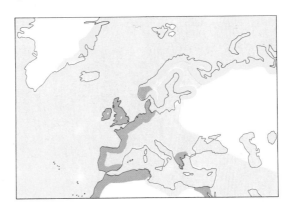

(Above) Juvenile Turnstone (foreground) and adults. (Left) Breeding areas (yellow), wintering areas (magenta) and areas where the Turnstone may be seen all year round (orange) and on passage (pink)

ORDER Charadriiformes
FAMILY **SCOLOPACIDAE:**

J. Wightman/Ardea

(Above) Waders on the seacoast: Knot *Calidris canutus*, Redshank *Tringa totanus* and Oystercatchers *H. ostralegus*

The family Scolopacidae consists of birds ranging from 12 to 60 cm in length with fairly long, pointed wings and short or medium-length tails. Often the legs and the anterior toes are long. The hind toes, on the other hand, are short and in the case of one species, the Sanderling *Calidris alba*, they are lacking altogether. There are about eighty-one species in this family (depending upon the authority consulted) consisting of snipe, woodcock and sandpipers.

The general coloration of the plumage of their upper parts is protective and serves as camouflage. The underparts are pale and may have a variety of markings and bars. Almost invariably there is a combination of colours: reddish, grey, chestnut, brown (black in some species) and white. The pattern in flight of the wing and tail is distinctive. The winter plumage is usually much more drab:

the upper parts turn grey in many species. This makes identification difficult. In contrast to these marked seasonal variations in plumage, there is usually no difference between the plumage of the two sexes.

Members of the Scolopacidae generally frequent open, boggy ground or areas near water. Most species are gregarious except during the nesting season. They join with other species to form mixed flocks, especially on the coasts, which are their favourite wintering areas. Some species however remain in swampy regions or even in woods throughout the year.

Although they consume plants, their diet consists mainly of small vertebrates. Prey is usually captured in mud, sand or shallow water. The Scolopacidae are to some extent crepuscular and nocturnal in habit, and each species therefore has

34

Snipe, Woodcock and Sandpipers

a fairly distinctive call. This serves as a link between individuals in a group, just as field marks of plumage serve the same purpose.

Members of this family perform elaborate courtship and other ceremonies, often accompanied by sounds which may be non-vocal as well as vocal. Snipe in particular have developed such sounds to a remarkable extent: during the display flight they will dive with their tails fanned out and the air which is forced through the rectrices produces a characteristic 'bleating' sound. Many species of snipe differ from each other only, or mainly, in the shape of the outer rectrices, which in turn determines the particular quality of the nuptial 'bleating'.

The nest is almost always built on the ground in the shelter of vegetation or, sometimes, in the open. A few species take advantage of the nests which other species have abandoned in trees, and one species lays its eggs in burrows scraped out by other birds. As a rule four eggs are laid (two or three in some species); the coloration is cryptic, as is that of the newly-hatched downy young who are ready to follow their parents as soon as they hatch. When danger threatens they are protected not only by their cryptic coloration but also by their habit of crouching down and remaining immobile.

The Scolopacidae appear to have originated in the northern hemisphere: most species nest in high latitudes and in some cases the breeding range is circumpolar. Almost all species migrate: those breeding in arctic and sub-arctic areas tend to perform trans-equatorial migrations. Populations breeding in temperate zones undertake shorter journeys and may even winter within the southern limits of the breeding range.

Although the classification of the various species (about eighty-one) is still a subject of some argument, for convenience the traditional subdivision into three sub-families is followed here: Scolopacinae, Tringinae and Calidritinae.

The sub-family Tringinae includes the curlews and a group of large sandpipers often loosely called 'shanks'. The curlews all belong to the genus *Numenius* and include the giants of the family: the Common or Eurasian Curlew *N. arquata* which has a Palearctic distribution and its Nearctic counterpart the Long-billed Curlew *N. americanus*. Smaller species are the Whimbrel *N. phaeopus*, the Slender-billed Curlew *N. tenuirostris*, the Bristle-thighed Curlew *N. tahitiensis* (which nests in Alaska and winters in the Pacific islands), and the possibly extinct Eskimo Curlew *N. borealis* with its Siberian counterpart the Little Curlew *N. minutus* which winters in Australia. All curlews have a long or very long, markedly decurved bill.

The genus *Tringa* comprises nine species, mostly

(Left) Greenshank *T. nebularia*: this species is larger and paler than the Redshank and, as may be deduced from their names, the green instead of red legs are another distinguishing feature

A. Lindau

A. Christiansen

(Right) Ruff *Philomachus pugnax* males at a lek in elaborate summer or nuptial plumage. (Below) World distribution of the Scolopacidae family

Palearctic, of which the best known are the Green Sandpiper *T. ochropus*, the Wood Sandpiper *T. glareola*, the Redshank *T. totanus*, the Greenshank *T. nebularia* and the Spotted Redshank *T. erythropus*. Of the Nearctic species the Greater Yellowlegs *T. melanoleuca* and the Lesser Yellowlegs *T. flavipes* are the most widespread. Among the smaller representatives, the Common Sandpiper *T. hypoleucos* and the Spotted Sandpiper *T. macularia* are considered by some authorities conspecific, the former being the Palearctic race and the latter the Nearctic one.

The sub-family Scolopacinae consists of woodcock and snipe, both characterised by their very long, straight bills with a remarkably flexible tip. Indeed, the tips of the mandibles may even be opened below ground or in mud in order to catch food. The presence of numerous sensitive and tactile nerve-ends contributes to the efficiency of this mechanism. The eyes, especially in woodcock, are set very far back and the ear opening is beneath rather than behind the orbit. These anatomical peculiarities enable the bird to locate predators rapidly both by means of hearing and vision, even when it is probing the earth with its bill. Indeed, woodcock and snipe have excellent vision, both posterior and anterior. Woodcock differ from other Scolopacidae in preferring damp, wooded ground. Snipe (genus *Gallinago*) include various species distributed through most of the world. The Common Snipe *Gallinago gallinago* is widely distributed and numerous. The more primitive forms are represented by the so-called sub-Antarctic snipe, all considered races of the Sub-Antarctic Snipe *Coenocorypha aucklandica* which is found in the lesser islands of New Zealand. This is primarily a nocturnal species, which flys infrequently and nests in burrows dug by other birds.

The third sub-family, Calidritinae, consists of the Ruff, sandpipers, godwits and dowitchers. Godwits (genus *Limosa*) are, after the curlews, the largest in size of the Scolopacidae. There are two Palearctic and two Nearctic species of godwit. The dowitchers, or red-breasted snipe (genus *Limnodromus*), are similar in shape to snipe, but have more vivid nuptial plumage. The female alone

evolved in association with social behaviour during courtship, when several males take part in symbolic fighting and posturing in special arenas or leks near the breeding-ground. This behaviour is in turn linked with sexual promiscuity and complete absence of any link between father and offspring, which are cared for entirely by the female who also undertakes all the incubation. The Ruff nests in much of Europe east across Asia and winters in the Mediterranean south to South Africa.

(Below) African Snipe *Gallinago nigripennis*. (Below left, top) Spotted Redshank *T. erythropus* in nuptial plumage and (bottom) Spotted Sandpiper *T. macularia*

apparently incubates though the male also has an incubation patch, while it is the male alone that cares for the young. Two species nest in North America and a third in Siberia. This last, the Asian Dowitcher *L. semipalmatus*, is sometimes classified in a separate genus, *Pseudoscolopax*. The largest group of the sub-family are the sandpipers belonging to the genus *Calidris* and including the Knot *C. canutus*, the Purple Sandpiper *C. maritima*, the Dunlin *C. alpinus* and the Sanderling *C. alba* among others. The smaller species are known as stints.

The Ruff *Philomachus pugnax*, is a unique species. The male is considerably larger than the female. In nuptial plumage he has a large erect ruff and two tufts which resemble ears whose coloration varies greatly; in fact no two identical males are ever found. These ornaments have

G. Hansson

G. R. Jones/Ardea

G. J. Brockhuysen/Ardea

A. P. Rossi

(Above) Snipe *G. gallinago* and (right) Bar-tailed Godwit *Limosa lapponica.* Both species have long and almost straight bills adapted to finding food in deep mud

J. B. Bottomley/Ardea

Western Sandpiper
Calidris mauri

French: BÉCASSEAU D'ALASKA
Italian: PIRO-PIRO OCCIDENTALE
Spanish: CORRELIMOS DE MAUR
German: ALASKA—SANDSTRAND-
LÄUFER

(Above) Western Sandpiper in autumn plumage (foreground) and summer plumage

HABITAT Tundra, sea coasts, coastal marshes and muddy beaches.

IDENTIFICATION Length: 16 cm. One of the most difficult of small American shore birds, collectively called 'peeps', to identify. Smaller than the Dunlin but larger than the Little Stint, although its fairly long bill recalls the former. In winter plumage resembles the Semi-palmated Sandpiper with grey, indistinctly-striped upper parts. Breast white with some markings. Light 'eyebrow' is fairly conspicuous. White wing stripe is less distinct than in Dunlin. When visible the reddish patches on nape, crown and ear coverts distinguish it from the Semi-palmated Sandpiper. In nuptial plumage upper parts turn reddish-buff like Little Stint and breast is streaked. In autumn edges of scapulars are often reddish, unlike the Semi-palmated, from which it may also be distinguished by the length of the bill. See also page 112.

CALL A thin, wavering 'chee-et'.

REPRODUCTION Number of eggs varies from three to five, whitish-yellow in colour, mottled brown and dark red.

FOOD Molluscs and crustaceans.

DISTRIBUTION AND MOVEMENTS Nests in Alaska and winters from the southern coasts of the United States to Venezuela. Accidental in Europe in Scotland and Ireland.

French: BÉCASSEAU MINUTE
Italian: GAMBECCHIO
Spanish: CORRELIMOS MENUDO
German: ZWERGSTRANDLÄUFER

Little Stint
Calidris minutus

(Above) Little Stint in summer plumage (foreground) and winter plumage. (Right) Breeding areas (yellow), wintering areas (magenta) and areas where the Little Stint may be seen on passage (pink)

HABITAT Swamp, moor and open forest in the tundra zone. On migration and in winter frequents shorelines and salt marshes.

IDENTIFICATION Length: 13 cm. The standard stint against which all others are identified. Is the smallest of the regular European shorebirds, about the same size as a sparrow. Generally speckled brownish above and whitish below with considerable streaking on the breast and flanks. In winter the brown turns grey. Dark bill is short and stout, and the legs are also dark. Is an active bird and always appears busy feeding. In all plumages has a distinctive light 'V' across the wings which meets at the tail. See also page 112.

CALL A clear 'tick' or 'timi-tit-tit'.

REPRODUCTION Breeds near the coast among grassy marshes but also on high ground some distance inland. The nest is lined with dead leaves and a few grasses. Four eggs are laid in late June and the first half of July. Both sexes incubate the eggs although the male may take the dominant role.

FOOD Insects and their larvae, molluscs and some vegetable matter.

DISTRIBUTION AND MOVEMENTS Breeds in the Arctic tundra from northernmost Scandinavia across northern Siberia. Migrant, wintering in Africa south of the Sahara, Egypt, the Persian Gulf and India. In Britain is a passage migrant, generally most numerous in the autumn.

S. C. Brown/Aquila

(Left) A group of waders including Knot, Turnstone and Dunlin. (Below) Dunlin: in winter plumage they lose the black markings on the belly

A. Faulkner Taylor/Aquila

French: BÉCASSEAU DE TEMMINCK
Italian: GAMBECCHIO NANO
Spanish: CORRELIMOS DE TEMMINCK
German: TEMMINCK-STRANDLÄUFER

Temminck's Stint
Calidris temminckii

HABITAT Generally breeds on tundra and moorland. Winters on marshland and by lakes.

IDENTIFICATION Length: 14 cm. Appears greyer than the Little Stint. Legs usually greenish-yellow and outer tail feathers white. Like other stints the legs and bill are moderately long and the wings and neck are fairly short. In shape resembles the Common Sandpiper. See also page 112.

CALL A short trilling 'tirr'.

REPRODUCTION Mid-June to the beginning of July. Nest consists of a hollow in the ground in which four eggs are laid. Both sexes incubate the eggs.

FOOD Mainly insects which are picked from the water's edge. Also other invertebrates.

DISTRIBUTION AND MOVEMENTS Northern Eurasia. Winters in the eastern Mediterranean south to equatorial Africa and east to southeast Asia. Occurs on migration on coasts of North Sea and the Baltic. Has bred on several occasions in Scotland and once in Yorkshire. Is a passage visitor to Britain and occurs annually in very small numbers mainly in southeast England.

(Above) Temminck's Stint in winter plumage (foreground) and summer plumage. (Below) Breeding areas (yellow), wintering areas (magenta) and areas where Temminck's Stint may be seen on passage (pink). (Facing page) Purple Sandpiper *Calidris maritima:* its plumage blends well with the tundra on which it breeds

French: BÉCASSEAU DE BAIRD
Italian: GAMBECCHIO DI BAIRD
Spanish: CORRELIMOS DE BAIRD
German: BAIRD-STRANDLÄUFER

Baird's Sandpiper
Calidris bairdii

HABITAT Breeds mainly in arid regions of Arctic tundra. Winters on coasts but also high in the Andes in South America.

IDENTIFICATION Length: 18 cm. Largest of the small waders, and resembles a small American Pectoral Sandpiper but bill is more slender and streaking on underparts fainter and not so extensive. Distinguished from Semi-palmated Sandpiper and other small waders by buff head and breast and less streaked upper parts. In summer appears fairly dark but winter plumage is lighter. Blackish or dark legs. Lacks a white wing bar. Behaviour and habits very similar to those of other species of the genus *Calidris*. See also page 114.

CALL Similar to that of Semi-palmated Sandpiper.

REPRODUCTION Early June onwards. Nest is a hollow in the ground, lined with grass and sometimes leaves. Eggs: normally four eggs are laid which vary in colour from pinkish-buff to ochre and are densely spotted chestnut or dark brown. Both sexes incubate the eggs.

FOOD Crustaceans and insects.

DISTRIBUTION AND MOVEMENTS Arctic regions of North America from Alaska to Baffin Island and northwest Greenland and extreme northeastern Siberia. Winters in South America from Ecuador south to Argentina. Accidental in Britain, Ireland and Finland. In Britain is a scarce visitor (several each year) from August to October.

French: BÉCASSEAU SEMI-PALMÉ
Italian: PIRO-PIRO SEMIPALMATO
Spanish: CORRELIMOS
SEMIPALMEADO
German: SANDSTRANDLÄUFER

Semi-palmated Sandpiper
Calidris pusillus

HABITAT Breeds on grassland or near marshes. Outside breeding season frequents seashores, sandy estuaries and brackish waters.

IDENTIFICATION Length: 14 cm. Very similar to the Least Sandpiper but distinguished by greyer plumage and dark olive, almost black legs. Is also slightly larger and bill is broader.
  Habits and behaviour similar to the Little Stint. Lives in small or large flocks which may become enormous on migration. During courtship flights rises to considerable heights. See also page 112.

CALL A rapid 'chrruk' in flight and a 'cher' or 'che' or 'chip'. Shorter call note than the Least Sandpiper.

REPRODUCTION Mid-June to July. Nest is a depression in the ground, lined with leaves. Eggs: normally four, varying in colour from olive-buff to olive-brown, with sepia spots and streaks especially towards the wider end. Eggs may have finer, more uniform speckling. Both sexes incubate the eggs for eighteen to nineteen days.

FOOD Insects, larvae, crustaceans; also vegetable matter.

DISTRIBUTION AND MOVEMENTS Arctic regions of North America. Winters in Central and South America. Accidental in France, Ireland and Britain where it is a scarce visitor mainly in July to October.

French: BÉCASSEAU MINUSCULE
Italian: GAMBECCHIO AMERICANO
Spanish: CORRELIMOS MENUDILLO
German: AMERIKANISCHER-
ZWERGSTRANDLÄUFER

Least Sandpiper
Calidris minutilla

HABITAT Breeds near ponds and marshes as well as dry uplands. Outside breeding season frequents mud-flats and swamps.

IDENTIFICATION Length: 13 cm. Smaller than Little Stint and distinguished from it by darker, less rufous plumage and pale yellowish or greenish legs. In winter breast is more streaked than Little Stint's and it resembles a miniature Dunlin. The bill is also narrower. Lives in flocks. See also page 112.

CALL A 'kreep' in flight. Also a 'quee-quee-quee-quee' when excited.

REPRODUCTION Early June to early July. Nest is a depression scraped out in moss or earth, lined with grass and leaves. Eggs: usually four, pale olive to yellow-buff, with many chestnut spots.

FOOD Insects, small crustaceans, worms and molluscs. Also vegetable matter although like most sandpipers feeds mainly on animal matter.

DISTRIBUTION AND MOVEMENTS Arctic regions of North America from central Alaska to Newfoundland. Winters from the western and southern United States south to Brazil and Peru in South America. Accidental in Britain, Ireland, France and Finland. In Britain is a rare vagrant principally to southwest England from August to October, and, although it does not occur annually it is certainly increasing in its reported appearances. Also a rare vagrant to Ireland.

(Above) Baird's Sandpiper in
summer plumage (left) and
winter plumage (right).
(Far left) Semi-palmated
Sandpiper in winter plumage
(top) and summer plumage
(bottom). (Below) Least
Sandpiper in winter plumage
(top) and summer plumage
(bottom)

(Above) Marsh Sandpiper
Tringa stagnatilis in winter
plumage. (Right) Greenshank
T. nebularia

M. D. England/Ardea

S. Roberts/Ardea

A. Faulkner Taylor/Aquila

(Left) Baird's Sandpiper *C. bairdii* and (below) Purple Sandpiper *C. maritima*

R. Kennedy/Aquila

Sharp-tailed Sandpiper
Calidris acuminata

HABITAT Breeds in the Arctic tundra and on grassy flats. Winters on coasts near estuaries and on the shores of lakes.

IDENTIFICATION Length: 19 cm. Very similar to the Pectoral Sandpiper but is distinguished by absence of clear-cut breast band. Also crown is more rufous than the Pectoral Sandpiper's. In winter plumage the spots on the breast are less distinct than in summer. Legs are greenish-grey rather than yellowish. See also page 114.

CALL A metallic 'pleep-pleep'.

REPRODUCTION No definite information available.

FOOD Insects, crustaceans and molluscs.

DISTRIBUTION AND MOVEMENTS Breeds in northeastern Siberia. Winters in Melanisia, New Zealand and Australia. Accidental in Britain and in Belgium: in Britain is a very scarce visitor.

(Below) Juvenile plumage of the Sharp-tailed Sandpiper (left), adult in winter plumage (centre) and summer plumage (right)

French: BÉCASSEAU À QUEUE POINTUE
Italian: PIRO-PIRO SIBERIANO
Spanish: CORRELIMOS ACUMINADO
German: SPITZSCHWANZ-STRANDLÄUFER

Pectoral Sandpiper
Calidris melanotos

French: BÉCASSEAU TACHETÉ
Italian: PIRO-PIRO PETTORALE
Spanish: CORRELIMOS PECTORAL
German: GRAUBRUST-
STRANDLÄUFER

HABITAT Breeds on tundra and on grassy flats. Winters by grassy meadows and pools.

IDENTIFICATION Length: 19 cm. Distinguished by black and rusty-red streaking on crown, neck and upper parts, and by buff stripes on back like those of Snipe. The streaking on neck and breast ends abruptly, making a clear-cut contrast with pure white of belly. Legs ochre. In flight the tail is light grey except for the very much darker central feathers. In summer appears more rufous and in winter more greyish. When seeking food, in a group or alone, moves slowly, probing the ground with its bill. When necessary will swim short distances. See also page 114.

CALL A reedy 'keek-keek'.

REPRODUCTION End of May and June. Nest is well hidden in the grass in a depression in the ground and is lined with grass and leaves. Eggs: usually four, light olive to pale brown, with dark spots. The female alone incubates the eggs for twenty-one to twenty-three days. Young are cared for by the female alone.

FOOD Insects, larvae, crustaceans and other invertebrates.

DISTRIBUTION AND MOVEMENTS Northeastern Siberia, Arctic regions of North America. Winters in South America and in Australia and New Zealand in small numbers. Accidental in Britain, Ireland, Iceland, Norway, France, Switzerland and Germany. It is the most common of the transatlantic vagrant waders.

(Above) Pectoral Sandpiper in winter plumage (foreground) and summer plumage. Like many sandpipers the winter plumage is much greyer

49

A. Lowry/Photo Researchers

(Above) Marbled Godwit *Limosa fedoa*, (right) Sanderling *Calidris alba* and (below) Redshank *Tringa totanus*. (Facing page) Knot *C. canutus* in winter plumage: it is a highly gregarious species in the winter

J. B. Bottomley/Ardea

A. Lindau

S. Roberts/Ardea

French: BÉCASSEAU DE
 BONAPARTE
Italian: PIRO-PIRO DORSOBIANCO
 O DI BONAPARTE
Spanish: CORRELIMOS DE
 BONAPARTE
German: WEISSBÜRZEL-
 STRANDLÄUFER

White-rumped Sandpiper
Calidris fuscicollis

HABITAT Nests in Arctic tundra. Winters on beaches, marshes and mud-flats.

IDENTIFICATION Length: 17 cm. White patch on rump conspicuous against darker tail and narrower than the Curlew Sandpiper's white patch. In spring back is brown, becoming greyish in autumn: in autumn the White-rumped closely resembles the Curlew Sandpiper but may be distinguished by its smaller size and shorter bill (and narrower white patch on rump). Breast is streaked and spotted. Juveniles similar to adults in summer plumage. Legs dark greenish or blackish-grey.
  Habits and behaviour similar to those of the Dunlin. See also page 114.

CALL A characteristic 'jeet'.

REPRODUCTION Mid-June to mid-July. Nest is a depression in moss or grass. Eggs: usually four, buff to pale green with darker spots. The female alone incubates the eggs and cares for the young.

FOOD Molluscs, insects, other invertebrates and also seeds.

DISTRIBUTION AND MOVEMENTS Arctic regions of North America. Winters in southern South America. Is a scarce visitor to Britain, recorded almost annually. Occurs mainly from July to November in southern England and Wales. Also accidental in Ireland.

(Above) White-rumped Sandpiper in winter plumage (foreground) and summer plumage

Purple Sandpiper
Calidris maritima

French: BÉCASSEAU VIOLET
Italian: PIOVANELLO VIOLETTO
Spanish: CORRELIMOS OSCURO
German: MEERSTRANDLÄUFER

HABITAT Breeds mainly on the Arctic tundra. In winter frequents rocky coasts.

IDENTIFICATION Length 21 cm. In winter distinguishable from other sandpipers by dark brownish-grey head, breast and upper parts, contrasting boldly with the white belly and spotted flanks. In summer upper parts appear lighter. Short, yellow legs and yellow base of bill. White wing-bar. Frequently associates with Turnstones. Is a bird of rocky coasts and is seldom found elsewhere. See also page 116.

CALL A 'weett-weett' or 'tritt-tritt'.

REPRODUCTION Beginning of June. Nest is a depression in the ground. Eggs: usually four, pale olive blotched and speckled with brown. Incubation carried out mostly by the male.

FOOD Vegetable matter, crustaceans and molluscs.

DISTRIBUTION AND MOVEMENTS Northern Europe, Arctic regions of Asia and North America: breeding distribution is circumpolar. Populations breeding in northernmost Europe winter on coasts of North Sea, Baltic and Atlantic, exceptionally also in the Mediterranean region. However in breeding areas where the coasts remain free of ice, populations are sedentary. In Britain is a winter visitor chiefly to rocky shores: thus most numerous in the west and north of Britain. Also a passage visitor.

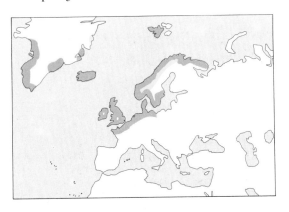

(Above) Purple Sandpiper in summer plumage (foreground) and winter plumage. (Left) Wintering areas (magenta) and areas where the Purple Sandpiper may be seen all year round (orange)

French: BÉCASSEAU COCORLI
Italian: PIOVANELLO
Spanish: CORRELIMOS ZARAPITÍN
German: SICHELSTRANDLÄUFER

Curlew Sandpiper
Calidris ferruginea

HABITAT Breeds in the tundra and steppe. Frequents coastal plains, lagoons, marshland. On migration is found on sea coasts, in estuaries and also in inland waters, water-meadows, sewage farms, etc.

IDENTIFICATION Length: 19 cm. Summer plumage rufous—similar to the Knot. Crown and upper parts are variegated black and chestnut; rump has blackish bars; sides of head and neck and underparts are deep russet. In grey-brown winter plumage can be distinguished from Dunlin by white rump (mainly visible in flight), longer legs, less spotted breast and more distinct 'eye-brow'. Another distinguishing feature is the bill which is longer, more slender and more decurved than that of Dunlin. The markedly curved bill is a useful field mark at all times. White rump also distinguishes it from most other waders of the genus *Calidris* (except the White-rumped). Immature Curlew Sandpiper has a buffish tinge.

Habits and behaviour similar to Dunlin. Generally lives alone or in small groups. In the breeding season the male performs a nuptial flight. See also page 114.

CALL A soft 'chirrip'. Also an alarm note 'week-week-week' or a 'pit-pit'.

REPRODUCTION End of June and July. Nest is a depression in grassy ground, sometimes lined with grasses and lichens. Eggs: usually four, sometimes three, varying in colour from light olive to grey-green with numerous dark spots. Both sexes incubate the eggs, but the period of incubation is not known.

FOOD Small crustaceans and molluscs, worms, insects; sometimes also vegetable matter.

DISTRIBUTION AND MOVEMENTS Nests in Arctic regions of Asia. Migratory in Europe and Asia, occurring both on coasts and inland. Winters in tropical and southern Africa, southern Asia, the Malaysian archipelago and Australian coasts. In Britain is a passage visitor mainly to the east and south coasts of England in most months, being most numerous in autumn, although numbers vary from year to year. Is also a passage visitor to Ireland.

(Above) Curlew Sandpiper in summer plumage (foreground) and winter plumage. (Right) Wintering areas (magenta) and areas where the Curlew Sandpiper may be seen on passage (pink)

Dunlin
Calidris alpina

French: BÉCASSEAU VARIABLE
Italian: PIOVANELLO PANCIANERA
Spanish: CORRELIMOS COMÚN
German: ALPENSTRANDLÄUFER

HABITAT Breeds on tundra, coastal marshes and wet heaths. On migration and in winter found on estuaries, marshes, sea coasts and meadows.

IDENTIFICATION Length 19 cm. Most common small wader of the shore. In winter plumage upper parts grey brown and underparts whitish. Sides of tail and rump whitish. Bill slightly decurved. Unlike Sanderling has no black shoulder spot. In summer plumage is the only small wader with a black belly. See also pages 112 and 114.

CALL A weak 'treep'.

REPRODUCTION May. Nest is a scrape in the ground and is lined with grass or leaves. Eggs: usually four, buff or blue-green with dark brown blotches. Both parents incubate the eggs for twenty-one or twenty-two days. Both parents also tend the young which leave the nest after a few days and fly after about three weeks.

FOOD Molluscs, worms, insects and vegetable matter.

DISTRIBUTION AND MOVEMENTS Breeding distribution circumpolar: northern Europe, Arctic regions of Asia and North America. Populations breeding in Europe winter on the southern shores of the North Sea, on northwestern and southwestern European coasts, on the shores of the Mediterranean and northwestern Africa. In Britain is a resident breeder mainly on moorland in Scotland and northern England although locally in Wales and southwest England. Also a passage and winter visitor to Britain. Resident breeder and winter and passage visitor to Ireland.

SUB-SPECIES *C.a. alpina* Norway, northern Scandinavia and the northern USSR. *C.a. schinzii* (smaller): Britain, Netherlands, northern Germany, southern Scandinavia, Soviet shores of the Baltic, Iceland, the Faeroes and southeast Greenland. *C.c. arctica:* northeast Greenland. Other sub-species present in North America.

(Below) Dunlin in juvenile plumage (top), summer plumage (centre) and winter plumage (bottom). (Left) Breeding areas (yellow), wintering areas (magenta), areas where it may be seen all year round (orange) and on passage (pink)

French: BÉCASSEAU MAUBÈCHE
Italian: PIOVANELLO MAGGIORE
Spanish: CORRELIMOS GORDO
German: KÜSTENSTRANDLÄUFER

Knot
Calidris canutus

(Above) Knot in summer plumage (foreground) and winter plumage. (Below right) Breeding areas (yellow), wintering areas (magenta) and areas where the Knot may be seen on passage (pink)

HABITAT Breeds on stony ground with little vegetation in the high Arctic. Winters on sandy or muddy beaches, near estuaries. Rare inland.

IDENTIFICATION Length: 25 cm. Distinguishable by habit of feeding with head well down in closely-packed groups. Larger than the Dunlin and appears rather dumpy, due mainly to the short neck, bill and legs. In summer upper parts are spotted black and chestnut, with rufous head and underparts. In winter upper parts are ash-grey, underparts white. Distinguished from Dunlin and Sanderling by uniform grey tail. On the wing, in winter plumage, appears virtually completely grey: this distinguishes it from the larger Redshank.
Habits and behaviour similar to the Dunlin. Is seen in dense flocks. During the courtship flight the male rises to great heights and flies in circles. See also page 116.

CALL A 'tooit-ooit' uttered in flight. Also a low 'not'.

REPRODUCTION June–July. Nest is a depression in the ground lined with lichens. Eggs: usually four, grey-green or olive-buff, closely mottled and streaked brown or smoke-grey. Both sexes incubate the eggs for twenty to twenty-five days. The young leave the nest as soon as they are dry.

FOOD Crustaceans, insects and molluscs. The Knot also feeds on some vegetable matter.

DISTRIBUTION AND MOVEMENTS Northern regions of Old and New World. Winters from Britain south to the Mediterranean, on the shores of the Black Sea and the western shores of Africa, in South America, southern Asia, Australia and New Zealand. In Britain is a winter and passage visitor to most coasts.

SUB-SPECIES The sub-species *C.c. canutus*

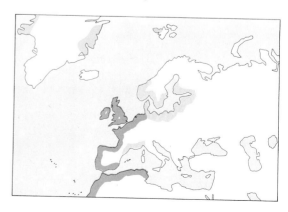

French: BÉCASSEAU SANDERLING
Italian: PIOVANELLO TRIDATTILO,
O CROCEZIA
Spanish: CORRELIMOS TRIDÁCTILO
German: SANDERLING

Sanderling
Calidris alba

(Above) Sanderling in summer plumage (foreground) and winter plumage. (Below right) Breeding areas (yellow), wintering areas (magenta) and areas where the Sanderling may be seen on passage (pink)

HABITAT Breeds on stony, sparsely vegetated regions of the Arctic tundra, often near water. Prefers to winter on flat sandy beaches, mudbanks and estuaries. Rare inland.

IDENTIFICATION Length 20 cm: slightly larger than the Dunlin. Chiefly distinguished by its very pale appearance in autumn and winter, due to the underparts and most of the head being completely white. In flight is distinguished from other shore birds by the white wing-bar contrasting boldly with the dark wing (in other species the wing-bar is much fainter). In winter plumage upper parts are pale grey with some darker spots and a dark shoulder-patch (this patch being a diagnostic field mark); the tail has white sides with dark central feathers. In summer, head, neck, upper parts and upper breast are variegated rufous and black, contrasting with the white underparts. White underparts distinguish it from the Dunlin and the larger Knot. Legs and bill are black.

Of all the small waders seen most often feeding along the edge of the tide. When approached generally runs rather than flying away. Lives in groups which are more or less continuously active. During courtship the male rises with rapid wingbeats and then begins a short downward flight, uttering a song as he descends. See also page 114.

CALL A short 'twick' or 'kwit'.

REPRODUCTION Mid-June. Nest consists of a depression in the ground, lined with dried leaves. Eggs:

usually four, generally dark olive-green irregularly scattered with small brown spots. Eggs are probably incubated by the female for twenty-three to twenty-four days. The young leave the nest a few hours after hatching and are looked after by both parents for about a fortnight.

FOOD Small crustaceans and molluscs, insects and larvae.

DISTRIBUTION AND MOVEMENTS The Arctic: breeding distribution circumpolar. Highly migratory: virtually cosmopolitan, wintering in the Americas, Asia, southern Africa, Australia and Europe (North Sea, Atlantic and Mediterranean coasts). In Britain is a widespread passage visitor. Winters on most coasts and has also been recorded irregularly in most inland counties.

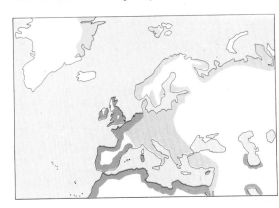

French: CHEVALIER COMBATTANT
Italian: COMBATTENTE
Spanish: COMBATIENTE
German: KAMPFLÄUFER

Ruff
Philomachus pugnax

HABITAT Nests in northern tundra and, in the more southerly part of its range, in damp grassland, water-meadows and marshes. In winter and on migration occurs on marshland and on shallow margins of fresh and salt water.

IDENTIFICATION Length: male 25 cm, female 23 cm. Male in breeding plumage is unmistakable, due to two erectile ear-tufts and a huge collar or 'ruff' in various combinations of black, chestnut, buff and white; this however only appears late in the season and for a short period. The dark brown and sand-coloured upper parts have a 'scaly' look, the breast is golden-buff and the belly white. However coloration of plumage highly variable—many combinations of black, white rufous and

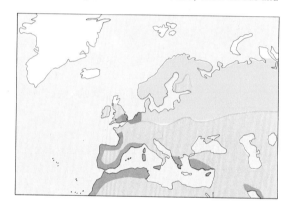

(Below) Female Ruff (foreground), male in winter plumage and (facing page) variations in the nuptial plumage of the male Ruff. (Right) Breeding areas (yellow), wintering areas (magenta), areas where the Ruff may be seen all year round (orange) and on passage (pink)

buff. Bill and leg colour varies: bill is red, yellow, brown or blackish and legs green, yellow or flesh-coloured. Outside the breeding season appears a medium-sized wader somewhat similar to the Redshank, but with a thicker neck, dark wings and bill and a dark tail with an oval white patch on either side. The female (called the Reeve) is similar but noticeably smaller. Juveniles similar to the female (both have thinner necks than the male), but upper parts more spotted.

Flight like that of Redshank. When standing still appears more erect than other waders. Polygamous. See also page 116.

CALL Generally silent, but during breeding season sometimes utters a hoarse 'uk'. Also a flight note 'too-i'.

REPRODUCTION Mid-May and early June. Nest is a hollow in grassy ground and completely hidden from sight. Eggs: usually four, varying in colour from pale grey or ochre to pale green, with dark sepia spots and blotches. The female incubates the eggs for twenty-one days and tends the chicks until they fly.

FOOD Mainly insects, but also worms.

DISTRIBUTION AND MOVEMENTS Northern Eurasia. Winters from the Mediterranean south to southern Africa, also southern Asia and locally in western Europe. In Britain is a very scarce breeder although since 1963 has bred probably annually in very small numbers in the Ouse Washes. Also occurs regularly as a passage visitor on or near most coasts of Britain and Ireland. Small numbers winter with increasing regularity mainly near the coasts but also inland in Britain.

(Above right) Sanderling *C. alba* and (far right) Black-tailed Godwit *L. limosa*. The Sanderling scurries over the sand, keeping pace with the retreating tide and picking up tiny marine organisms. The Black-tailed Godwit, thanks to its long legs, wanders into shallow water and probes at leisure in the mud. (Right) Immature Ruff *P. pugnax*

M. Brosselin/Jacana

Jane Burton/Bruce Coleman

R. A. Hume/Aquila

Buff-breasted Sandpiper

Tryngites subruficollis

French: BÉCASSEAU ROUSSET
Italian: PIRO-PIRO FULVO
Spanish: CORRELIMOS CANELO
German: GRASLÄUFER

HABITAT Breeds on dry regions of Arctic tundra. On migration found on dry grassy fields rather than shore-lines.

IDENTIFICATION Length: 20 cm. Female is smaller than male. Crown and back are mottled dark; eye-ring pale; throat, sides of head and underparts entirely buff. Unlike other species of the same family, the rump lacks a black centre and white margins. Underwing white with marbled tips to the flight feathers. Bill relatively short: legs yellow. Juveniles similar to adults. Gregarious and flies with its neck drawn back, with zig-zags and many turns, in large and compact flocks. During courtship the male performs a complex nuptial flight. See also page 114.

CALL A low, tremulous 'poo-rreet'.

REPRODUCTION Beginning of June to mid-July. Nest consists of a slight depression in the ground, lined with grasses, moss and dried leaves. Eggs: four to five, light blue-green or buff, densely spotted with sepia which the female incubates.

FOOD Predominantly insects and other invertebrates, like that of other sandpipers.

DISTRIBUTION AND MOVEMENTS Arctic regions of North America. Winters in southern South America. Accidental in Britain more or less every year in varying numbers and in France, Germany and Switzerland.

(Below) The Buff-breasted Sandpiper is the only small wader which has all-buff underparts

French: BÉCASSEAU FALCINELLE
Italian: GAMBECCHIO FRULLINO
Spanish: CORRELIMOS FALCINELO
German: SUMPFLÄUFER

Broad-billed Sandpiper
Limicola falcinellus

HABITAT Breeds on tundra and on moors and winters mainly on coasts.

IDENTIFICATION Length: 16 cm. Resembles a small dark Dunlin in winter plumage although the bill is longer and broad at the base and the legs are shorter. The bill is decurved at the tip and the throat is white. Markings on the mantle resemble those of a snipe and the two white lines on each side are a distinguishing feature as is the conspicuous white eyestripe which forks behind the eye. When seen at close quarters the coppery edges of the secondaries are visible. See also page 110.

CALL The flight note is a low-pitched 'chrr-eek' and it emits a trilling song in the breeding season.

REPRODUCTION June. Lays four to five eggs which both sexes incubate.

FOOD Molluscs, worms, insects and seeds.

DISTRIBUTION AND MOVEMENTS Breeds in Norway and Sweden to northern Finland and east to the Kola Peninsula and probably also on tundra in northern Siberia. Winters in the eastern Mediterranean and southern Asia and south to Australia. In Britain is a rare autumn and occasionally spring passage migrant which is mostly recorded in southeast England. Also passage visitor to Ireland.

SUB-SPECIES *L.l. falcinellus* breeds in Scandinavia and on the Kola peninsula.

(Below) Breeding areas (yellow), wintering areas (magenta) and areas where the Broad-billed Sandpiper may be seen on passage (pink)

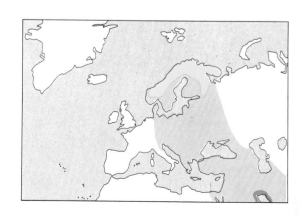

Stilt Sandpiper
Micropalama himantopus

(Left) Stilt Sandpiper in winter plumage (foreground) and summer plumage

French: CHEVALIER ÉCHASSE
Italian: PIRO-PIRO ZAMPELUNGHE
Spanish: CORRELIMOS ZANCOLÍN
German: BINDENSTRANDLÄUFER

HABITAT Nests on marshy Arctic tundra; on passage and in winter frequents seashore and coastal marshland and freshwater areas.

IDENTIFICATION Length 21 cm. Long dark green legs and long slender bill. Summer plumage dark grey, and underparts are strongly barred with darker grey. Rust-red patch at sides of head. In winter plumage, paler and with white underparts and rump. Has no wingbar. In flight the legs extend well beyond the tail. See also page 116.

CALL A gentle 'chuu', like the Knot's but slightly harsher.

REPRODUCTION Nests in a depression in the ground, in tundra. Nest is sometimes lined with leaves and grass. Eggs: four, pale grey-green with brown spots.

FOOD Mainly small water creatures similar to other sandpipers.

DISTRIBUTION AND MOVEMENTS Coastal regions from north-east Alaska to Manitoba and possibly to north Ontario. Wintering area not known precisely, but probably from Bolivia through Brazil and Paraguay to Argentina and Uruguay. Accidental in Britain and Ireland, and one or two visitors are now identified almost every year.

(Right) Short-billed Dowitcher *Limnodromus griseus* and (below) Long-billed Dowitcher *L. scolopaceus*. The Long-billed has a higher-pitched call

W. Stirling/Ardea

J. B. & S. Bottomley/Ardea

J. B. & S. Bottomley/Ardea

G. K. Brown/Ardea

(Above) Buff-breasted Sandpiper *Tryngites subruficollis* and (left) Broad-billed Sandpiper *Limicola falcinellus*: the white eyestripe is a conspicuous feature of this species

French: LIMNODROME À LONG BEC
Italian: PIRO-PIRO
PETTOROSSICCIO
Spanish: AGUJETA ESCOLOPÁCEA
German: SCHLAMMLÄUFER

Long-billed Dowitcher
Limnodromus scolopaceus

(Above) Long-billed Dowitcher in winter plumage (left) and summer plumage

HABITAT Nests on marshes and near pools. Winters on mudbanks, seashore, banks of pools and lagoons. Also found more frequently on fresh water than the Short-billed Dowitcher.

IDENTIFICATION Length 28–31 cm. Slightly larger than the Short-billed Dowitcher and has a longer bill. Like the Snipe the lower back and rump are white. On the flanks the plumage is barred rather than spotted. Otherwise is almost identical to the Short-billed with which it was long confused, the two being sometimes regarded as a single species. See also page 116.

CALL A single squeaking note: 'keek' which is higher pitched than the Short-billed Dowitcher's.

REPRODUCTION Nests in a depression in the ground among grass or moss, usually near water. Eggs: four, green-brown, with dark spots and streaks. Incubation period is not known.

FOOD Water insects and their larvae and probably also small marine invertebrates.

DISTRIBUTION AND MOVEMENTS Nests in northeast Siberia, the coasts of Alaska, parts of Canada. Winters south from the Californian coast to Texas and Florida, southwards as far as Guatemala. Accidental in Antilles, Argentina and Europe. In British Isles is an accidental visitor in autumn occurring slightly more frequently than the Short-billed Dowitcher.

Short-billed Dowitcher
Limnodromus griseus

HABITAT Nests on marshland and near water with rich vegetation. Winters on sand and mudbanks in bays and estuaries, on lakesides, marshes and pools.

IDENTIFICATION Length: 25 cm. One of the few shore-birds with a long bill and a narrow white stripe at the centre of a dark back. Adult plumage dark: crown and back black with tawny markings; pale tawny eye stripe; sides of head, neck and underparts chestnut with black spots; flanks and under-tail coverts barred; legs short and greenish. Winter plumage: ash-grey upper parts with few spots, white underparts with faint stripes, flanks spotted, and tail less strongly barred than that of the Long-billed. Juveniles: upper parts similar to adult's in summer; underparts tawny, breast striped and spotted with brown.

Flies with head drawn back and bill slightly downwards, the whole flock manoeuvring together. On land, moves gracefully, and probes the mud with its bill, immersing it to its full length to seek for food. See also page 116.

CALL A short 'tu-tu-tu'.

REPRODUCTION June. Nests in a hollow in moss. Eggs: normally four, almost pear-shaped, resembling Snipe's. Incubated for about three weeks.

FOOD Insects, larvae, worms and molluscs.

DISTRIBUTION AND MOVEMENTS Northern regions of North America. Winters in Central and South America. Accidental in Britain, France, Denmark and Sweden. In Britain and Ireland the Short-billed has been recorded only a few times in the last hundred years, but many dowitchers have not been specifically identified and the Short-billed may be more regular than the records suggest.

French: MACRORHAMPHE GRIS
Italian: PIRO-PIRO PETTOROSSICCIO MINORE
Spanish: AGUJETA GRIS
German: SCHLAMMLÄUFER

(Left) Short-billed Dowitcher in summer plumage (foreground) and winter plumage

French: CHEVALIER ARLEQUIN
Italian: TOTANO MORO
Spanish: ARCHIBEBE OSCURO
German: DUNKLER
WASSERLÄUFER

Spotted Redshank
Tringa erythropus

HABITAT Nests near marshes and in swampy places in forest, heath and tundra. In winter frequents muddy areas of sea coasts, shores of large lakes, salt-marshes and swamps.

IDENTIFICATION Length 30 cm. In summer plumage, distinguished from all other shorebirds by its deep black plumage with white speckles on the upper parts. Rump is white and tail barred. In winter plumage resembles the Redshank, but may be distinguished by the lack of a wing bar, slender, longer bill, and longer legs which extend beyond the tail in flight. Upper parts are more densely speckled with white than the Redshank's, and the pattern on the head is less speckled. Legs are red in summer, orange in winter. Red based bill distinguishes it from other shanks as does all dark coloration and white wedge-shaped rump.

Flight, behaviour and habits much like Redshank; differs however in its more erect stance on land, and its more active searching for food. In summer perches on branches and bushes, also rocks and posts. See also page 122.

CALL A diagnostic loud 'to-itt' or 'tchu-eet', and a 'chick-chick-chick'. This call note distinguishes it from the Redshank and Greenshank.

REPRODUCTION End of May to early June. Nests in a hollow in the ground which is lined with grass, pine-needles and dry leaves. Eggs: normally four, pear-shaped, ranging in colour from creamy olive to olive-grey or pale marine grey, with dense speckled markings. Incubated probably only by the male. Young are initially reared by both parents, but soon abandoned by the female.

FOOD Insects, molluscs, crustaceans and small amphibians.

DISTRIBUTION AND MOVEMENTS Northern Europe, northern Siberia. Winters in the Mediterranean area and on the Black Sea. Passage visitor in central Europe, where it very occasionally spends the summer. In Britain is a regular double passage migrant, more common in the autumn, and it also winters in small numbers. The Spotted Redshank is also a winter and passage visitor to Ireland.

(Below) Spotted Redshank in summer plumage (foreground) and winter plumage. (Right) Breeding areas (yellow), wintering areas (magenta) and areas where the Spotted Redshank may be seen on passage (pink)

Redshank
Tringa totanus

HABITAT During the nesting season frequents marshy grassland, moorland, grassy lakesides and salt water. Winters by estuaries, on mudbanks and along open shores.

IDENTIFICATION Length: 28 cm. A medium-sized wader, recognisable in flight by its white back and rump and dark wings with a broad white trailing edge. On land, recognisable by its orange-red legs. The long red bill has a black tip. Brown upper parts have thick black and grey markings; tail has black and white bars; underparts have fine stripes and small speckles. Juveniles: more tawny upper parts, and yellow legs.
   Very active and noisy. Flight powerful, often erratic. When it suspects danger, bobs in a characteristic way, moving its neck rapidly up and down with the bill held horizontal, while the back end of the body moves in the opposite direction, so that the tail dips as the head rises. On landing, stands for an instant with the wings raised over the back. Hunts for food in the mud and in the water at low tide; well able to swim if necessary. During courtship the male follows the female with the tail fanned out and both birds hold their heads down. If the female accepts the male, she stops in her tracks and the male slowly comes up to her, holding his wings raised over his back and waving them gently; at the same time he calls. See also page 122.

CALL A call note 'tleeoo-hoo-hoo'. The song consists of various musical phrases that are repeated, particularly a 'tau-eeoo'.

REPRODUCTION Mid-April to June. The nest is a depression among tall grass lined with dried grasses; the tall grass-stems are woven together to hide the eggs. Eggs: normally four, buff with dark brown blotches and spots. Incubated by both sexes, for twenty-three or twenty-four days. The chicks leave the nest as soon as they are born, and are reared by both parents.

FOOD Insects, molluscs, crustaceans, worms, also some plant matter.

DISTRIBUTION AND MOVEMENTS Iceland, Faeroes, Britain and Ireland, central and southeast Europe, southern Iberian peninsula, north Italy: central Asia. Winters in the Mediterranean area, on west European coasts and northwest African coast. In Britain is a fairly numerous and widely distributed resident breeder. Also occurs as a passage and winter visitor.

SUB-SPECIES *T.t. totanus:* continental Europe and western Siberia. *T.t. robusta* (larger): Iceland and Faeroes. *T.t. britannica* (less barred and spotted): Britain. *T.t. eushinus:* Asia.

French: CHEVALIER GAMBETTE
Italian: PETTEGOLA
Spanish: ARCHIBEBE COMÚN
German: ROTSCHENKEL

(Left) Breeding areas (yellow), wintering areas (magenta), areas where the Redshank may be seen all year round (orange) and on passage (pink)

(Right) Spotted Redshank *Tringa erythropus* in winter plumage and (below) Spotted Redshank in summer plumage on the nest. (Facing page, top) Dowitchers, Willets and Marbled Godwits. Dowitchers are vagrants from North America to Europe. (Facing page, below) Marsh Sandpiper *T. stagnatilis*

K. W. Fink/Ardea

M. D. England/Ardea

French: CHEVALIER STAGNATILE
Italian: ALBASTRELLO
Spanish: ARCHIBEBE FINO
German: TEICHWASSERLÄUFER

Marsh Sandpiper
Tringa stagnatilis

(Above) Marsh Sandpiper in summer plumage. (Right) Breeding areas (yellow), wintering areas (magenta) and areas where the Marsh Sandpiper may be seen on passage (pink)

HABITAT Nests on grassy and marshy country. Winters on marshy freshwater margins.

IDENTIFICATION Length: 23 cm. Very similar to Greenshank. Distinguished both by smaller size, and by straight and more slender bill, white forehead, and thinner, greenish legs; more agile and graceful in movement. In flight the legs extend beyond the tail to a greater extent than in the Greenshank. In summer plumage upper parts are more darkly spotted.

Very active, and quick in movement. When seeking for food, often moves its bill from side to side like the Greenshank. During courtship the male executes an undulating flight. See also page 122.

CALL A 'ti-u, tiu, tia' which is not as loud as that of other shanks. Also tremulous trilling notes.

REPRODUCTION May–June. Nests in a hollow in grassy ground. Eggs: normally four, ranging in colour from cream to tawny grey or yellowish-brown, with purplish-brown spots. Probably incubated by both sexes.

FOOD Water-insects and their larvae; also molluscs.

DISTRIBUTION AND MOVEMENTS Eastern Europe and southwest Siberia. Winters in tropical and southern Africa and southern Asia. Passage visitor to the eastern Mediterranean region. Accidental in Britain, Belgium, France, Spain, Switzerland, Germany, Finland.

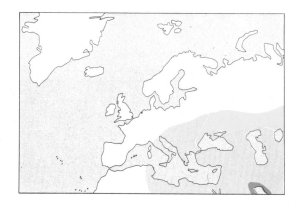

Greenshank
Tringa nebularia

HABITAT Nests on heathland, marshland, or in swamp clearings in forests. Winters on banks of lakes and rivers and on seashore by estuaries and salt-marshes.

IDENTIFICATION Length 30 cm. Distinguished from Redshank by slightly larger size, greyer plumage, greenish legs which are slightly longer and extend beyond the end of the tail in flight, whiter head and underparts, and absence of wing-bar. The blackish bill is slightly up-turned; the white area on the back, rump and tail is larger than in the Redshank.

Flight rapid and erratic. Perches on trees and rocks in summer. See also page 122.

CALL A shrill thrice repeated 'tiu-tiu-tiu' less strident than the Redshank; a repeated 'tooip'. Song: a repeated 'tiu-ee'.

REPRODUCTION Early May and June. Nests in a depression in the ground, excavated by the female. Eggs: normally four, oval, tawny olive or buff with irregular dark streaks and other markings. Incubated by both sexes for twenty-four or twenty-five days. Young are reared by both parents and fly about four weeks after hatching.

FOOD Water insects and their larvae, crustaceans, worms, molluscs and sometimes amphibians.

DISTRIBUTION AND MOVEMENTS Northern Europe and northern Asia as far as Kamchatka peninsula. Winters in the Mediterranean region, Africa, southern Asia, Australia. Occasionally summers where it is known as a passage visitor, and very occasionally winters there. A sparse breeder in Scotland, but comparatively common further south on passage.

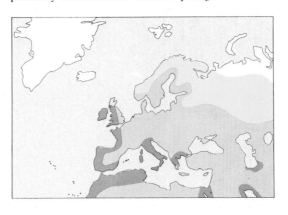

(Left) Breeding areas (yellow), wintering areas (magenta) and areas where the Greenshank may be seen on passage (pink)

(Right) Redshank *T. totanus*
in summer plumage on the
nest. (Facing page, top)
Redshank in winter plumage
and (below) Greenshank
T. nebularia at the nest

F. V. Blackburn

R. J. C. Blewitt/Ardea

E. Soothill/Aquila

French: GRAND CHEVALIER À
PATTES JAUNES
Italian: TOTANO ZAMPEGIALLE
MAGGIORE
Spanish: ARCHIBEBE PATIGUALDO
GRANDE
German: GROSSER
GELBSCHENKEL

Greater Yellowlegs
Tringa melanoleuca

HABITAT Nests on marshland among trees and on tundra. On migration and in winter is found by lakes, pools, saltmarshes and mudflats. Not frequently found on open shore.

IDENTIFICATION Length 30 cm. Very similar to Lesser Yellowlegs, but about one-third larger. A distinguishing feature is the black bill with olive base which is longer and more massive and slightly upturned. Distinguished from Greenshank by the shape of the bill, more spots on upper parts, and the absence of the wedge-shaped patch of white on the lower back. Legs strongly built and deep yellow in colour. Juveniles in winter have more white on rump and underparts. See also page 122.

CALL 'Hiu-hiu-hiu', rather like the Greenshank.

REPRODUCTION From early May onwards. Nest made in a depression in the ground in tree-growing terrain, never far from water. Eggs: normally four, ranging in colour from pale cream to creamy olive, with chestnut spots which are sometimes grouped at the broad end. Incubated probably only by the female for about three weeks.

FOOD Insects, molluscs and worms. Very little plant matter.

DISTRIBUTION AND MOVEMENTS Breeds in North America from Alaska to Newfoundland. Winters in southern North America, and in South America. Accidental in Britain where it is less frequently identified than Lesser Yellowlegs.

Lesser Yellowlegs
Tringa flavipes

HABITAT Nests in sparse forest generally near water. On migration and in winter is found by lakes, pools, saltmarshes and mudflats. Not frequently found on open shore.

IDENTIFICATION Length: 25 cm. Very similar to Greater Yellowlegs: also similar to Spotted Redshank, but smaller, with longer bright yellow legs. Upper parts dark blackish-brown with light spots and feather-margins. Winter plumage is lighter and less spotted. In flight, the underside of the wings is uniform dark grey, and the tail white (though with bars). Head, neck and breast greyish with black stripes; underparts white. See also page 122.

CALL A 'yew' or 'yew-yew' which is not as loud as the Greater Yellowleg's.

REPRODUCTION Mid-May to mid-June (in Arctic regions nests in June). Nest is a hollow in the ground which is lined with dry leaves, grass and other pieces of vegetation; built near water. Eggs: normally four, ranging in colour from pale grey to warm cream, but also yellow-brown with red-brown or chestnut spots and streaks. Incubated probably by both sexes. The young leave the nest shortly after hatching.

FOOD Crustaceans, molluscs and various insects.

DISTRIBUTION AND MOVEMENTS North America. Winters in South America. Accidental in Britain—a handful each year—and in the Netherlands.

French: PETIT CHEVALIER À PATTES JAUNES
Italian: TOTANO ZAMPEGIALLE MINORE
Spanish: ARCHIBEBE PATIGUALDO CHICO
German: GELBESCHENKEL

J. A. Bailey/Ardea

M. E. J. Gore/Ardea

K. W. Fink

(Left) Stilt Sandpiper
Micropalama himantopus: the
underparts are barred in
summer plumage. (Below)
Grey-rumped Sandpiper *T.
brevipes*. (Facing page, top)
Lesser Yellowlegs
T. flavipes (left) and Greater
Yellowlegs *T. melanoleuca*:
The Greater Yellowlegs has a
louder call than the Lesser and
is substantially larger. (Facing
page, below) Marsh
Sandpiper *T. stagnatilis*

A. D. Trounson & M. C. Clampett/Ardea

Grey-rumped Sandpiper
Tringa brevipes

(Above) Grey-rumped Sandpiper in winter plumage (foreground) and summer plumage

HABITAT By mountain streams, even in or near snow-covered regions, during nesting season. On migration, stops over in plains, near areas flooded by great rivers. Prefers to winter on inland waters.

IDENTIFICATION Length: 25 cm. Uniform grey-brown above, with barred underparts in summer plumage. Easily confused with its North American counterpart the Wandering Tattler *Tringa incana*, of which it is sometimes considered a sub-species. Lower belly and under-tail coverts white. In autumn, identification becomes difficult, but the upper parts appear generally less grey and the light eyebrow-stripe may be less marked than in summer plumage.

CALL An irregular screech which varies in intensity.

REPRODUCTION Little is known of this species; its eggs have not yet been described. It is known that the chicks moult and take on juvenile plumage about the end of July.

FOOD During the nesting season, the bird's sole food appears to consist of the larvae of certain flies.

DISTRIBUTION AND MOVEMENTS Nests on eastern Siberian mountains, from Taimyr peninsula to Tunguska river, Lake Baikal and Anadyr mountains. Accidental in Europe.

French: CHEVALIER À CROUPION GRIS
Italian: PIRO-PIRO DORSOGRIGIO
German: GRAUBÜRZELWASSER-LAÜFER

J. B. & S. Bottomley/Ardea

(Above) Wood Sandpiper
Tringa glareola: this individual
is occupying a Redwing's nest
although Wood Sandpipers
also nest in depressions on the
ground. (Left) In winter the
Wood Sandpiper frequents
fresh-water margins

G. Hakansson

(Bottom) Green Sandpiper in summer plumage and (below) a detail of the tail. (Right) Breeding areas (yellow), wintering areas (magenta) and areas where the Green Sandpiper may be seen on passage (pink)

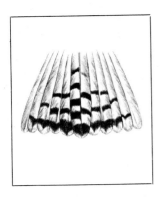

Green Sandpiper
Tringa ochropus

HABITAT Breeds in wooded or marshy country near pools, rivers and lakes. Outside the breeding season lives on lakesides, water meadows, marshes and by rivers. Is only occasionally found on estuaries.

IDENTIFICATION Length: 23 cm. Larger and darker above than Common and Wood Sandpipers. In flight recognisable by dark upper parts contrasting sharply with white rump, tail and belly although the Wood Sandpiper has similar pattern. Underwing black. Neck and breast brownish-grey. No wing bar; tail has a dark bar near the tip. In summer plumage the Green Sandpiper has cream-coloured patches on upper parts, which become very faint in winter. Legs greenish. See also page 124.

CALL Emits a 'tlooitt-ooitt-ooitt' on taking flight, also has a musical song.

REPRODUCTION Mid-April to July (May in Sweden, June in central Europe, July in Siberia). Generally uses an abandoned nest of other species, but sometimes heaps up pine-needles among tree-branches to form a nest. Eggs: normally four, greenish or olive-cream, with a few brown spots and grey tinges. Incubation is carried out mainly by female for about twenty-two days. Young are first reared by both parents then by the male alone.

FOOD Insects and their larvae. Also worms, crustaceans, spiders and molluscs: sometimes eats berries.

DISTRIBUTION AND MOVEMENTS Palearctic. Breeds in northern and central Europe east across Asia. Winters mainly in the Mediterranean area south to tropical Africa and also in southeast Asia. Commonly encountered singly or in small parties on passage in Britain. Has bred in Scotland.

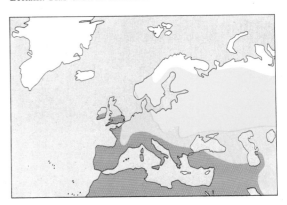

French: CHEVALIER CULBLANC
Italian: PIRO-PIRO CULBIANCO
Spanish: ANDARRÍOS GRANDE
German: WALDWASSERLÄUFER

Wood Sandpiper
Tringa glareola

French: CHEVALIER SYLVAIN
Italian: PIRO-PIRO BOSCHERECCIO
Spanish: ANDARRÍOS BASTARDO
German: BRUCHWASSERLÄUFER

HABITAT Nests in woodland and scrub and in marshy areas. Also nests on tundra. Winters mainly on freshwater margins.

IDENTIFICATION Length: 20 cm. In summer plumage the dark brown upper parts are thickly speckled with white. Neck, head and breast have narrow white markings: broad eye stripe. Distinguished in flight by its white rump, and grey-white areas under the wings. No wing bar. In winter the white speckles become less distinct, giving it an appearance closer to the Green Sandpiper, though the latter is larger and has a more strongly contrasting dark and light appearance. Long yellow-green legs which project beyond the tail in flight distinguish it from the Common and Green Sandpipers.
  Excitable and noisy; flies over the water in flocks, emitting shrill cries. Behaviour is otherwise similar to the Green Sandpiper's. See also page 124.

CALL A high-pitched 'wit-wit-wit' in flight. Also a shrill alarm note 'chip-chip'. Song: a musical 'tleea-tleea-tleea' which resembles the Redshank's.

REPRODUCTION May to July. Nests in a hollow in the ground lined with leaves and grass. Eggs: four, olive-brown or buff, with many spots. Both sexes incubate the eggs. Young are reared initially by both parents, then by the male alone as the female soon abandons the brood.

FOOD Worms, insects (especially flies), spiders, molluscs, small fish and plant matter.

DISTRIBUTION AND MOVEMENTS Northern Europe, Asia. Winters in the Mediterranean region, Africa, southern Asia and Australia. In Britain is a rare breeder in the extreme north and is also a regular passage migrant.

(Above) Wood Sandpiper in summer plumage and (below) a detail of the tail: the more strongly barred tail distinguishes it from the Green Sandpiper. (Left) Breeding areas (yellow), wintering areas (magenta) and areas where the Wood Sandpiper may be seen on passage (pink)

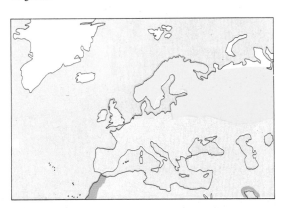

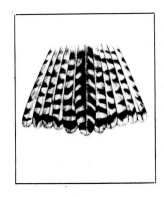

French: CHEVALIER SOLITAIRE
Italian: PIRO-PIRO SOLITARIO
Spanish: ANDARRÍOS SOLITARIO
German: EINSAMER
WASSERLÄUFER

Solitary Sandpiper
Tringa solitaria

(Above) Solitary Sandpiper in summer plumage. (Right) Detail of half of the Solitary Sandpiper's tail: it appears dark in the centre whereas the barring on the sides is lighter

HABITAT Nests in mainly coniferous forests and on marshland. At other times lives near water in open or wooded country.

IDENTIFICATION Length: 19 cm. Very similar to Green Sandpiper but distinguished by lack of white on the rump. The broad tail appears white at the sides with a dark centre. Legs olive-coloured, rarely yellow. Behaviour and habits as the Green Sandpiper. During courtship, takes flight slowly with the tail outspread; moves wings rapidly, uttering a variety of cries; then alights again. See also page 124.

CALL Similar to the Common Sandpiper's but higher and less varied: a 'peet-weet' or 'peet-wit-wit' in flight.

REPRODUCTION May and June. Generally makes use of abandoned nests of birds of other species. Eggs: normally four, ranging from pale green to greeny-blue or cream in background, with chestnut and violet spots. Other information regarding incubation is not available.

FOOD Insects and their larvae; small molluscs, worms and small crustaceans.

DISTRIBUTION AND MOVEMENTS Breeds in North America and winters in Central and South America. Accidental in Britain, Ireland, Iceland, Belgium, France and Germany.

Common Sandpiper
Tringa hypoleucos

French: CHEVALIER GUIGNETTE
Italian: PIRO-PIRO PICCOLO
Spanish: ANDARRÍOS CHICO
German: FLUSSUFERLÄUFER

HABITAT Breeds by the shores of freshwater lakes and streams and also in sheltered inlets by the sea. In winter is found mainly by fresh water.

IDENTIFICATION Length: 20 cm. A small grey-brown wader about the size of a Starling. Underparts, sides of the rump and tail white. Conspicuous white wing-bar. Light buff-grey area on sides of the neck. Best distinguished from other waders, such as the similar winter Dunlin, by characteristic call and flight: generally flys low over the water alternately flicking its wings and briefly gliding, and as it flies it emits a shrill 'twee-wee-wee'. Also has a circular display flight. Tends to perch on low objects, bobbing its head. Like many other birds the Common Sandpiper will lure intruders away from its nest and eggs by trailing a 'broken' wing. See also page 124.

CALL A high-pitched 'twee-wee-wee' emitted in flight and a trilling song heard during courtship.

REPRODUCTION Nest is a depression in the ground lined with grass and leaves, often close to water. Eggs: generally lays four eggs, buff or sometimes grey with red-brown patches. Both parents incubate the eggs for about twenty-two days. The chicks are tended by both parents, and leave the nest within a few hours and fly in approximately four weeks after hatching.

FOOD Mainly insects. Also snails, worms and some vegetable matter.

DISTRIBUTION AND MOVEMENTS Palearctic: breeds from Britain, Iberia and Scandinavia east across Asia and north to the Arctic Circle. Winters mainly from the Mediterranean south to South Africa, India, southeast Asia and Australia. In Britain and Ireland is a widespread breeder, resident from April to August. Also occurs in Britain as a passage and rare winter visitor.

(Above left) Common Sandpiper in summer plumage and (above) a detail of its tail. (Below) Breeding areas (yellow), wintering areas (magenta), areas where the Common Sandpiper may be seen on passage (pink)

(Above) Black-tailed Godwit *Limosa limosa* in flight: the conspicuous white wing-bar is a diagnostic feature. (Right) Black-tailed Godwit on the nest

T. Porsne

(Left) Curlew *Numenius arquata* with chick. (Below) Long-billed Curlew *N. americanus*. The long decurved bills of the curlews makes them easily distinguishable

R. Kinne/Bruce Coleman

French: CHEVALIER GRIVELÉ
Italian: PIRO-PIRO MACCHIATO
Spanish: ANDARRÍOS MACULADO
German: AMERIKANISCHER
          UFERLÄUFER

Spotted Sandpiper
Tringa macularia

HABITAT Nests in habitat similar to the Common Sandpiper's but is sometimes found in areas far from water such as farmland. Winters in swamp areas, by lagoons or on the banks of rivers and streams. Occasionally winters on sandy beaches.

IDENTIFICATION Length: 19 cm. Very similar to Common Sandpiper, from which it is distinguished in summer plumage by the black spots on its underparts, and the yellow bill with dark tip. In winter plumage almost identical to Common Sandpiper: some authorities regard it as a sub-species of the Common Sandpiper.

Behaviour is similar to Common Sandpiper's. Perches on rocks, stone walls, occasionally trees and electric cables. See also page 124.

CALL Call resembles the Common Sandpiper's. Song: a repeated 'weet-weet-weet'.

REPRODUCTION Mid-May to June. Nest is a hollow in the ground, lined with grass and moss. Eggs: four (occasionally three or five), pale olive with brown spots. Eggs are incubated mainly by the male, for about twenty-one days; incubation begins when laying is complete. The young leave the nest shortly after hatching and are reared by the male.

FOOD Chiefly insects; also worms and molluscs.

DISTRIBUTION AND MOVEMENTS Breeds in North America. Winters in southern North America, Central and South America. Accidental in Britain, Ireland, Belgium, Germany and Switzerland, but easily overlooked in winter plumage.

(Right) Spotted Sandpiper in summer plumage

Terek Sandpiper
Tringa cinereus

HABITAT Nests mainly in marshy areas and in forest and scrub by water. In winter found by fresh and salt water.

IDENTIFICATION Length: 22 cm. Appears uniformly grey on upper parts although is marked with black streaks. Underparts white. Distinctive features are the long slender upturned bill and yellow legs. In winter the upper parts, rump and tail are pale grey. Underparts white, sides of the head, neck and breast pale with dark stripes. Secondaries and inner primaries have a broad white tip; the stripes are more apparent in summer. Two black stripes form a rough 'V' on the back. In flight resembles a small Redshank, but the bill, less white on the wings and rump, shorter yellow legs and stripes on the back distinguish it from the Redshank.

Lives in small groups. During courtship flies obliquely upwards to a considerable height and then descends, holding its wings motionless. See also page 124.

CALL Rather noisy, especially during the breeding season. Emits a trilling note 'du-du-du-du', an alarm note and a varied and musical song.

REPRODUCTION End of May and June. Nest is a depression in the ground near water. Eggs: four, green-brown with numerous dark streaks and spots. The eggs are incubated probably only by the male.

FOOD Mainly water-insects.

DISTRIBUTION AND MOVEMENTS Breeds in eastern Europe and Asia east to the Anadyr and Amur rivers. Passage and winter visitor to southeast Europe, the Middle East, southeast Asia and southern Africa. Accidental in Britain, France, Spain and Italy.

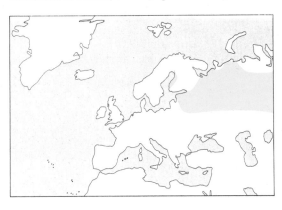

French: BARGETTE DE TÉREK
Italian: PIRO-PIRO TEREK
Spanish: ANDARRÍOS DEL TEREK
German: TEREK-WASSERLÄUFER

(Below) Terek Sandpiper in summer plumage (foreground) and winter plumage. (Above) Breeding areas (yellow) of the Terek Sandpiper. (Overleaf) Common Sandpiper *Tringa hypoleucos* on the nest

French : BARGE À QUEUE NOIRE
Italian : PITTIMA REALE
Spanish : AGUJA COLINEGRA
German : UFERSCHNEPFE

(Bottom) Black-tailed Godwit in summer plumage (foreground) and winter plumage. (Below) A detail of the tail. (Right) Breeding areas (yellow), wintering areas (magenta) and areas where the Black-tailed Godwit may be seen all year round (orange) and on passage (pink)

Black-tailed Godwit
Limosa limosa

HABITAT During the nesting season frequents marshy or very damp terrain. Less common on heathland and sand-dunes. Outside the nesting season is found on beaches, muddy coasts, estuaries, deltas and salt-water marshes.

IDENTIFICATION Length: 40 cm. In flight, distinguished from Bar-tailed Godwit by the broad white wing-bar, the long legs which extend beyond the end of the tail, the dark (rather than white) rump and white tail; the tail has a broad black band at the tip. The bill is also straighter and longer. Winter plumage: upper parts brown-grey, darker and more uniform than Bar-tailed Godwit; underparts washed with buff, not white as Bar-tailed. Summer plumage: chestnut colour which is darker than Bar-tailed's confined to upper parts of breast: broad dark stripes on the breast. Underside of the breast and the flanks are white with broad black bars and irregular markings. Female is darker in colour than male. Both sexes have black-tinged pink bill; legs blackish-green. Young resemble adults in winter, with neck and breast tinged with tawny colour. In flight the conspicuous white wing-bar is a diagnostic feature.

Feeds in the water, wading with the water up to its abdomen, and often immersing its whole head. See also page 118.

CALL In flight: a loud 'weeka-weeka-weeka'. During feeding, sometimes calls 'keek' or 'keeoo'.

REPRODUCTION April and throughout May. Eggs: generally four, often slightly pointed, dull or only slightly shiny. Eggs are a greenish-blue or olive or grey colour with few spots and are incubated by both partners for twenty-four days. Young reared by both parents.

FOOD During nesting: insects, larvae, worms, fish, tadpoles and molluscs. On migration and in winter: crustaceans, marine molluscs and plant matter.

DISTRIBUTION AND MOVEMENTS Palearctic: breeds in Iceland, Britain, Ireland and the Netherlands east across Eurasia. Winters from the British Isles and the Mediterranean area south to tropical Africa and in southeast Asia and Australia. In Britain has returned to breed in East Anglia after an absence of many years. Is also a spring and autumn migrant in Britain.

SUB-SPECIES *L.l. limosa:* North-central Europe. *L.l. islandica* (darker red in summer plumage): Iceland. Another sub-species is present in Asia.

Bar-tailed Godwit

Limosa lapponica

French: BARGE ROUSSE
Italian: PITTIMA MINORE
Spanish: AGUJA COLIPINTA
German: PFUHSLCHNEPFE

HABITAT Breeds on marshy parts of tundra and ponds and marshy country on edge of conifer forests. Outside the nesting season is found on muddy or sandy beaches on coast or estuary: seldom occurs inland.

IDENTIFICATION Length: 37 cm. Like the Black-tailed Godwit it is a fairly large wader, and both are distinguished from the curlews by their straighter, slightly upturned bills and rufous summer plumage. Larger than Redshank and smaller than Curlew. Distinguished from Black-tailed Godwit by lack of white wing-bar, strongly barred tail, more striped plumage and shorter legs. In winter plumage, upper parts resemble the Curlew's, ranging from grey to grey-brown with dark stripes. The wings are darker, with black-brown primaries and pronounced stripes on back. Tail darker, barred with brown, grey and off-white; rump dull white, underparts whiter, with faint stripes on breast. In summer plumage male's head, neck, back and under-parts are rufous; dark stripes on head and back. Female is duller in colour and browner. Juveniles have a tawny breast with varying amounts of spots and stripes. Bill black with pink base; legs grey.

Flight: rapid and direct with neck drawn back. Flocks fly in irregular formation, sometimes in a 'V' although sometimes in more compact formation. Bar-tailed God-wits occasionally perform aerobatics like Knot and Dunlin. Feed in groups in shallow water on beaches left uncovered by the tide. See also page 118.

CALL Outside the nesting season is rather silent. Call in flight: a low-pitched 'kirrick', and a more strident alarm-note: 'krick'.

REPRODUCTION May and June. Nests in marshy areas, occasionally on dry ground near or beyond the

tree-line. Eggs: usually four, elongated, sometimes pointed; shinier than Black-tailed Godwit's. Eggs are greenish in colour with darker spots and streaks. They are incubated by both sexes for about three weeks. The young are reared by both parents.

FOOD During the nesting season eats mainly water-insects, larvae and worms. On migration and in winter feeds on crustaceans, small molluscs, small fish and insects.

DISTRIBUTION AND MOVEMENTS Breeds from Scandinavia east across the USSR to Alaska. Winters in Britain south to South Africa, southeast Asia and Australia. In Britain occurs as a passage and winter visitor to the coasts of most maritime counties. Also occurs on most coasts of Ireland.

SUB-SPECIES *L.l. lapponica:* Scandinavia and northern USSR. *L.l. baueri* (larger and has darker rump): eastern Siberia and Alaska.

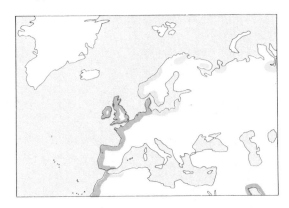

(Top) Bar-tailed Godwit in summer plumage (foreground) and winter plumage. (Above) A detail of half of the Bar-tailed Godwit's tail: the strongly barred rather than banded tail distinguishes it from the Black-tailed Godwit. (Left) Breeding areas (yellow), wintering areas (magenta) and areas where the Bar-tailed Godwit may be seen on passage (pink)

French: COURLIS CENDRÉ
Italian: CHIURLO
Spanish: ZARAPITO REAL
German: GROSSER BRACHVOGEL

Curlew
Numenius arquata

(Above) Curlew in summer plumage with chick. (Right) Breeding areas (yellow), wintering areas (magenta), and areas where the Curlew may be seen all year round (orange) and on passage (pink)

HABITAT During nesting season found on moorland, marshy areas, water-meadows, sand-dunes and other open damp country. Winters mainly on muddy shores, estuaries, also rocky coasts.

IDENTIFICATION Length: 57 cm. The largest and one of the most common white-rumped waders in Britain. Characteristic features are the long, strongly decurved bill and striped brown plumage. Distinguished from Whimbrel by its larger size, longer bill, and absence of well-marked stripes on crown. Dark, red-tinged bill; head, neck and breast pale brown, with streaks of dark chestnut and transverse markings on flanks; back more strongly striped; white rump; legs grey-green. Winter plumage paler than summer, but otherwise very similar. Juveniles resemble adults, with warmer brown on upper parts, tawnier underparts and shorter bill. Generally shy and timid. Flight: rapid, with slow wingbeat, sometimes at a considerable height. Legs project beyond the tail in flight. Feeds by probing deeply into mud and sand. Swims well. Gregarious, and sometimes associates with other species on the beach. See also page 126.

CALL Variety of calls, including a song which begins with a succession of liquid low notes, in crescendo, then a long gurgling scream. Also a shrill, high-pitched 'cor-lee' from which its English name is derived, and a rarely heard Whimbrel-like titter.

REPRODUCTION April–May. Eggs: four or five, buff, olive or brown with darker spots. Both sexes incubate the eggs for twenty-nine or thirty days. The young leave the nest a few hours after hatching.

FOOD Molluscs, crustaceans, fish, worms and sometimes plant matter. Inland: insects, larvae, molluscs, berries, seeds and occasionally grain.

DISTRIBUTION AND MOVEMENTS Central and northern Europe, central and northern Asia. Winters in Mediterranean area, Africa, and on western and south-western European coastlines. Also winters on North Sea and exceptionally on southern Baltic coasts. Common shorebird in Britain and breeds in most upland areas.

SUB-SPECIES *N.a. arquata*: central and northern Europe. *N.a. orientalis* (paler): USSR.

94

Slender-billed Curlew
Numenius tenuirostris

HABITAT Breeds on marshland and also on marshy country near coniferous forests. At all times prefers damp country.

IDENTIFICATION Length: 39 cm. Similar to Whimbrel in size; bill also similar but more slender. Differs from Whimbrel in lack of dark stripes on head. Smaller and paler than Curlew. Underparts white with heart-shaped spots; rump also white. Well-marked narrow dark bars on the tail stand out against white background. Underparts more spotted in winter. Juveniles have warm tawny upper parts, and lack adult's heart-shaped spots on flanks. Bill brown with flesh-coloured base; legs lavender grey. See also page 126.

CALL Similar to Curlew's but more high-pitched and shorter: 'crruee'. Also an alarm note 'kew-ee'.

REPRODUCTION May-June. Nest is a hollow in marshy ground, lined with grass. Generally four eggs are laid: olive-grey or brown, with brown or ash-grey spots. The female alone incubates the eggs.

FOOD Insects, worms and small molluscs.

DISTRIBUTION AND MOVEMENTS Southwest Siberia. Passage visitor to southeast Europe and southwest Asia. Winters in Mediterranean area and in Morocco. Accidental in western Europe.

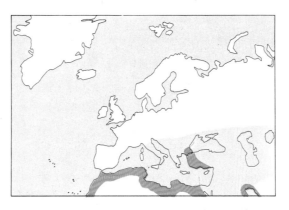

(Below) Slender-billed Curlew in summer plumage. The dark heart-shaped spots of the feathers of the underparts (bottom) are a distinguishing feature. (Left) Wintering areas (magenta) and areas where the Slender-billed Curlew may be seen on passage (pink)

French: COURLIS À BEC GRÊLE
Italian: CHIURLOTTELLO
Spanish: ZARAPITO FINO
German: DÜNNSCHNABEL-
BRACHVOGEL

(Right) Black-tailed Godwit
L. limosa. (Facing page)
Curlew *N. arquata* with young

Ralf Richter/Ardea

French: COURLIS CORLIEU
Italian: CHIURLO PICCOLO
Spanish: ZARAPITO TRINADOR
German: REGENBRACHVOGEL

Whimbrel
Numenius phaeopus

HABITAT Breeds on heathland, moors and peat-bogs. At other times is found in similar habitats to the Curlew, especially on coasts and even in rocky areas.

IDENTIFICATION Length: 39 cm. Resembles the Curlew but may be distinguished by its voice, smaller size, shorter bill, and bold brown and white stripes on crown. Wingbeats are quicker than the Curlew's. Upper parts are darker than the Curlew's, underparts light and tinged with red-brown, and with fine dark streaks. Legs are grey-green. Female is slightly larger than the male and upper parts of the juvenile are darker than the adult's.

In behaviour similar to the Curlew but less shy and easier to approach. In courtship flight performs acrobatics, tumbling and descending in circles. See also page 126.

CALL A rippling, tittering cry which is unlike any of the Curlew's normal calls. Song is similar to the Curlew's. Also has an alarm note 'gook-gook'.

REPRODUCTION Late May and June. Nest is a scrape in heather or rough grass on moorland. Eggs: four or five, pale olive to brown or sometimes pale green-blue with heavy dark spots. Both sexes incubate the eggs for twenty-four days. The chicks leave the nest a few hours after hatching and fly after five or six weeks.

FOOD Insects and their larvae, molluscs, crustaceans and plant matter.

DISTRIBUTION AND MOVEMENTS Breed in Iceland and northern Europe east to northeast Siberia. Also breeds in northern North America. Passage visitor to European and west Asian coasts. Winters in northwest Africa, eastern and southern Africa and south Asia. In Britain breeds in northernmost Scotland and is a regular passage migrant further south. A few winter in western Britain and Ireland.

SUB-SPECIES Sub-species are present in North America and Asia.

(Right) Breeding areas (yellow), wintering areas (magenta) and areas where the Whimbrel may be seen on passage (pink)

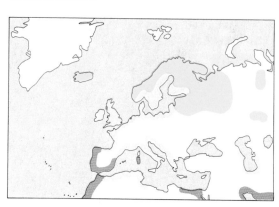

Eskimo Curlew
Numenius borealis

French: COURLIS ESQUIMAU
Italian: CHIURLO ESQUIMESE OR BOREALE
Spanish: ZARAPITO ESQUIMAL
German: ESKIMO-BRACHVOGEL

HABITAT During nesting season frequents damp terrain. On migration, can be found by water, also in fields and pastures, ploughed land and sand-dunes.

IDENTIFICATION Length: 36 cm. Similar to Whimbrel but smaller: close to the Lapwing in size. Bill is shorter and the back is darker. Distinguishing feature is the uniformly dark primaries, without bars. Pale central stripe on crown; upper parts striped brown; upper side of tail olive-brown; underparts pale, almost white, with tawny belly. Legs bluish-grey. See also page 126.

CALL Harsh notes in flight: 'tr-tr-tr'. Also a variety of whistles and musical notes.

REPRODUCTION June. Nests on the ground in treeless areas. Eggs: four, olive-brown to tawny, with dark patches and spots. No information is available on length of incubation.

FOOD In summer feeds on berries and seeds; at other times eats larvae, insects and molluscs.

DISTRIBUTION AND MOVEMENTS North America: breeds very rarely in the northern Mackenzie in Canada. Accidental in Britain and Iceland although not for many years. Once thought to be extinct, the Eskimo Curlew has been noted on passage on the Texas Gulf coast in recent years. However it is unlikely that it will appear again in Europe.

Little Whimbrel
Numenius minutus

French: COURLIS PYGMEE
Italian: CHIURLO MINIMO
German: ZWERGBRACHVOGEL

HABITAT Breeds in sparse woodland in mountainous areas and alpine tundra. Outside the breeding season found in steppe, plains and river valleys with marshy areas.

IDENTIFICATION Length: 28 cms. Overall body shape similar to other curlews, but smaller with a short and straighter bill. Very similar to the Eskimo Curlew, and considered by some to belong to the same species. Crown dark brown, divided by a white streak in the centre; pale eye stripe as in the Whimbrel. Lower part of the back and rump dark with whitish edges to the feathers. Axillaries pale ochre (not russet), with narrow dark bars.

CALL Never carefully studied or described by reliable observers: probably similar to that of the Eskimo Curlew.

REPRODUCTION Little is known of this bird's habits or reproductive cycle because of its rarity and because it breeds in such inaccessible territory.

DISTRIBUTION AND MOVEMENTS Northeastern Siberia; more precisely, in the catchment-basins of the Monero and Katanga rivers, the Verkhoyansk massif and perhaps in the northern Stanovoy mountains.

(Above) Upland Sandpiper
Bartramia longicauda
and (right) Whimbrel
N. phaeopus

French: BARTRAMIE À LONGUE
          QUEUE
Italian: PIRO-PIRO CODALUNGA
Spanish: CORRELIMOS DE
          BARTRAM
German: BARTRAMS UFERLÄUFER

Upland Sandpiper
Bartramia longicauda

(Preceding page) Woodcock
Scolopax rusticola: its subdued
colouring resembles that of
dead leaves

HABITAT At all seasons frequents broad open fields, grassland, damp terrain with luxuriant vegetation and pastures.

IDENTIFICATION Length: 26 cm. Plumage brown, bill and legs rather short. Slender neck, long rufous tail give it a characteristic shape. Upper parts brown, striped, spotted and barred; brown feathers have a tawny edge; axillaries and undertail strongly barred. Centre of tail dark ash-grey, sides paler; primaries very dark; breast has black spots and arrow-like markings; flanks barred. Juveniles lack bars on scapulars, and their primaries have broader tawny edges. Bill black; legs yellowish. Similar in habits to the plovers. Often perches on posts. See also page 116.

CALL During the nesting season emits a delicate trilling whistle. Also a rapid, emphatic alarm-note: 'quip-ip-ip-ip'.

REPRODUCTION End of April to early May. Nests in open grassland or in fields in a depression in the ground. Eggs: four or five, oval, slightly translucent, cream or tawny, with a pinkish tinge, or sometimes greenish-white with ash-grey patches and speckles. Both parents incubate the eggs for about thirty days and both parents rear the young.

FOOD Insects, larvae, molluscs and seeds.

DISTRIBUTION AND MOVEMENTS North America. Winters in southern South America. Accidental in Britain, Ireland, the Netherlands, Denmark, Germany and Italy.

Woodcock
Scolopax rusticola

HABITAT Mainly open woodland with dense, damp undergrowth, heathland and swampy areas. On passage seen in more open country.

IDENTIFICATION Length: 34 cm. A medium-sized plump bird, with rounded wings and a long straight bill. Its subdued colouring resembles that of dead leaves, which provide it with excellent cover: thus it is difficult to observe. When taking wing from the undergrowth, it makes no cry, but its wings make a distinctive sound like the rustling of paper. More stumpy in shape than the Common Snipe, larger and with a thicker bill. Upper parts marbled brown, tawny and black; underparts finely barred with dark brown. Transverse bars on crown and neck. Eyes brown-black, rather large, placed well back on the round head. Bill dark flesh-colour, browner near the tip. Juveniles resemble adults.
   Flight varies: strong and rapid, or light and undulating if disturbed; bill held downward. Neck is retracted, even when on the ground. Characteristic territorial

flight known as 'roding' in which the male flies a circuit at dusk and dawn. At this time the flight is owl-like and he flies with interrupted wing-beats, uttering two distinct calls. Rarely alights on trees. Active at dusk. Not gregarious: usually alone except in nesting season. Behaves independently even when other Woodcock are in the vicinity. A characteristic feature is the way the young are carried between a parent's legs in order to remove them from danger or take them to feed. See also page 128.

CALL Two notes are heard during the slow nuptial flight or roding over the trees at dawn or dusk: a high-pitched 'tsiwick' uttered with the bill open, and a low-pitched grating note emitted with the bill closed.

REPRODUCTION Mid-March to May also June and occasionally July. Nests in a depression in the ground in wooded areas, usually at the foot of a tree. Eggs: generally four, very shiny, varying in colour from grey-white to light brown, speckled with chestnut-brown. Very occasionally the eggs are white with no markings. Incubation is carried out only by the female for twenty or twenty-one days. Female alone cares for the young.

FOOD Mainly earthworms, also insects and grubs, molluscs, crustaceans, seeds and grasses.

DISTRIBUTION AND MOVEMENTS Breeds in Britain and western Europe east across Eurasia to Japan. Also breeds in the Canaries and Corsica. Migrant and sedentary: winters mainly in the Mediterranean region and in southern Asia. In Britain and Ireland is a fairly numerous resident breeder and it also occurs as a winter and passage visitor.

French: BÉCASSE DES BOIS
Italian: BECCACCIA
Spanish: CHOCHA PERDIZ
German: WALDSCHNEPFE

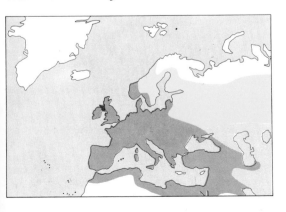

(Left) Breeding areas (yellow), wintering areas (magenta), areas where the Woodcock may be seen all year round (orange) and on passage (pink)

103

French: BÉCASSINE DES MARAIS
Italian: BECCACCINO
Spanish: AGACHADIZA COMÚN
German: BEKASSINE

Common Snipe
Gallinago gallinago

HABITAT Breeds in marshes, damp meadows, wet moors and heaths. Winters by freshwater margins. Occasionally found by estuaries.

IDENTIFICATION Length: 26 cm. Distinguished by its very long, straight bill, and markedly striped dark plumage. Crown black with tawny central stripe; sides of head brown, with tawny stripes above and below the eye; neck and breast tawny with dark brown markings; flanks cream with more or less distinct dark bars. Upper parts boldly spotted and striped with black, brown, russet and tawny. Tail has irregular black and bronze bars, and some white at the sides. Legs pale greenish. Juveniles have much narrower pale stripes along the back.

May be seen taking wing from the ground, uttering a raucous call and zig-zagging low at great speed before rising into the air, when it flies up to a great height. Flies quickly with rapid wingbeats. Will dive at a very steep

angle (45°). Active at dusk. Walks over ground holding body almost horizontal, with neck drawn back and bill inclined downward. See also page 128.

CALL When flushed, utters a raucous guttural 'shap', once or several times in rapid succession. Sometimes emits a cheerful-sounding 'tchoo-ee-tchoo-ee'. In springtime, also when alarmed: 'chip-per-chip-per' (a rapid, insistent, rhythmical note). During territorial flight, the outer tail-feathers are spread wide and produce a vibrating sound like a rapidly repeated 'hu-hu-hu'.

REPRODUCTION Very occasionally in March; usually from April onwards. Eggs: four, generally shiny, background colour ranging from olive-grey to olive-brown, or pale blue, blue-grey, tawny-yellow; generally with dark or black spots. Female incubates the eggs for twenty days. The young leave the nest as soon as they are dry, and are reared by both male and female.

FOOD Worms, insects, larvae, molluscs and crustaceans. Also plant matter.

DISTRIBUTION AND MOVEMENTS Breeds in west, central and northern Europe, central and northern Asia and North America. Winters in Africa and in eastern and southern Europe. In Britain and Ireland is a resident breeder although some birds winter south of the English Channel. Also occurs as a passage and winter visitor.

SUB-SPECIES *Gallinago gallinago gallinago:* Europe. except Iceland and Faeroes. *G.g. faeroensis:* Iceland and Faeroes. The sub-species *G.g. delicata* inhabits North America and is accidental in Scotland.

(Right) Breeding area (yellow), wintering areas (magenta), areas where the Common Snipe may be seen all year round (orange) and on passage (pink)

Great Snipe
Gallinago media

HABITAT During the nesting season frequents marshes and grassy swampland, water-meadows or dense undergrowth. In winter frequents drier areas.

IDENTIFICATION Length: 28 cm. Distinguished from Common Snipe by larger size, darker wings, large areas of white at sides of tail, less marked parallel bands on crown, darker back and scapulars, more strongly barred sides. The tawny tail has more conspicuous white markings. Bill dark brown, pale yellow at base, legs grey or yellowish. The bill is somewhat shorter than the Snipe's, and the flight is slower. In flight appears darker and heavier than the Common Snipe. See also page 128.

CALL Emits collective 'hihi-orr' at display ground.

REPRODUCTION From early May onward in central Europe. Further north in June and July. Eggs: four, ranging from grey to tawny red. Female alone incubates for twenty-two to twenty-four days.

FOOD Feeds on earthworms, molluscs, insects and grubs.

DISTRIBUTION AND MOVEMENTS Northern Europe east across Asia. Winters in eastern and southern Africa. Is a passage-migrant through southeast Europe: rare further west. However has occurred irregularly in Britain and Ireland, recorded mainly in the autumn and winter.

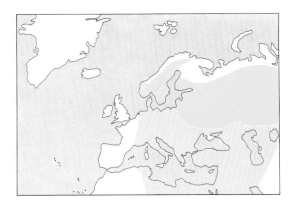

(Left) Breeding areas (yellow) and areas where the Great Snipe may be seen on passage (pink)

French: BECASSINE DOUBLE
Italian: CROCCOLONE
Spanish: AGACHADIZA REAL
German: DOPPELSCHNEPFE

French: BÉCASSINE DES FORÊTS
Italian: BECCACCINO DI SWINHOE
German: WALDBEKASSINE

(Left) Swinhoe's Snipe

Swinhoe's Snipe
Gallinago megala

HABITAT Wet grassland, at the edges of forests and marshy areas.

IDENTIFICATION Length: 27 cm. Very similar to the Common Snipe and to the Pin-tailed Snipe, but somewhat larger. Coloration of tail feathers is mainly dark brown, with ochre or whitish tips. Juveniles have tawny margins to scapulars. There is a complex aerial courtship display, accompanied by swooping dives during which the air passing between the modified tail-feathers produces a whistling sound. See also page 128.

CALL Rather silent except in the mating season, when it utters a 'chiping' note similar to that of the Common Snipe.

REPRODUCTION Nest is a hollow in the ground; generally four eggs (occasionally anything from two to five) are laid. Incubation lasts probably the same length of time as in the Common Snipe but reliable data is lacking. It appears that incubation varies in length depending on the altitude at which the birds breed. The breeding season begins after the first week in May and continues into June, depending on location.

FOOD Small insects and plant matter in summer.

DISTRIBUTION AND MOVEMENTS Nests in south central Siberian forests. Winters in Indo-China, the Philippines, and northern coastal regions of Australia. Accidental in areas west of the Caspian.

French: BÉCASSINE À QUEUE
          POINTUE
Italian: BECCACCINO STENURO
German: STIFTBEKASSINE

Jack Snipe
Lymnocryptes minimus

HABITAT During the nesting season frequents water-meadows, marshes and pools in northern regions. Nests in grass and wet terrain. Outside the breeding season found in similar country to the Common Snipe.

IDENTIFICATION Length: 19 cm. Resembles Common Snipe, but is distinguished easily by its smaller size, shorter bill, and slow, straight flight. Other distinguishing features are the absence of cream stripe on crown, more metallic colour of plumage, indistinct striped markings on sides (instead of well-marked bars), and absence of white on tail. Legs greenish. See also page 128.

CALL Rather silent, but sometimes makes a sort of dull drumming noise.

REPRODUCTION Beginning of June to August. Nest is a hollow in the ground lined with grass and moss. Eggs: normally four, colour ranging from cream, olive-cream, to olive-brown, with numerous sepia and chestnut spots. Only female appears to incubate the eggs for twenty-four days.

FOOD Worms, molluscs and insects; sometimes plants.

DISTRIBUTION AND MOVEMENTS Northeast Europe and north Asia. Winters in central Europe, northwest and east Africa. Commonly winters in Mediterranean area south to tropical Africa and in western Europe. Eastern populations winter in southern Asia. In Britain and Ireland is a widespread winter and passage visitor, but never in large numbers.

French: BÉCASSINE SOURDE
Italian: FRULLINO
Spanish: AGACHADIZA CHICA
German: ZWERGSCHNEPFE

Pin-tailed Snipe
Gallinago stenura

HABITAT Wet tundra with rocks and birch thickets.

IDENTIFICATION Length 27 cm. Distinctive feature is the short, narrow and stiff outer tail-feathers. Coloration similar to that of the Common Snipe, from which it can be distinguished not only by the tail-feathers and the shorter bill, but also by less white on the outer side of the first flight-feather, the white tips to the secondary flight-feathers and the grey or brown colouring of the short tail-feathers. See also page 128.

CALL A harsh 'scape' when flushed.

REPRODUCTION There is little reliable information available on the nest or breeding, but the eggs are dingy olive-green and covered with brown markings.

FOOD Insects and molluscs.

DISTRIBUTION AND MOVEMENTS Northwest and northeast Siberia, Urals, extending southwards perhaps as far as Outer Mongolia. Migrant species, wintering in India and southern Asia.

(Above) Jack Snipe and (left, facing page) Pin-tailed Snipe. (Right) Breeding areas (yellow), wintering areas (magenta) and areas where the Jack Snipe may be seen on passage (pink)

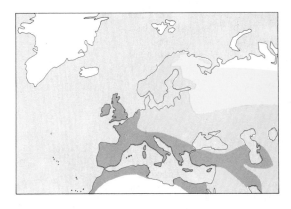

Plovers in flight

1: RINGED PLOVER *(Charadrius hiaticula)* Characteristic features of adults are the pattern of the head (a) and tail (b). Main distinctive feature of juveniles (c) is dark collar and no black on head. At all ages, relatively dark plumage and white wing-bar are distinctive features.

2: KENTISH PLOVER *(Charadrius alexandrinus)* Distinguishable at all ages by dark bill, short tail (a) with distinctive pattern, and less marked pale wing-bar (b). Adults (especially males) further distinguished by pattern of face and by russet head (c).

3: LITTLE RINGED PLOVER *(Charadrius dubius)* This species is distinguished mainly by the absence of a wing-bar (a) and the yellow-green legs (not yellow, as Ringed, nor black, as Kentish). Eye-ring is yellow (b).

4: LESSER SANDPLOVER *(Charadrius mongolus)* The Lesser Sandplover, also known as the Mongolian Plover, is a vagrant to Europe from the east. It has been included here only for comparison purposes as it closely resembles the Greater Sandplover. Much the same size as Ringed Plover. Has a narrow wing-bar outlining the wing coverts near the secondaries, and a more marked bar on the primaries. In nuptial plumage, male is recognisable by his black mask and russet pectoral bar (a); female has tawny orange collar (b). In autumn/winter plumage (c, d) and in juveniles, tawny orange colouring and mask are not present, making it difficult to distinguish from the Greater Sandplover. Pattern of tail (e) is typical, with two indistinct oval patches at the base.

5: GREATER SANDPLOVER *(Charadrius leschenaultii)* Heavy bill is characteristic; also, in male, face markings with black mask and white patch above base of bill (a), lacking in winter plumage (b, c). Tail markings (d) distinguish it from similar Lesser Sandplover.

6: CASPIAN PLOVER *(Charadrius asiaticus)* Bill is shorter and lighter, face white, and there is no wing-bar, merely a white patch on the primaries; these features (a, b) distinguish this species from Greater Sandplover in autumn and winter. Pattern of tail (c) and upper tail also distinctive. In nuptial plumage male is easily recognised by his orange-red pectoral band which has a black band underneath (d).

7: KILLDEER *(Charadrius vociferus)* This transatlantic vagrant is the only plover found in Europe with a double black pectoral band, a conspicuous white wing-bar and orange rump. Tip of tail also orange: white patches at the end of the tail are sometimes visible.

8: DOTTEREL *(Eudromias morinellus)* Easily recognised in nuptial plumage by white eyestripes and chestnut breast. In juvenile and winter plumage has characteristic white eyebrow stripe, dark sub-terminal bar and pale tip on tail, no trace of wing bar, and brown-black plumage on back with pale edges. Crown has dark stripes. When visible, the striking white colour of the first primary flight feather is also a distinguishing feature. Tawny stripes on breast are reminiscent of the underparts of the Lesser Golden Plover.

(Below) Ringed Plover and Dunlin in flight

John Wightman/Ardea

(Above) Spur-winged Plover in flight. Like the Lapwing and the Sociable Plover, when seen from below the black and white pattern of the wing is distinctive

9: LESSER GOLDEN PLOVER *(Pluvialis dominica)* In juvenile and winter plumage (a, b) the two sub-species *P.d. dominica* and *P.d. fulva* are practically indistinguishable. Both differ from Golden Plover in their much less yellow coloration on upper parts; also lack white wing-bar. From below (b, c) the two sub-species differ from Golden Plover in their dark underwing. In summer (c) they have broad black markings on throat and on the breast.

10: GOLDEN PLOVER *(Pluvialis apricaria)* Juvenile (a) and winter plumage (b): yellowish above, with a narrow but distinct white wing-bar; uniform rump. In summer plumage, the black of throat and breast varies in extent depending on sub-species, but is never as extensive as in Lesser Golden or Grey Plover. The white underwing is a characteristic feature at all times.

11: GREY PLOVER *(Pluvialis squatarola)* Winter and juvenile plumage (a, b): upper parts greyer than in preceding species; bill heavier; upper side of tail white, tail bears distinct dark transverse bars. Juveniles slightly yellower than adults. In nuptial plumage (c) the black of underparts is very extensive. Black axillaries which contrast with white underwing are distinctive at all ages.

12: LAPWING *(Vanellus vanellus)* From below (a): black and white wing, pectoral band present in all adult and juvenile plumages, russet undertail. From above (b): upper parts bottle-green, wings black with pale tips, rump white, tail black. The black crest on the head is also a distinctive feature. In display flight wings make a throbbing sound, and the broad rounded wings are characteristic.

13: SOCIABLE PLOVER *(Vanellus gregarius)* Adult, from below (a): white of wing extends to posterior edge; crown is dark. In nuptial plumage has black ventral band with reddish lower belly. Juvenile, from above (b) has characteristic dark crown (black in adult), pale face, and eyebrow stripes joining to form 'V' on nape; the rump is white.

14: SPUR-WINGED PLOVER *(Vanellus spinosus)* From below (a): black-and-white wing has different pattern from those of the two preceding species; white face; underparts black except undertail. From above (b): characteristic markings on head, black with white cheeks; upper side of tail white, tail black, white on wing limited to a central diagonal band. Flies rather slowly.

Sandpipers and allies in flight

J. B. & S. Bottomley/Ardea

(Above) Dunlin and Knot in flight

1: DUNLIN *(Calidris alpina)* Illustrated here in winter plumage as a standard reference for the size of stints and sandpipers. Summer and juvenile plumage are described on page 114.

2: LITTLE STINT *(Calidris minuta)* Nuptial or summer plumage (a): upper parts russet; no white on tail; legs black. Juvenile in autumn (b): wing-bar always present as are the 'V' marks on the back. Winter plumage (c): distinguished by pattern of tail and wing bar.

3: BROAD-BILLED SANDPIPER *(Limicola falcinellus)* Winter plumage (a): white face and eyebrow stripe; dark crown; pale area on wing, pale wing-bar, dark anterior border of wing. In nuptial plumage (not illustrated) appears very dark above, reminiscent of the Jack Snipe. Juvenile and autumn plumage (b); stripes on head, upper parts like Little Stint, pale area on wing contrasting with dark anterior border and short wing-bar.

4: TEMMINCK'S STINT *(Calidris temminckii)* Nuptial plumage (a): dark bars on back edged with tawny yellow. In overall shape, has a longer and much whiter tail than Little Stint. Legs greenish-yellow. Juvenile plumage (b): recognisable by white on tail and characteristic pattern of feathers on upper parts (c). Winter plumage (d): uniformly grey, like Little Stint; distinguished from latter by tail markings.

5: LEAST SANDPIPER *(Calidris minutilla)* Figures (a), (b), (c), show nuptial, juvenile and winter plumage respectively. Note short wing-bar. Generally similar to Little Stint but smaller and less rufous.

6: SEMI-PALMATED SANDPIPER *(Calidris pusillus)* Nuptial plumage (a): black above, with no russet. Juvenile plumage (b): duller above than that of the Western Sandpiper. Winter plumage (c): like Western, hard to distinguish. Bill (d) is shorter than in Western Sandpiper, though individuals vary.

7: WESTERN SANDPIPER *(Calidris mauri)* Nuptial plumage (a): note russet on upper parts. Juvenile plumage (b): russet areas above. Winter plumage (c): grey and white, with no distinctive features. Figure (d) shows bill, which may vary in length.

R. Vaughan/Ardea

(Above) Sanderling in flight

8: DUNLIN *(Calidris alpina)* In summer (a): russet on back; the black patch on the belly appears and then slowly disappears. Juveniles in autumn (b) have bill like adult's. Back heavily marked; very evident wing-bar and strong markings on tail. In winter there are always russet stripes on the breast. Adults, seen from below: in summer plumage (c) the large black patch is visible: in autumn, variable spotted markings (d). Complete winter plumage (illustrated on page 113, figure 1) much greyer all over above; white below. Figure (e) shows flight profile of these small waders.

9: SANDERLING *(Calidris alba)* Transitional plumage preceding nuptial is russet on body and breast (a). Juveniles (b) have shorter and straighter bill than Dunlin, and are paler above. In winter plumage, back is pale grey. Distinctive features: dark carpal patch and forewing, tail markings, pure white underparts, white wing bar (the most distinct of all these small waders).

10: BAIRD'S SANDPIPER *(Calidris bairdii)* In nuptial plumage (a) note tawny-edged dark plumage on back and scapulars; this disappears at the end of the breeding season. Tail (b) has no distinctive pattern; white edges bear dark brown spots. Juveniles in autumn (c) are recognisable by shortish bill, narrow but easily visible white and cream edge of back feathers, and striped breast, the rest of the underparts being white; no wing bar.

11: CURLEW SANDPIPER *(Calidris ferruginea)* Adult in nuptial plumage (a) is russet above and below, with a rather smudged white rump; bill rather long and curved; pale wing-bar. Juveniles in autumn and adults in winter recognisable by shape of bill, white rump, black tail and constant wing bar. Upper parts very grey in winter, but juveniles still show faint pale crescents on back feathers, and a reddish tan colour on the breast.

12: SHARP-TAILED SANDPIPER *(Calidris acuminata)* Similar to the Pectoral Sandpiper, especially from above (a), with back feathers showing clear-cut markings and a bar that is perhaps more marked than in Pectoral. From below (b) easily distinguished from Pectoral by absence of sharp contrast between breast and remainder of underparts, the latter often bearing unmistakable arrow-shaped markings never seen in Pectoral. Under-tail coverts are striped.

13: PECTORAL SANDPIPER *(Calidris melanotos)* From above (a): slightly curved bill; often well-marked pattern on crown; stripes on back and nape of juveniles warm tawny colour outlined in paler shade. Indistinct wing-bar. As in Sharp-tailed Sandpiper, back and rump are dark. From below (b) shows a characteristic pattern on underwing, though this is hard to make out in the wild. Adults and juveniles always show well-marked coloration of breast contrasting with white of remaining underparts—a distinguishing feature from Sharp-tailed.

14: WHITE-RUMPED SANDPIPER *(Calidris fusci-collis)* Adults in nuptial plumage (a) recognisable by dark upper parts, curved white patch on rump and black tail; also short bill. Juveniles (and adults in winter) (b) have eye-brow stripe, indistinct wing-bar, and dark tail with white upper tail.

15: RUFF *(Philomachus pugnax)* Male in nuptial plumage, with multicoloured ruff and ear tufts, is unmistakable. In winter plumage, from above (a), has a strongly marked back, indistinct but visible wing-bar, and—most importantly—a characteristic pattern on the tail which is also present in the female. Female (b) is much smaller, some individuals being barely larger than Buff-breasted Sandpiper. Reeve's head shown in (c). From below (d) male often has sharply outlined breast markings; female slightly less so.

16: BUFF-BREASTED SANDPIPER *(Tryngites subruficollis)* Very similar to a female Ruff, and the two species are easily confused. From above (a) has strongly marked upper parts, but lacks the characteristic tail markings and wing-bar, while the tips of the remiges are slightly darker in autumn and quite black (b) in summer. From below (c) has a black patch at base of primaries, with a characteristic shape (d). Posterior wing edge is dark. Figure (e) shows the head.

17: UPLAND SANDPIPER *(Bartramia longicauda)* Head is small and bill is rather short. From above (a) has dark back, long tail with white and pale orange outer edges. No wing-bar. Other distinguishing marks are the longish rufous tail and the markings at the base

of the wings. From below (b) note barred underwing and flanks.

18: KNOT *(Calidris canutus)* In winter (a) is rather a plump bird, with long wings and no particular distinguishing features; the bill is quite short and heavy; little to note except white wing-bar and rump and remaining predominantly grey plumage. Juveniles (b) have crescent-shaped markings on back feathers which can be seen at close quarters. In summer (c) the area of red is larger, as in Curlew Sandpiper. Figure (d) shows adult in transitional phase.

19: TURNSTONE *(Arenaria interpres)* Juveniles (a) lack the bright coloration of adults (b), but show the same pattern of white. Main distinctive feature is the white patch on the rump with white upper tail; legs are orange. Adult from below is shown in winter (c) and summer plumage (d).

20: PURPLE SANDPIPER *(Calidris maritima)* In winter generally dark grey with yellowish bill and typical sandpiper-like tail markings. Remiges very dark, and wing-bar visible only on inner half of wing. Underparts are shown in figure (b).

(Below) Turnstone and Dunlin in flight: the Turnstone is larger than the Dunlin and the black and white pattern of the plumage is conspicuous

John Wightman/Ardea

(Above) Bar-tailed Godwits: their flight is fast and direct. (Overleaf, page 120) Woodcock in flight at dusk

21: BLACK-TAILED GODWIT *(Limosa limosa)* Distinguishing features from Bar-tailed Godwit are the straighter, longer bill, and legs extending well beyond the tail in flight. In winter (a) coloration is dark, but wing markings do not change (has a broad white wing-bar); nor do tail markings (black with white trailing edge). In summer (b), underwing is white and black, flanks russet with pronounced bars.

22: BAR-TAILED GODWIT *(Limosa lapponica)* From above, in juvenile or winter plumage (a), shows patchy grey markings, with whitish rump and indistinct wing-bar. In summer plumage (b), head, neck and breast are russet. Tail always barred. Flocks of Bar-tailed Godwit sometimes perform aerobatics.

23: STILT SANDPIPER *(Micropalama himantopus)* In winter plumage, seen from above, has a white eye-stripe, white rump and indistinct wing-bar; from below (b), underparts are pale and striped. In nuptial plumage,

from above (c), has russet head, dark striped back, pale barred rump and part of tail. From below (d) has stripes on neck, remainder of underparts strongly barred with dark grey.

24: LONG-BILLED DOWITCHER *(Limnodromus scolopaceus)* and **SHORT-BILLED DOWITCHER** *(Limnodromus griseus)* The Long-Billed and Short-billed Dowitchers are very hard to distinguish in the field, and in flight they are virtually indistinguishable. In summer, seen from above (a), both have russet neck, very white upper rump, and pale edge to secondaries; stripes and bars vary markedly between individuals. From below (b), have russet breast. In winter, from above (c), retain the white rump, the flanks being spotted and barred (white markings on wings and coloration of upper parts varying between individuals). From below (d), neck, breast and abdomen are white. Short-billed Dowitcher in autumn plumage (e) has dark brown and buff-coloured stripes on neck.

A. & E. Bomford/Ardea

(Left) Oystercatchers *Haematopus ostralegus* (foreground) and Knot *Calidris canutus* in flight. (Below) Sanderling *C. alba:* the white belly and white wing-bar distinguish it from other similar-sized waders

R. J. C. Blewit/Ardea

Sandpipers in flight

1: **MARSH SANDPIPER** *(Tringa stagnatilis)* Adult in summer (a): long slender bill, well-marked spots on back; very long legs; white markings on rump similar to Greenshank. Some individuals show a pale border on the posterior edge of the wing. In autumn and winter (b) upper parts are pale grey, almost uniform; some individuals may have a pure white head. May be distinguished at all seasons by its slender body, bill, and legs, the latter extending beyond the tail. Head and bill are illustrated in (c).

2: **SPOTTED REDSHANK** *(Tringa erythropus)* In winter (a) is very grey. In summer is the only dark wader with a wedge-shaped white rump. Bill longer and thinner than the Redshank's. No bars or other markings on wings. In summer (b) the plumage is quite dark with pale spots. Legs dark red, and they trail well behind in flight. Underside of wing white, contrasting with smoke grey of rest of plumage.

3: **REDSHANK** *(Tringa totanus)* The most easily identifiable species, being the only one with a white posterior wing edge and white rump at all seasons. Flight is fast and direct with quick wingbeats.

4: **GREENSHANK** *(Tringa nebularia)* May be distinguished by shape of bill (a), the large white 'V' on back and rump (b) and green legs. Coloration of upper parts may be greyish or dense grey (in winter), spotted and striped with black (summer), with considerable individual variations. No white on wings.

5: **GREATER YELLOWLEGS** *(Tringa melanoleuca)* Bill slightly upturned like the Greenshank's, white on rump ends squarely, legs are yellow: these are the chief characteristics of this species. Dark and spotted in summer; may be very grey in winter. In general similar to the Greenshank but larger with white on rump and tail only.

6: **LESSER YELLOWLEGS** *(Tringa flavipes)* Bill quite long and straight (a). White on rump ends squarely. Yellow legs project well beyond the tail in flight (b). Similar in size to the Redshank but more slender.

(Right) Spotted Redshank *T. erythropus:* the white underside of the wing contrasts with the smoke-grey plumage

7: SOLITARY SANDPIPER *(Tringa solitaria)* Seen from above (a) two important features may be observed: the dark rump and pale eye-ring. Seen from below (b) is very similar to the Green Sandpiper, except that the underwing is lighter, the rump dark and the sides of the tail white.

8: GREEN SANDPIPER *(Tringa ochropus)* Seen from above (a) is very dark with a white rump. Seen from below (b) its almost black underwing is conspicuous. White rump most striking feature.

9: WOOD SANDPIPER *(Tringa glareola)* Seen from above (a) upper parts are generally paler than the Green Sandpiper's and the legs protrude further beyond the tail. Seen from below (b) a pale patch can be discerned on the wing. The speckles on the Green Sandpiper and the Wood Sandpiper vary considerably according to their age and to the time of year, so they are not reliable features for identification purposes, and in any case they are almost impossible to detect in flight.

10: SPOTTED SANDPIPER *(Tringa macularia)* In summer plumage (a) markings on the white underparts are visible. The pattern on the underside of its wing is similar to that of the Common Sandpiper's: some authorities regard the Spotted Sandpiper as a subspecies of the Common Sandpiper. In winter, seen from above (b) the pattern of white on the trailing edge of its wing (c) extends much further than it does on the Common Sandpiper. Wing coverts (d) are also much more noticeably barred than the wing coverts of the Common Sandpiper's.

11: COMMON SANDPIPER *(Tringa hypoleucos)* Both the Common and the Spotted Sandpiper have a characteristic way of holding their wings when flying over water (a). Seen from above (b) the Common Sandpiper can be distinguished from the Spotted Sandpiper by the different pattern (c) of its white wing-bars and by its coloration which is perhaps slightly greener. This small grey-brown wader is best distinguished from similar waders (such as Dunlin in winter plumage) by its characteristic flight and call-note. Flies low over the water with flickering wings calling 'twee-wee-wee'.

12: TEREK SANDPIPER *(Tringa cinereus)* Resembles a small Redshank in flight but may be distinguished by upturned bill (a). Its tail is entirely grey. In summer has characteristic dark streaks (b) on the sides of its back. The white on the wings (c) varies among individuals of this species.

(Below) Common Sandpiper
T. hypoleucos

S. Dalton/NHPA

Curlews in flight

1: CURLEW *(Numenius arquata)* One of the largest European shorebirds. It can be identified by its long curved bill, large size, its white rump and its characteristic call: 'cur-lee cur-lee'. Long curved bill and legs projecting beyond the tail in flight distinguish the curlews from the somewhat similar immature gulls in flight.

2: SLENDER-BILLED CURLEW *(Numenius tenuirostris)* Considerably smaller than the Curlew: like the Curlew lacks the marked head stripes of the Whimbrel. More extensive white on its rump (a) than any other curlew. Its bill is similar in appearance to the Curlew's but shorter. Its underwing (b) is even whiter than the Whimbrel's. However the most reliable characteristic for the purpose of identification is undoubtedly the large dark spots (c) on its flanks.

3: WHIMBREL *(Numenius phaeopus)* Markedly smaller than the Curlew and the bill is much shorter. The dark and pale stripes on its head and a white rump are characteristic. The curved bill distinguishes it from the godwits.

4: ESKIMO CURLEW *(Numenius borealis)* The Eskimo Curlew has a pale, indistinct supercilium, and its rump is dark, not white like the Curlew's (a). It also lacks white coloration on the tail. Flank feathers (b) and axillaries (c) are distinctive. Seen from below (d) its primaries and secondaries are uniform. Note the distinctive colour of its underwing.

5: LITTLE WHIMBREL *(Numenius minutus)*. Its bill is unusually small for a curlew and fairly straight. Pattern on the head is sharply defined like the Whimbrel's, but its rump and upper tail-coverts (a) are dark like the Eskimo Curlew's. Little Whimbrel may be distinguished from the Eskimo Curlew by the coloration of its underwing (b) and by the pattern and colour of its flank feathers (c) and axillaries (d).

(Right) Whimbrel *Numenius phaeopus.* It flies with fast wingbeats and the long curved bill is a distinguishing feature

A. & E. Bomford/Ardea

Snipe and Woodcock in flight

(Below) The Woodcock *Scolopax rusticola* spends much of the day concealed in woodland undergrowth. (Overleaf, pages 130–131) Black-winged Stilt *Himantopus himantopus* settling on its eggs. The extremely long pink legs make this species easily identifiable. The long dark bill is also a distinctive feature

1: SNIPE *(Gallinago gallinago)* Seen from above (a) the streaks on its back are clearly visible; the tips of its flight feathers vary in colour from white to dirty white. In display flight (b) its outer tail feathers are fanned out and vibrate. It has bars and pale lines on the underside of its wing (c). The shape and pattern of the tail is the most useful clue for distinguishing the various species of the genus *Gallinago*. The Snipe's tail (d) has white tips to the feathers.

2: JACK SNIPE *(Lymnocryptes minimus)* Smaller than the Snipe and its bill is shorter. Seen from above (a) it also has streaks on its back. Its flight (b) is slower and straighter than the Snipe's. There is no white on the tail.

3: GREAT SNIPE *(Gallinago media)* Seen from above (a) it has white bars on its tail and streaks and markings on its wings which vary in intensity. Its silhouette in flight (b) resembles the Snipe's. Its wing, seen from below (c), has barred coverts. The tail of the male (d) has a broad white area which is less extensive in the female Great Snipe.

4: PIN-TAILED SNIPE *(Gallinago stenura)* Very similar to the Snipe but the wing-bars (a) are slightly wider. It has very narrow outer tail feathers (b).

5: SWINHOE'S SNIPE *(Gallinago megala)* Similar in size to the Great Snipe and the pattern of its plumage is very similar, though there is less white on some parts of its wings. Its most characteristic feature is its tail (b) which has a few bars.

6: WOODCOCK *(Scolopax rusticola)* Unmistakable in flight due to large size and long rounded wings. Unlike most other waders the bill is held downwards in flight. Flies fast and twistingly among trees. Territorial flight very distinctive: male flies a circuit at dusk and dawn. Flight somewhat resembles an owl's and the Woodcock utters two distinct notes—a croak and a 'twisick' in flight.

A. Christiansen

R. T. Peterson

Although its distribution is cosmopolitan, the family Recurvirostridae includes few genera. In fact the family consists of the Black-winged Stilt *Himantopus himantopus*, the Banded Stilt *Cladorhynchus leucocephalus* and the Ibisbill *Ibidorhyncha struthersii* in addition to avocets of the genus *Recurvirostra*. They all have long or very long legs except the Ibisbill. The Black-winged Stilt has the longest legs of all and looks as though it is literally walking on stilts. Avocets have partially webbed toes and long, slender, characteristically upturned bills. The Ibisbill has a curved bill rather like that of an ibis or curlew.

Most species are elegantly coloured, with black and white plumage sometimes combined with vivid chestnut markings on the head, neck or breast. The coloration of the Ibisbill, however, is dull and rather plover-like. Members of this family frequent marshy ground, lagoons and salt and fresh-water pools: indeed they sometimes show a marked preference for fairly salty water. They hunt for food, wading in water deep enough to reach halfway up their legs or more. Some species—particularly avocets—also swim.

They nearly always nest in colonies, which vary in size, and lay their eggs in a hollow in the mud or sand or among low marsh vegetation. However they sometimes build proper nests—most notably in the case of Black-winged Stilt. The social and breeding habits are particularly complex. Avocets, for

(Above and facing page) Black-winged Stilt *H. himantopus*. (Below) The long trailing legs and black underwing of the Black-winged Stilt make it easy to distinguish in flight

J. S. Wightman/Ardea

(Above right) Melanic form of the Black-winged Stilt which is found in New Zealand and Australia. (Above, far right) American Avocet *R. americana* and (right) Red-necked Avocet *R. novaehollandiae*

example, perform elaborate ceremonies involving a number of individuals. They form a circle with their bills lowered and pointing towards the centre like oystercatchers. The 'circle ceremony' often leads to scuffles and the birds fight with their wings.

The distribution of the various species belonging to this family is cosmopolitan. The Avocet *Recurvirostra avosetta* belongs to the Palearctic and Ethiopian regions and is found as far north as Scandinavia and the North Sea and as far east as northern China; it is basically a migrant, and winters in Africa and southeast Asia. The drainage of the fens and hunting pressure wiped out the last breeding colony of Avocets in Britain in 1825. However after the Second World War a few birds began to nest on Minsmere and Havergate Islands in Norfolk: both were made into RSPB reserves and the species is thus protected.

The American Avocet *R. americana* nests from southern Canada south through the United States, wintering as far south as Central America. Its head and neck are cinnamon coloured. The salt lakes of the Chilean Andes have their own species, the Andean Avocet *R. andina*, and Australia is the home of the Red-necked Avocet *R. novaehollandiae* which also occurs in New Zealand. The Black-winged Stilt with its five sub-species (regarded by some authorities as species in their own right) is truly cosmopolitan: one form is typically Palearctic, but its distribution area extends to Africa, southern Asia and Madagascar. North and South America have a sub-species of their own and the sub-species *H.h. leucocephalus* of the Black-winged Stilt nests in Australia and New Zealand where a melanic—that is completely black —variety is also found. The Banded Stilt, which has a chestnut-coloured breast band and yellow legs, but otherwise resembles the Black-winged Stilt, is exclusive to Australia where it frequents salt lakes in the outback and feeds on crustaceans. The Ibisbill differs from the other members of the family not only in the shape of its bill and in its coloration, but also in its habitat—it is found on the central Asian plateaus and lives in swift-flowing mountain rivers and streams.

C. K. Mylne/Ardea

(Above and left) Avocet *R. avosetta:* the upcurved bill is swept from side to side when feeding

L. Norstrom

French: ECHASSE BLANCHE
Italian: CAVALIERE D'ITALIA
Spanish: CIGUENUELA
German: STELZENLAUFER

Black-winged Stilt
Himantopus himantopus

HABITAT Nests by lakes, pools, lagoons and flooded areas. Winters in similar areas and on the banks of slow-flowing rivers.

IDENTIFICATION Length: 38 cm. Unmistakable due to its long pink legs which protrude beyond the tail in flight. Distinctive long black bill and black upper parts contrast sharply with its pure white underparts. In winter, male and female are similar with white heads and necks. However in spring and summer back of the male's

(Below) Male in summer plumage (foreground) and female. (Right) Breeding areas (yellow), wintering areas (magenta), areas where the Black-winged Stilt may be seen all year round (orange) and on passage (pink)

head is black. Juveniles browner, with pale margins to the back and wing feathers. It is a noisy bird and has a habit of nodding when disturbed. See also page 144.

CALL A shrill 'queep-queep-queep'.

REPRODUCTION April–May. The shape of the nest varies. It is built of vegetation and mud near water. The Black-winged Stilt usually lays three eggs. Incubation is carried out by both sexes for twenty-five or twenty-six days. The chicks leave the nest as soon as they have hatched and are cared for by both parents. See also page 144.

FOOD Insects, larvae and plants from the surface of the water.

DISTRIBUTION AND MOVEMENTS Southern Europe, central and southern Asia, North and South America and Australia. It is a migrant in the northern regions, wintering in Africa and southern Asia. Occasionally found in Germany, Denmark, Poland and in Britain where two pairs bred in 1945 at Nottingham Sewage Farm. It is now accidental almost every year.

SUB-SPECIES In addition to the nominate sub-species described here, there are sub-species in North and South America, the Hawaiian Islands, the Philippines, Indonesia, New Guinea, Australia and New Zealand.

Avocet
Recurvirostra avosetta

French: AVOCETTE
Italian: AVOCETTA
Spanish: AVOCETA
German: SABELSCHNABLER

HABITAT Nests in areas with little vegetation, in river deltas, close to shallow water, on sandbanks and in water-meadows. At other times of the year it frequents sandy and muddy coasts, sandbanks, estuaries and the low banks of inland lakes.

IDENTIFICATION Length: 43 cm. Snow-white plumage with black markings and long, black upcurved bill are unmistakable. Blue-grey legs. The juvenile's plumage is tinged with irregular brown coloration.

In flight its neck and legs are held out front and rear: the legs protrude well beyond the tail. It moves gracefully on the ground, holding its body horizontally with its neck curved. When startled, it stands erect with its neck stretched up. It hunts for food in the mud or in shallow water, sweeping its bill from side to side. Swims readily and also up-ends. See also page 144.

CALL A clear, liquid 'cleep' or 'cloo-eet'.

REPRODUCTION April–May. It nests in colonies on sandy or muddy ground. The nest is situated on bare sand or in a furrow. The Avocet usually lays four rufous-coloured eggs with irregular black speckles. Incubation is carried out by both sexes for twenty-two to twenty-four days. The young birds are able to feed themselves as soon as they are hatched, but are tended by both parents.

FOOD Insects, molluscs and crustaceans.

DISTRIBUTION AND MOVEMENTS Southern Sweden, the southern coasts of the Baltic, northern Italy, southeast Europe, central and south western Asia and southern, northwest, and east Africa. In Britain returned to breed in Suffolk in 1947 after an absence of one hundred years. Regular colonies now exist at Minsmere and Havergate, both reserves of the Royal Society for the Protection of Birds. Otherwise it is a passage migrant in small numbers and a winter visitor to the Tamar estuary in Devon. In the northern regions it is migrant and winters in Africa and southern Asia.

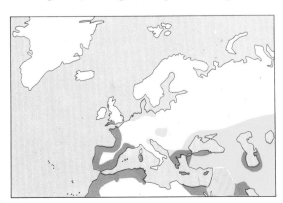

(Left) Breeding areas (yellow), wintering areas (magenta), areas where the Avocet may be seen all year round (orange) and on passage (pink)

ORDER Charadriiformes
FAMILY PHALAROPODIDAE: Phalaropes

(Above) Male Red-necked Phalarope *Phalaropus lobatus* and (right) female Red-necked Phalarope. In summer the red patches on the throat are diagnostic field marks

The family Phalaropodidae consists of three species. They are similar to sandpipers but are expert swimmers. They all have very dense plumage, reminiscent of a duck's, especially on the underparts; air is trapped between the skin and the feathers, making the birds very buoyant. The toes are slightly webbed at the base and the sides are lobed or edged with a series of small, flattened scales. They are more aquatic in their habits than any other shorebird and are among the smallest birds to be seen swimming except for a few all-dark petrels. In fact two of the three species spend most of the year at sea and can survive without fresh water for long periods. Their flight is rather weak.

Phalaropes, all of which nest at high northern latitudes, adopt reversed sexual roles: the males incubate the eggs and tend the young. The females' plumage is much brighter and more striking than the males which are smaller and duller. The females take the lead during courtship.

During the nesting season they are sociable and form scattered colonies which are often spread over large areas. In keeping with their unusual role, the females are the first to reach the nesting grounds where violent squabbles ensue over the allocation of the best sites. Despite their colonial habits, each female defends her own territory and it is there that the males are courted. It is not known whether the female mates with one male or with several.

Three or four eggs are laid, and although incubation is carried out exclusively by the male, it appears that the female, who always stays near the nest, helps to care for the offspring in some cases. However, a great many females abandon the nesting sites shortly after reaching them, although it is not known for certain whether it·is immature or adult

(Above) Male Red-necked Phalarope *P. lobatus* on the nest

J. Grahn

(Above right) Grey Phalarope *P. fulicarius* in summer plumage and (right) in winter plumage

females who choose not to devote themselves to family duties after the eggs have been laid. Whatever the case may be, these females gather in large numbers not far from the coast and wait to be joined by the males and newly-hatched birds before setting off on the journey south. If migrating phalaropes run into a storm they are often driven off course, like small storm petrels, and may sometimes be far inland.

At one time each species was allocated to a separate genus because of the differences among them, but at present the three species are included in the single genus *Phalaropus*. Wilson's Phalarope *P. tricolor* is the largest species. Its long legs and bill are almost needle-shaped. Its toes are only slightly lobed since it is less marine in its habits than the other species and is much more prone to feed on land. In summer it is restricted to the arctic regions of North America, but it winters in the tropical and southern parts of South America, along the coasts and to a certain extent on inland waters. It is a transatlantic vagrant to Europe. During the breeding season, the Red-necked Phalarope *P. lobatus* and the Grey Phalarope *P. fulicarius* are distributed in the arctic and do not travel far from coastal regions, remaining within easy reach of the small lakes or fresh-water pools where they find most of their food. They have a strange way of feeding, spinning round rapidly in circles in the water. This is believed to disturb the small creatures on which they feed—such as crustaceans—and bring them to the surface. Sometimes they half submerge themselves like surface-feeding ducks. At the end of the breeding season they migrate towards the open sea of tropical oceans where they live on plankton and remain far from the shore. In fact their distribution in the open sea appears to be dependent upon the seasonal availability of plankton.

The Red-necked Phalarope is a rare species, and is a very scarce breeder in Britain and Ireland. In the nineteenth century its numbers fell rapidly due to intensive collecting of its eggs, but the RSPB has helped preserve it in nesting sites in the Shetlands, and in the northern and western islands of Scotland.

Grey Phalarope
Phalaropus fulicarius

French: PHALAROPE À BEC LARGE
Italian: FALAROPO BECCOLARGO
Spanish: FALAROPO PICOGRUESO
German: ROSTROTER
WASSERTRETER

HABITAT Nests on wet open grassland near pools or lagoons and on coasts. Winters at sea.

IDENTIFICATION Length: 20 cm. Along with the Red-necked Phalarope, the only small shorebird which regularly swims in the open sea. Summer plumage: yellow bill with a black tip, dark crown, white face, wide cream and chestnut-coloured streaks on its upper parts and dark chestnut underparts. In winter upper parts are pale blue-grey and its underparts become white, so that it resembles a Sanderling, from which it can be distinguished by a dark marking across the eyes. Female is larger and her plumage more brightly coloured.

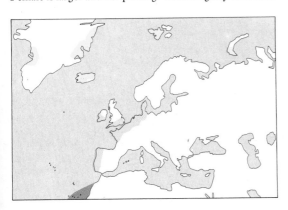

Its flight is fast. Swims on the surface, moving its head rapidly from side to side to catch insects. When hunting for food in shallow water, it spins round, possibly in order to bring larvae and other creatures floating to the surface. Usually lives alone or in pairs in its breeding grounds, but is gregarious at sea. See also page 144.

CALL 'Weet' or 'pee-eep' like the Sanderling's call.

REPRODUCTION Late June to early July in Spitsbergen; slightly later elsewhere. The nest consists of a small depression in moss, among stones or in grass. It usually lays four eggs, ranging in colour from cream to olive-brown or amber, with brown or chestnut markings or streaks. Incubation is carried out by the male only for nineteen days. The young are cared for by the male alone.

FOOD Crustaceans, molluscs, worms and insects.

DISTRIBUTION AND MOVEMENTS The Arctic: breeding distribution circumpolar. It winters on the coasts of the south Atlantic and the west coasts of the Americas from California to Chile. It is a passage visitor on North Sea coasts and is accidental in various parts of Europe. In Britain is an annual passage visitor in highly variable numbers mainly from August to December.

(Above) Grey Phalarope in summer plumage (foreground) and winter plumage. (Left) Breeding areas (yellow), wintering areas (magenta) and areas where the Grey Phalarope may be seen on passage (pink)

French: PHALAROPE À BEC ÉTROIT
Italian: FALAROPO BECCOSOTTILE
Spanish: FALAROPO PICOFINO
German: HALSBANDWASSER-
TRETER

Red-necked Phalarope
Phalaropus lobatus

(Above) Red-necked Phalarope in summer plumage (foreground) and winter plumage. (Below) Breeding areas (yellow) and areas where the Red-necked Phalarope may be seen on passage (pink)

HABITAT Nests on water-logged grassland, by marshes or lagoons. Like the Grey Phalarope winters at sea.

IDENTIFICATION Length: 16 cm. Is similar to the Grey Phalarope from which it can be distinguished, in summer by its smaller size, slender black bill, slate grey head and neck and brown-striped upper parts. Orange patches on the throat of this species are diagnostic in summer plumage. In winter it can be distinguished by its dark grey back with less uniform coloration and off-white streaks, and by the contrasting white wing-bar on its dark wings. Juveniles resemble adults in winter plumage but the upper parts and crowns are darker. In winter it can be distinguished from the Sanderling by the dark marking across its eye and by its thinner bill.

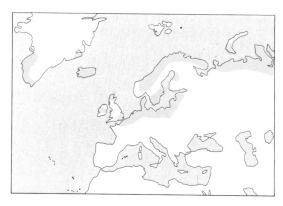

During courtship the female searches for a site and then sings and flies around to advertise her presence. She then returns to the water where she swims, holding her neck erect and emitting various call notes. Although her initial approach to the male may be hesitant, she heads straight for him, with her neck lowered between her shoulders; then she starts swimming again, holding her neck high and beating her wings rapidly. Once a pair has been formed, the two birds create the nest, either separately or together. See also page 144.

CALL Its most frequent call is a 'tweet' or 'weet'.

REPRODUCTION Late May to early June. It nests in loose colonies on marshy ground. The nest consists of a depression in the ground close to water, and it is lined with grass. The Red-necked Phalarope usually lays four eggs ranging in colour from cream to creamy-olive with sepia or chocolate-coloured markings. Incubation by male for eighteen to twenty days.

FOOD Insects and larvae: also molluscs and seeds.

DISTRIBUTION AND MOVEMENTS Breeds in northern Europe and the northern regions of Asia and America. Winters in West Africa, on the coasts of the Indian Ocean, in the Malaysian archipelago and in the Molucca Islands. In Britain is a very scarce breeder mainly restricted to Scottish islands. Also a rare breeder in Ireland. Occurs as a rare passage visitor annually in small numbers in Britain and Ireland.

Wilson's Phalarope
Phalaropus tricolor

HABITAT Tundra, boggy meadowland and arctic and sub-arctic water-meadows during the nesting season. In winter frequents lakes and coasts, preferably close to marshes and water-logged fields. Unlike other phalaropes it avoids the open sea.

IDENTIFICATION Length: 23 cm. Fairly easy to distinguish at all seasons because of its white rump and the absence of a white wing-bar which is present in the Grey or Red-necked Phalaropes. In summer the female has colourful plumage, with a pattern of dark and russet broad stripes down the neck and along the back. Black line runs through the eye. Pale blue-grey extends from the crown to the back. The underparts, eye-stripe and part of the cheeks are white. The front of the neck is often 'washed' with red. Male has paler chestnut streaks than the female and a dark crown and back. In winter the sexes are similar with grey upper parts and white underparts. In flight the tail and rump are white. The black bill is particularly slender and its overall appearance is more like that of a 'shank' than a phalarope. Wilson's Phalarope is far less aquatic than other phalaropes and though it is an expert swimmer, it frequently hunts for food on banks like a typical shorebird. See also page 144.

CALL A nasal note: 'aang'. Call note in flight: 'chew'.

REPRODUCTION The nest is a depression in the ground, well hidden among vegetation in marsh or tundra and it is often lined with blades of grass. Three or four pale, yellow-brown eggs densely covered with brown and black markings are laid. Incubation lasts for twenty-one days and is carried out by the male alone.

FOOD Mainly insects and small shellfish, but also the seeds of aquatic plants.

DISTRIBUTION AND MOVEMENTS An American species, nesting from Canada south to the central United States. Winters in southern South America. Accidental in Britain and Ireland with increasing frequency since it was first identified in 1954.

French: PHALAROPE DE WILSON
Italian: FALAROPO DI WILSON
Spanish: FALAROPO DE WILSON
German: WILSONS WASSERTRETER

(Below) Female Wilson's Phalarope in summer plumage (foreground), male in summer plumage (centre) and winter plumage

Phalaropes and other waders in fligh

1: AVOCET *(Recurvirostra avosetta)* The strikingly upturned black bill and its bold black and white plumage are distinctive. Emits a soft grunting note in flight.

2: OYSTERCATCHER *(Haematopus ostralegus)* May be distinguished by its large size, black upper parts, white underparts and the white wing-bar. Its thick orange-pink bill is also very distinctive as are its longish pink legs.

3: GREY PHALAROPE *(Phalaropus fulicarius)* Female in summer plumage (a): reddish throat and underparts. Adult in winter plumage (b): the crown and head may still have dark patches although the forehead has already turned white; the white wing-bar on its grey upper parts is a conspicuous feature. Many individuals seen from September to November (c) still show vestiges of summer plumage on their backs and on the tops of their heads, but as a rule the red coloration fades before they reach Europe. Prior to the winter moult, the wings lose their grey colour and turn darker. The black coloration of the crown gradually disappears in August and September; the base of the bill is yellow in adults but greenish in juveniles.

4: RED-NECKED PHALAROPE *(Phalaropus lobatus)* Adult winter plumage (a): dark greyish back; dark wings (not pale like the Grey Phalarope's). Juvenile in autumn plumage (b): note the head pattern which can be seen more clearly in (c). On the wings there is a principal wing-bar and a second, less clearly defined one; the markings on the back are like those of the Little Stint; the wings are very dark. Like other phalaropes flight is rather weak.

5: WILSON'S PHALAROPE *(Phalaropus tricolor)* Female in summer plumage (a): the pattern running from the sides of the head down the back, and the white rump are distinctive features. Adult in winter plumage (b): pale supercilium, blurred and insignificant wing-bar, and white rump. At any age and in any plumage, the long, very slender bill is a distinctive feature of Wilson's Phalarope.

6: BLACK-WINGED STILT *(Himantopus himantopus)* The exceptionally long pink legs make it unmistakable. The long, straight black bill and black wings are also distinctive. In flight the legs trail well beyond the tail.

(Below) Oystercatchers *Haematopus ostralegus* in flight

C. R. Knights/Ardea

BURHINIDAE: Thick-knees

P. Jackson/Bruce Coleman

(Above) Stone Curlew
Burhinus oedicnemus: the
large yellow eye is a
conspicuous feature

The nine species of the family Burhinidae have huge eyes, which gives them an owl-like look. The iris is generally yellow. The body resembles a bustard's in shape and the coloration is similar to a curlew's. Thick-knees are mainly crepuscular birds (hence the large eyes) and live on stony or sandy ground, often on river shores. When danger threatens they will run rather than fly, or else crouch down: hence the long, three-toed legs, like a bustard's, and the mimetic coloration like a curlew's.

Although much of their anatomical structure, as well as to some extent their behaviour, places them in the order Charadriiformes at first glance they resemble bustards. This has led some authorities to classify them in the order Gruiformes.

It seems more likely, however, that this is yet another example of evolutionary convergence, due to the very similar surroundings in which the two families live. However, according to almost all systems of classification, Gruiformes and Charadriiformes are adjacent orders, so that those characteristics of thick-knees which are transitional between one order and another may be of evolutionary significance in that the position, or rather the degree of relationship, of these birds may be genuinely intermediate between the two orders.

Thick-knees vary in length from thirty-six to fifty-two centimetres. In the typical genus *Burhinus* the bill is relatively short, straight and strong, green or yellow with a black tip. The bill of the Beach Stone Curlew *Orthorhamphus magnirostris* is long and appears very heavy and swollen, as does the bill of the Great Stone Curlew *Esacus recurvirostris*. The bill of the Great Stone Curlew is laterally compressed as well.

The long legs of the thick-knees are reticulated: that is, they have a horny covering which resembles small round scales. The inter-tarsal joint, inaccurately known as the 'knee', appears very swollen, giving rise to the English name of thick-knee. There are only three toes (no hind toe) which are short and joined by a membrane at the base.

The shape of the wing varies with the different species although it is usually long and broad, but rounded or pointed depending upon the migratory habits of the species. The tail is of medium length.

The sexes are alike, although the female in each species tends to be smaller than the male. The plumage varies little according to the season and the general coloration of all species is sandy-brown, buff and greyish-brown, with a variety of streaking, barring and spotting. The chin and cheeks are generally white and there are one or two pale wing-bars as well as dark ones: the wing-bars are fairly conspicuous in flight. In both species of the monotypic genera and in two species of the genus *Burhinus* (which has seven species in all) the coloration of the upper parts is fairly uniform, with a dark 'eyebrow' visible even at some distance. The young have soft, cryptically coloured down; indeed, difficult though it is to pick out adults from their background, the chicks are even better camouflaged.

When in danger thick-knees crouch down with their heads extended so they appear quite flat— another feature which helps them remain inconspicuous. Thick-knees are shy birds: during the day they remain in the shelter of dense bushes and even here although they are relatively numerous, their presence may be unsuspected. Sometimes, however, they can be remarkably trusting: the Senegal Thick-knee *Burhinus seneglalensis* is wary and suspicious in Uganda, but in Egypt it readily nests on rooftops. The Double-striped Thick-Knee *B. bistriatus*, if reared in captivity, will sometimes become so trusting and affectionate towards its owner that it will serve as a watchdog at night, since in the night the usually silent thick-knees become noisy. During the breeding season in particular hootings, gruntings, croakings and pipings can be heard, each species having its own characteristic sequence. Also during the breeding season the males, particularly on moonlight nights, are much given to courtship displays.

The nest is a hollow or slight depression in the ground (the majority of observers report that no actual nest is built) in which two eggs are laid. The eggs are white to buff and blotched with brown so they blend in well with the surrounding environment. One species, the Water Thick-knee or Water Dikkop *B. vermiculatus*, often lays its eggs on the dried dung of elephant, buffalo or hippopotamus. In some areas the Water Thick-knee nests where crocodiles lay their eggs: this unusual association appears to be common and limited only by the availability of crocodiles!

All thick-knees are usually solitary, at least in

(Left) Beach Stone Curlew *Orthorhamphus magnirostris* and (below) Stone Curlew *Burhinus oedicnemus* on the nest

Eric Hosking

(Above) Spotted Thick-knee *Burhinus capensis* which is present in Africa. (Below) world distribution of the family Burhinidae

the breeding season, although the Stone Curlew *B. oedicnemus* has been observed on migration in groups of up to a hundred individuals.

Their diet consists of vegetable and animal matter, the former consisting mainly of seeds and small plant shoots. Animals eaten range from insects to molluscs, crustaceans, small amphibians and reptiles and even small rodents. Hunting for food generally takes place at night.

As has already been said, thick-knees dislike taking flight, but when they do they fly rapidly, despite the apparently slow wingbeat, although usually only for short periods. When running they hold their heads low and their necks retracted: like plovers they prefer to run rapidly for short distances and then pause, rather than cover the whole distance at once.

The family is fairly widespread in the Old World, with only two species in the Neotropical region. Of the seven species of the genus *Burhinus*, the commonest is still probably the European Stone Curlew which is found in much of Europe and also in North Africa and central and southern Asia. It is also the only species which is truly migratory.

The African species are almost all sedentary, the Senegal Thick-knee being the only one to perform some movements, albeit irregular, which also explains why this is the only species to occur accidentally in Europe. The Water Thick-knee, as its English name implies, prefers to be near water and may indeed be considered a species of river banks and lakesides, while the other African species, as well as the Peruvian Thick-knee *B. superciliaria* of South America and the Southern Stone Curlew *B. magnirostris* of Australia prefer dry areas, sometimes semi-desert, with or without scrubby vegetation.

The Great Stone Curlew or Reef Thick-knee is found on sand or gravel seashores or banks of the great rivers in India, while the Beach Stone Curlew is a typical shorebird, found almost exclusively on sea coasts, even cliffs, from the Andaman Islands to Australia and the Solomon Islands.

Stone Curlew
Burhinus oedicnemus

French: OEDICNÈME CRIARD
Italian: OCCHIONE
Spanish: ALCARVÁN
German: TRIEL

HABITAT Nests on open stony, sandy and chalky land, on barren hillsides, heathland with scanty vegetation, sparse pine woods, among crops and occasionally in marshes. In winter frequents similar habitats.

IDENTIFICATION Length: 40 cm. At close quarters the staring yellow eye makes this species easily identifiable. The short thick bill is yellow and black, breast and flanks are streaked; belly white; tail brown, white at the sides, and tipped black. Juveniles are similar to adults.

Flight direct, almost always close to the ground, with legs extended beyond the tail. The two white and one black wing-bars are distinctive in flight. One white bar is visible on the closed wing. On the ground takes small steps, but if necessary can run, with head lowered and neck retracted. When danger threatens, flattens itself with its head on the ground. Display ceremonies may be quite complex. See also page 156.

CALL The call-note in flight is a 'coo-eek'; also emits a twittering 'kitti-keerik-ditik-tik'.

REPRODUCTION April to beginning of May. The eggs, usually two in number, are laid on the ground. They vary from whitish to pale brown, with irregular brown mottling and streaking. Both sexes incubate for twenty-five to twenty-seven days. The young leave the nest a day after hatching and are tended by both parents.

FOOD Molluscs, worms and insects; sometimes the nestlings of other birds and rodents.

DISTRIBUTION AND MOVEMENTS Central and southern Europe, southwestern and southern Asia, northern Africa. Winters in western and southwestern Europe, northwestern and eastern Africa. Resident in southern Europe. In Britain is a scarce breeder confined southwards at a line drawn between the Severn and the Wash and to chalk downland and open heaths. It has declined in number in recent years and is only exceptionally seen in winter.

SUB-SPECIES *B. o. oedicnemus:* central and southern Europe except Greece. *B. o. barterti* (paler and with less barring): southern USSR. *B. o. saharae* (more rufous): Mediterranean islands, Greece. Other sub-species are present in southern Asia.

(Below) Breeding areas (yellow), wintering areas (magenta), areas where the Stone Curlew may be seen all year round (orange) and on passage (pink)

FAMILY GLAREOLIDAE: Pratincoles and Coursers

R. Gillmor/Bruce Coleman

(Above) Collared Pratincole *Glareola pratincola*. When seen on the ground, pratincoles are similar to plovers although in flight they resemble swallows or terns. (Facing page, top and bottom) Black-winged Pratincoles *G. nordmanni*

The family Glareolidae includes seventeen species which vary in length from 15 cm to 26 cm. The general coloration among members of this family ranges from olive to brown and chestnut, sometimes marked with black, white or rust although a few species have a glossy sheen or cryptic coloration. There are two groups: the Glareolinae or pratincoles and the Cursoriinae or coursers.

Pratincoles are generally smaller than coursers and differ in behaviour: coursers are more terrestrial and as the name implies are swift runners whereas pratincoles are strong fliers. Most species are gregarious. They are the size of a Starling or a little larger—roughly 20 to 25 centimetres. The wings are long and pointed. The tail is forked, like

that of the terns of the family Laridae. The legs of pratincoles are shorter than the coursers' legs.

Flight is light and swift and similar to that of the terns, though on the ground pratincoles can run rapidly, like plovers.

The coloration is mainly dull brown, and the belly and undertail coverts are often white. The tail is also white with a black tip. The sexes are alike, although sometimes differing in size. The bill is rather short, wide at the base and the tip is decurved. The legs are short, somewhat like a tern's. The hind toe is present and well developed; the claw of the middle toe is long and usually pectinated. A short web connects the middle toe to the other two front toes.

With the bill open, these birds have a very wide aperture indeed: their diet consists mainly of insects, taken on the wing. Indeed their diet is so specialised that, in African districts plagued with locusts, pratincoles are among the species locally known as 'locust birds', from their habit of converging upon swarms of these insects. Unfortunately such swarms of locusts can only be controlled by these natural means in the very early stages when the numbers are still comparatively small. Pratincoles are also able to capture insects on the ground, following them with short, swift pattering steps.

The eggs are laid on the ground, on dried mud in marshy districts (particularly salt-marshes), on sand and occasionally on bare rock; rarely in the shelter of bushes. Three eggs are generally laid which are cryptically coloured and very difficult to see. Although directly exposed to the heat of the sun, the shell is comparatively thin. However the egg is sometimes protected from the sun by a parent's outstretched wing. Both sexes incubate and care for the young.

Their surroundings—marshy seashores, areas liable to flooding, river banks, etc.—are inhospitable for much of the year, and nesting takes place after the rainy season. Such dependence on local conditions of great variability may explain to some extent the sporadic nature of breeding in some parts of Europe.

Pratincoles are widely distributed from Europe and Asia to Africa and Australia, but are not represented in the Americas. The main genera are *Glareola*, consisting of species which are almost always strongly migratory, and *Galachrysia* (not recognised as a genus by all authorities) which consists mainly of sedentary species. Australia has the monotypic genus *Stiltia*: the Australian Pratincole *Stiltia isabella* may be regarded as a half-way between the coursers and pratincoles as it has the long legs typical of the coursers.

The coursers comprise some ten species: one Australian, two Indian and six or seven African. They have a plover-like shape and call, the long legs lack the hind toe and the bill is pointed and often decurved. The coloration, apart from that of the Egyptian Plover *Pluvianus aegyptius*, is mainly sand-coloured or brown, perfectly suited to their habitat which is sandy, arid, desert or semi-desert areas, near the coast or inland.

Coursers are much less gregarious than pratincoles, and as their name indicates, they run with agility, pursuing their prey (insects and also small vertebrates) on the ground. In flight they are, however, sure and swift and one species, the Bronze-winged Courser *Rhinoptilus chalcopterus*, is mainly nocturnal in habit. The genus *Rhinoptilus* includes two other African species as well as one Indian one which is possibly now extinct.

The best-known genus is *Cursorius*, which includes the Cream-coloured Courser *C. cursor*, which occurs as an accidental visitor in Europe and is found on the borders of the Sahara, as well as from Kenya to Persia and the Cape Verde Islands.

R. Kinne/Photo Researchers

R. Gillmor/Bruce Coleman

The Australian species *Peltohyas australis* is known as the Australian Dotterel.

The most aberrant species among the coursers is undoubtedly the rare Egyptian Plover or Crocodile Bird which is confined to Egypt. Its coloration is distinct from all the other species: pearl-grey upper parts and light buff underparts with a striking pattern of dark green (appearing almost black) on the crown, a white eye-stripe and a greenish-black breast band. In flight a black wing-bar is visible. The popular name—Crocodile Bird—is derived from its habit of removing organic matter from the teeth of crocodiles: this statement, however, although constantly repeated, appears to have been made on the authority of travellers and explorers with little ornithological knowledge, and requires confirmation. The fact that these birds are found together with crocodiles may have given rise to what must be considered a myth, even if the possibility of its being true cannot be totally dismissed. One fact, equally interesting, has however been verified, and that is that these same birds do not incubate their eggs but cover them with sand. The parents regurgitate water on the covering sand, possibly in order to cool it down. It is possible that the young are also covered with sand to protect them both from the burning heat of the sun and from enemies.

(Above left) Cream-coloured Courser *Cursorius cursor* (Above right, top) Juvenile Collared Pratincole *G pratincola* and (bottom) Temminck's Courser *C. temminckii* which is present in Africa. (Left) World distribution of the family Glareolidae.

Cream-coloured Courser
Cursorius cursor

French: COURVITE ISABELLE
Italian: CORRIONE BIONDO
Spanish: CORREDOR
German: RENNVOGEL

HABITAT Inhabits desert and semi-desert regions.

IDENTIFICATION Length: 23 cm. Resembles a smaller slim sandy Golden Plover. Coloration basically sandy with completely black primaries and underwing: the dark underwings very conspicuous in flight. Slender, decurved bill; wide white eye-stripe edged with black, grey nape; short, rounded tail, with blackish sub-terminal band and white tip; yellow-cream legs. In flight wings appear long: flight is somewhat jerky. Behaviour is similar to that of Golden Plover. Runs rapidly and hides by crouching in the grass. Generally lives in pairs or small groups. Immature has brown-speckled upper parts. See also page 156.

CALL Call-note on the wing is a harsh 'praark'. Otherwise is usually a silent species.

REPRODUCTION Mid-April to July. Normally two eggs are laid on the ground which vary from sandy-grey to light brown, closely streaked and spotted with brown. Both sexes incubate the eggs although the length of the incubation period is not known. Both male and female tend the young.

FOOD Insects and their larvae.

DISTRIBUTION AND MOVEMENTS North Africa and southwest Asia. Sedentary and partially migratory south to Sudan and northwest India. In Europe is an accidental visitor to Britain, Ireland, Scandinavia, Germany and the USSR.

SUB-SPECIES A sub-species breeds in the Canary Islands and the Sahara east to Egypt.

153

French: GLARÉOLE À COLLIER
Italian: PERNICE DI MARE
Spanish: CANASTERA
German: BRACHSCHWALBE

Collared Pratincole
Glareola pratincola

HABITAT Present in a wide range of habitats, ranging from marshy areas, river deltas and lake shores to arid and semi-desert regions. Winters in the dry steppe and savannah regions of Africa.

IDENTIFICATION Length: 25 cm. Seen in flight, closely resembles a tern in shape and movements: has a deeply forked black tail which is white at the base. On the ground resembles a long-winged plover: the wings are also pointed. Short, slightly curved bill; upper parts olive brown; underparts light buff and belly white. Chin and throat are creamy; legs short and black. In flight the chestnut rather than black axillaries distinguish it from the Black-winged Pratincole. Juveniles have a pectoral band with dark streaks and the back feathers have paler edges, giving them a 'scaly' look.

Flocks are numerous, and spend most of their time in the air, becoming more active towards evening. Catches insects both in the air and on the ground. See also page 156.

CALL A 'kuik' like that of the terns; also a 'kitti-krrik-kitik-tik'.

REPRODUCTION Beginning of May to June. Eggs are generally laid on the bare ground often on sandy or loamy soil. Usually three eggs are laid, varying from stone-grey to buff. Both sexes incubate the eggs for seventeen to eighteen days.

FOOD Mainly insects: grasshoppers, beetles, locusts, flies and mosquitoes.

DISTRIBUTION AND MOVEMENTS Breeds from northwest Africa and southern Spain and Portugal through southern France, Hungary, the southern Balkan peninsula, Agean and Black Sea coasts, southwestern Asia. Also breeds south through much of Africa. Sedentary and migratory: where migratory winters in Africa south of the Sahara. In Britain and Ireland is a rare vagrant.

SUB-SPECIES Sub-species are present in Africa.

(Right) Breeding areas (yellow) and areas where the Collared Pratincole may be seen on passage (pink)

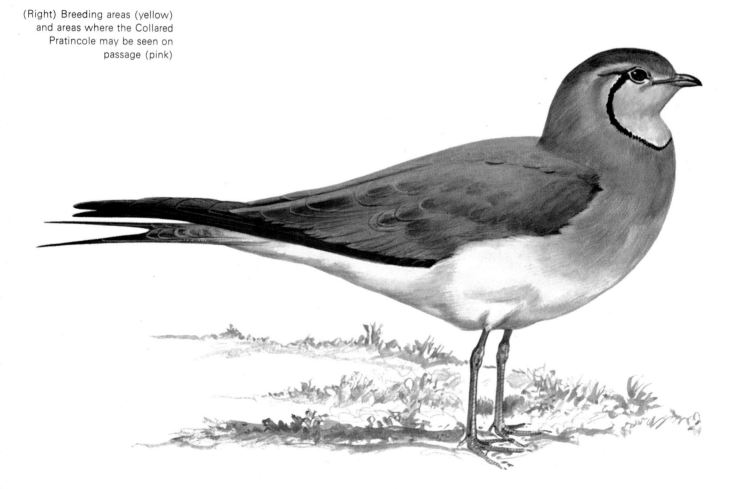

Black-winged Pratincole
Glareola nordmanni

HABITAT Nests on parched steppes, in salt-marshes with little or no grass, sometimes among crops.

IDENTIFICATION Length: 25 cm. Very similar to Collared Pratincole, but distinguished by the black, not chestnut underwing (particularly the coverts and axillaries). The general coloration is darker and less olive-coloured. Best distinguished from Collared Pratin-cole when the wing is lifted to reveal the black under-wing with dark rather than white-edged secondaries.

Habits and behaviour like Collared Pratincole's, but probably more inclined to nest in fairly numerous colonies. When the breeding season is over gathers in flocks consisting sometimes of more than 5,000 birds.

CALL A 'keerlik-keerlik' very similar to that of the Collared Pratincole.

REPRODUCTION Second half of May. Nests in colonies. The eggs, usually four in number, resemble those of Collared Pratincole and are laid on mud or sand; nest is a depression in the ground. Information on incubation and nestlings is not available.

FOOD Insects, principally locusts.

DISTRIBUTION AND MOVEMENTS Southeastern Europe east to southwest Asia. Winters in eastern and southern Africa. Accidental in Britain perhaps more regularly than formerly believed, Ireland, Norway, Denmark, Netherlands, and Italy.

French:	GLARÉOLE À AILES NOIRES
Italian:	PERNICE DI MARE ORIENTALE
Spanish:	CANASTERA ALINEGRA
German:	SCHWARZFLÜGEL BRACHSCHWALBE

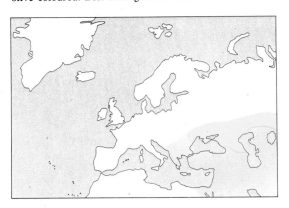

(Above) Adult Black-winged Pratincole (foreground) and immature. (Left) Breeding areas (yellow) and areas where the Black-winged Pratincole may be seen on passage (pink)

Thick-knees and pratincoles in flight

1: **STONE CURLEW** *(Burhinus oedicnemus)* From above (a) the head appears rounded and the eyes huge and yellow, conspicuous even in flight. The white wing-patch and the two white and one black wing-bars are characteristic. From below (b): the pure white under-wing, with dark trailing edge, is a diagnostic fieldmark. Flight is slow and direct and the legs trail behind.

2: **CREAM-COLOURED COURSER** *(Cursorius cursor)* From above (a): the pattern of the head is un-mistakable. In juveniles, however, the colouring is duller. The pattern of the wing is also characteristic: black wing-tips and axillaries. From below (b): very pale body and uniformly dark wings, appearing black at a distance. In flight the long legs project slightly beyond the tail.

3: **BLACK-WINGED PRATINCOLE** *(Glareola nordmanni)* In winter (a) breast is lightly mottled and the wings are uniformly dark. In summer (b), seen from above, back and wings are uniformly coloured, without contrasts. The white-edged secondaries are also lacking. Juveniles (c) may be recognised by the mottling on the throat and by the shape of the tail when open.

4: **COLLARED PRATINCOLE** *(Glareola pratincola)* In winter (a) seen from below, distinctive rufous axillaries and white border to the proximal part of wing. In summer (b): back and wing-coverts appear much paler than flight-feathers and the white trailing edge, absent in the Black-winged Pratincole, is still con-spicuous in flight. Flocks are noisy, with tern-like chattering, and sometimes perform aerobatics.

(Right, top and bottom) Upwards and downward stroke of the wings of the Collared Pratincole *Glareola pratincola*

J. S. Wightman/Ardea

ORDER Charadriiformes
FAMILY **STERCORARIIDAE: Skuas**

J. Grahn

R. T. Smith/Ardea

Skuas are dark gull-like seabirds: some authorities consider them merely a sub-family of the family Laridae but in general they are considered a separate family.

The plumage of the skuas is usually dark brown, at least on the upper parts. The Great Skua *Stercorarius skua* also has dark underparts with paler mottling, whereas among the other three species of the genus mottling and occasional barring are characteristic of immature or juvenile plumage. There is no sexual dimorphism among members of this family, but polymorphism does occur in the Pomarine Skua *S. pomarinus*, the Arctic Skua *S. paristicus* and in the Long-tailed Skua *S. longicaudus*. Among these species the underparts are white tinged with buff in the light phase and greybrown or chocolate-coloured in the dark phase. Most adult skuas do have these two colour phases, but the Great Skua is an exception, with no variation in coloration.

The Arctic and Long-tailed Skuas—in the latter the dark form is extremely rare—have two elongated and pointed central tail feathers in adult plumage. The Pomarine also has elongated central tail feathers but they are more twisted. In all species the bill is similar to that of a gull, but it is soft in the basal part—with separate plates covering the nostril areas—and hard and hooked at the tip. The toes are webbed and the claws hooked, and

these birds do indeed behave like birds of prey, being sometimes known as pirates of the air. Many species have a white wing patch. The Pomarine, Arctic and Long-tailed Skuas have developed to varying degrees the ability to force other birds to abandon or even disgorge food, which they then grasp and swallow on the wing. They fly down their victims with great persistence.

However skuas are not incapable of finding their own food. Especially during the breeding season, when a more varied diet is needed for the young, they take a great deal of prey, from seabirds and their eggs to rodents which they kill with strokes of their bills and grasp with the strong claws. Indeed the ferocity of the Great Skua is proverbial; while often feeding on refuse and carrion, it will not hesitate to attack animals much bigger than itself. It defends its nest and young from predatory carnivores and even from man, attacking with repeated swooping and diving. The other skuas also defend their eggs and young in the same way, but their smaller size renders them harmless, at least to man. Skuas breed on barren moorland and on tundra, on passage they occur on coasts, and winter well out to sea.

The Great Skua has a virtually bipolar distribution, when all the sub-species are taken into consideration. The nominate race is confined to the Atlantic, where it nests in a few well-defined

(Above) Great Skuas *Stercorarius skua* and (facing page) Arctic Skua *S. parasiticus* at the nest

(Right) Pomarine Skua *S. pomarinus:* this light phase is much more common than the dark colour form of the Pomarine Skua in which virtually all plumage is dark grey. (Below) World distribution of the family Stercorariidae

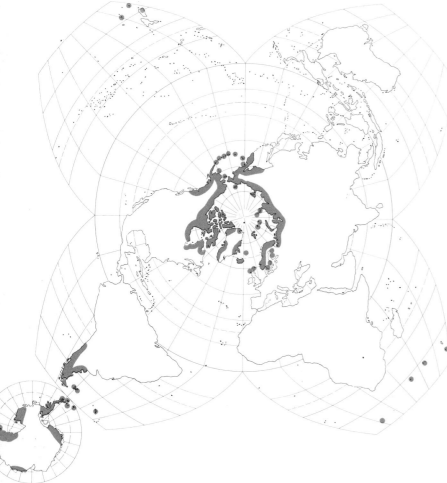

localities, from the Scottish islands to the Faeroes and Iceland. Outside the breeding season, or before reaching maturity, individuals disperse all over the Atlantic as far as the Tropic of Cancer. Other sub-species live in the Antarctic polar regions, where the Arctic sub-species may also have had its origins. The Antarctic Great Skuas (comprising four to six sub-species which are sometimes considered separate species) take a heavy toll of penguin colonies.

The Pomarine, Arctic and Long-tailed Skuas all have an exclusively northern and Arctic distribution. In many areas they are typical birds of the tundra even though they rarely nest far from the sea. The Pomarine Skua in particular is the least marine species of the four. It is affected by cyclical fluctuations of its prey, especially lemmings: only in years when the latter are abundant do all the eggs hatch and the young Pomarines survive to maturity.

Sexual maturity, or rather reproductive capacity, is reached between three and six years of age. This long maturation period may be linked to the birds' behaviour since, in order to provide for a family, they must first become adept hunters and pirates.

What particular adaptive significance the colour phases and their frequency may have, whether for different species or different populations of the same species, is not known: they could be a manifestation, more striking than usual, of a more general hereditary or genetic variation which may include physiological or behavioural advantages which still escape us.

(Left) Pale colour phase of the Arctic Skua *Stercorarius parasiticus* and (below) dark colour phase. (Bottom) MacCormick's Skua *S. maccormicki,* the Antarctic equivalent of the Great Skua *S. Skua,* together with Adelie Penguins *Pygoscellis adeliae.* Ornithologists are divided in opinion about the exact relationship between the northern and southern 'great' skuas

French: GRAND LABBE
Italian: STERCORARIO
         MAGGIORE
Spanish: PÁGALO GRANDE
German: GROSSE RAUBMÖWE

Great Skua
Stercorarius skua

(Above) Immature Great Skua (left) and adult. (Below right) Breeding areas (yellow), wintering areas (magenta) and areas where the Great Skua may be seen on passage (pink)

HABITAT Breeds on moorland and tundra: on passage found on coasts, and in winter frequents the open seas.

IDENTIFICATION Length: 58 cm. Similar in size to Herring Gull but more bulky. Plumage almost uniformly dark; tail rather short; bill large, black, hooked; legs blackish. Very conspicuous white wing patch at base of primaries. Wings are gull-like but broader. Upper parts streaked tawny-brown. On the ground its bulky build and shorter tail and bill than those of a similar-sized gull make it appear heavy and clumsy. Juveniles have less white on the wings so that their plumage seems nearly uniform; they keep this plumage until after their second winter. Flight is heavy but agile when pursuing other birds. Also has a harrier-like display flight.

During courtship the male throws back his head, puffs out his neck feathers and struts back and forth uttering an excited call in front of the female, who stands up and calls in answer. See also page 166.

CALL A low 'eh-eh-eh' in flight. Also a 'skirr' or 'took-tiik', or a combination of both notes.

REPRODUCTION Mid-May to early June. Nests in scattered colonies, usually on high ground near the sea. Nests in heather or moss. Eggs: usually two, varying in colour from olive-grey to reddish-brown, sometimes very pale greyish or light blue, with dark brown blotches. Both sexes incubate the eggs for twenty-eight to thirty days. The young are looked after by both parents for a period of six to seven weeks.

FOOD Fish, crustaceans, molluscs and beach refuse.

Often attacks gulls and other birds and forces them to drop or disgorge their food.

DISTRIBUTION AND MOVEMENTS Breeds in Iceland, Faeroes and northern Scotland. A related species breeds in southern South America and on islands in the southern oceans. Migratory: north Atlantic populations winter south to the Tropic of Cancer. In Britain, breeds mainly in Shetland and Orkney and is resident from March to August or September. Most British birds winter off coasts of Europe principally off Iberia. Is also a passage visitor to Britain and Ireland, mainly in March and April and August to October, from Iceland, Scotland and probably the Faeroes. Seen in largest numbers off western Ireland.

SUB-SPECIES The exact systematic relationship between the large skuas remains unsettled.

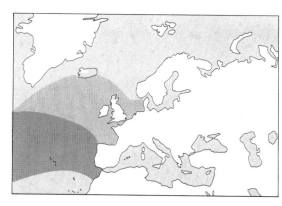

Pomarine Skua
Stercorarius pomarinus

HABITAT Breeds mainly on marshy tundra, but spends the rest of its life at sea. Regular pelagic migrant, but may also be found on migration in coastal waters during stormy periods.

IDENTIFICATION Length: 51 cm. Adults may be distinguished by the elongated central tail-feathers which, when not broken off, are blunt and twisted and give them a characteristic flight silhouette. Both pale and dark colour forms occur, but the pale form of this species is much more frequent. Pale form: crown and face blackish; ear-coverts and collar yellow; remaining upper parts grey-brown; throat and belly white; under-tail coverts and underwing grey-brown. Flanks usually streaked dark brown and a dark pectoral band is often visible. Plumage of the less common dark phase mainly dark brown. In both forms the base of the primaries is whitish, creating a pale patch on the wings when open. Immature Pomarine distinguishable from Arctic Skua only by larger size. See also page 166.

CALL Call-note is a harsh rapid 'whiic-yew' and occasionally a shrill 'week-week'.

REPRODUCTION Less sociable than the Great and Arctic Skuas: nests in scattered pairs on arctic tundra from the second half of June or early July. Nest is a depression in the moss, and two, exceptionally three, olive-green or brown eggs with dark markings are laid. Both sexes incubate the eggs, but the length of incubation is not known. Nor is any further information on reproduction available.

FOOD Birds and their eggs; fish, including dead fish; carrion (mammals and birds); ships' refuse and seaweed.

DISTRIBUTION AND MOVEMENT Breeding distribution is almost circumpolar: Breeds on the tundra of northern Europe, Asia and North America: Winters south to southwest Africa, Australia and Peru. In Britain is a passage visitor to most coasts, most frequently to the North Sea coasts. The Pomarine Skua is also a passage visitor to Ireland.

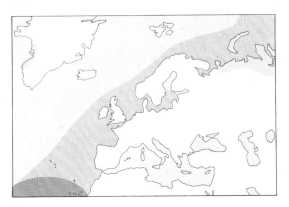

French: LABBE POMARIN
Italian: STERCORARIO MEZZANO
Spanish: PÁGALO POMARINO
German: SPATELRAUBMÖWE

(Below) Immature Pomarine Skua (left), pale colour phase (centre) and dark phase (right). (Left) Breeding areas (yellow), wintering areas (magenta) and areas where the Pomarine Skua may be seen on passage (pink)

French: LABBE PARASITE
Italian: LABBO
Spanish: PÁGALO PARÁSITO
German: SCHMAROTZERRAUB-
MÖWE

Arctic Skua
Stercorarius parasiticus

(Above) Immature Arctic Skua (left), adult in pale colour phase (centre) and dark colour phase (in flight). (Below right) Breeding areas (yellow), wintering areas (magenta) and areas where the Arctic Skua may be seen on passage (pink)

HABITAT Breeds on moorland and tundra near coasts. Also breeds on marine islands and marshy land near lakes and pools. Winters at sea.

IDENTIFICATION Length: 46 cm. Similar to the Common Gull in size, and in general is the most common skua. Smaller than Pomarine Skua and distinguished from it by straight, pointed tail feathers rather than blunt, twisted ones. Has light and dark phases and also many intermediate phases. In dark phase plumage is uniformly dark brown, with paler or more yellowish neck and sides of face. In light phase, ear coverts, neck and underparts are more or less whitish, so that there is a blackish cap on top of the head, separated from the back by a light collar. Under-tail coverts are dark brown and the brown of the back extends down to sides of breast and continues to form dark pectoral band. Dark form is commoner in southern parts of breeding range, light form in northern ones.

In winter plumage, light form has the whole of neck, throat, ear coverts and upper breast streaked or spotted brown and whitish, with some whitish streaks on back; upper and under-tail coverts and flanks broadly barred blackish and white. The dark form does not vary much from summer to winter. Legs black. Juvenile plumage varies greatly although central tail feathers much less conspicuous: adult plumage is not acquired until the third year. Flight rapid and graceful: somewhat hawk-like. Piratical behaviour: attacks other seabirds to make them disgorge food. See also page 166.

CALL A wailing 'ke-ayou' with variations and a deeper 'tuk-tuk' at the breeding grounds.

REPRODUCTION End of May onwards. Nests in colonies or isolated pairs on moorland or tundra. The nest is a depression in the moss, grass or heather, sometimes lined with vegetation. Eggs: usually two, sometimes only one and rarely three or four, greenish, olive-green or brown, exceptionally pale blue, with dark brown mottling. Both sexes incubate the eggs for twenty-four to twenty-eight days. The young are tended by both parents; they leave the nest after about three to four weeks.

FOOD Small mammals; birds and their eggs; carrion (mammals and birds). Also feeds on fish, molluscs, crustaceans, moss, berries and insects according to season.

DISTRIBUTION AND MOVEMENTS Arctic circle: breeds on the northern moors, coasts and islands of North America and Eurasia. Migratory: winters in southern South America and Africa; also in Australia and New Zealand. In Britain breeds in northern Scotland and is resident from April to September. Also occurs as a passage visitor to most coasts.

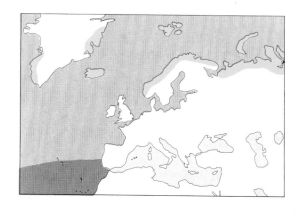

Long-tailed Skua
Stercorarius longicaudus

HABITAT Breeds on arctic tundra and winters at sea.

IDENTIFICATION Length: 53 cm. It is the smallest of the skuas although the long tail adds to the overall length. Immediately distinguishable by the very long central tail-feathers which are almost twice as long as the rest of the tail. Body less bulky than that of other skuas. Upper parts grey-brown with a well marked black 'cap' on the head. Underparts lighter: no pectoral band. Legs grey and bill black. Adults in the dark colour phase are extremely rare. In the immature the central tail-feathers are only slightly longer than the other tail-feathers. Immature is also more closely streaked and barred brown and black on the upper parts: bill smaller.

The Long-tailed Skua resorts to piracy less frequently than other skuas. See also page 166.

CALL Silent except at the breeding grounds when it emits a resonant 'kree'.

REPRODUCTION Begins late May or early June. Nest is a depression in the ground and is often lined with grass and twigs. Eggs: one to three, usually two, brown-green in colour with irregular dark markings. Incubation lasts approximately twenty-three days.

FOOD Fish and marine organisms. Also insects and lemmings in the breeding season.

DISTRIBUTION AND MOVEMENTS Breeds on islands in the Arctic Ocean and alpine tundra in North America and Eurasia. Winters at sea in the Atlantic and Pacific oceans south to about 50° South. Accidental in many parts of Europe. In Britain and Ireland is a scarce passage migrant on coasts.

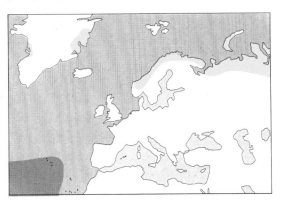

French:	LABBE À LONGUE QUEUE
Italian:	LABBO CODALUNGA
Spanish:	PÁGALO RABERO
German:	FALKENRAUBMÖWE

(Below) Adult Long-tailed Skua (foreground) and immature. (Left) Breeding areas (yellow), wintering areas (magenta) and areas where the Long-tailed Skua may be seen on passage (pink)

Skuas in flight

Identification of skuas in flight should be based mainly on their size and shape (remembering that the central tail-feathers may be broken off) and their method of flight, since species may vary greatly in coloration, especially the Arctic and Pomarine Skuas.

1: **GREAT SKUA** *(Stercorarius skua)* Unlike other skuas does not have two distinct colour phases. Its large size, awkward, heavy shape and white patch on both upper wing (a) and under-wing (b) are characteristic. The flight silhouette is shown in (e), illustrating the wings which are less angled than a gull's. Flight is heavier than a gull's and, when pursuing other birds, very agile.

2: **POMARINE SKUA** *(Stercorarius pomarinus)* Heavy and fairly bulky, reminiscent of a gull. When the central tail-feathers are present their shape is a diagnostic field mark. Even in immatures (a) lacking the elongated, twisted central tail-feathers, the white wing-patch is more extensive than the Arctic Skua. Adults are shown in the light phase (b) and dark phase (c and d). Flight is heavier than that of the Arctic Skua.

3: **LONG-TAILED SKUA** *(Stercorarius longicaudus)* The black cap, small size (about that of a Sandwich Tern), agile tern-like flight and especially the very elongated tail-feathers make this species easy to identify. Adults (a and b) are found almost always in the light phase. The tail of the immature is shown in (c); seen from above immatures are brown like immature Pomarines. From below (d) immatures may be recognised by the white wing-patch.

4: **ARCTIC SKUA** *(Stercorarius parasiticus)* Adult in light phase: upper parts (a) vary from greyish to brown; the white wing-patch is also very variable; some individuals have a white patch at base of neck; seen from below (b) the pectoral band is not always present. In immatures the central tail feathers are only slightly longer and more pointed (c) and the white wing-patch is fairly conspicuous. Immatures seen from below (d) and from the side (e). The flight is buoyant, graceful and rapid, like a hawk's. Three typical flight postures when hunting are illustrated in (f): like other skuas flies down other birds with persistence to obtain food.

(Right) Arctic Skua *S. parasiticus* alighting at the nest

Eric Hosking

LARIDAE: Gulls and Terns

B. Pettersson

Gulls and terns were formerly assigned to a separate order Lariformes: at present, however, in spite of the apparently considerable differences in shape, gulls and terns are classified along with the skuas in the order Charadriiformes. This order also includes the plovers and other waders and, with the gulls and terns, they share common features of skeletal and muscular structure and behaviour. Nonetheless, gulls and terns are a clearly distinct group. They can be separated into two well-defined sub-families: Larinae, consisting of the gulls, and Sterninae which is composed of the terns.

The distribution of gulls is worldwide, and they are among the best known of seabirds. Gulls frequent the coast and the open sea, although some species prefer to breed by inland waters such as lakes and swamps. Some species are small—about twenty centimetres long—but the majority are fairly large and may reach eighty centimetres in length.

They are powerful birds with long pointed wings, the tail is of medium length and usually square, and the bill is tough and hooked and used as a weapon by some species. The front toes are webbed and the hind toe is small or occasionally rudimentary. Adult plumage of most gulls is white on the underparts with a varying amount of grey or brown (sometimes almost black) on the upper parts. Most species have black wing-tips. There are only a few uniformly dark species such as the Lava Gull *Larus fulginosus* of the Galapagos Islands: its English name aptly describes its dark plumage. Several species have a dark hood or mask on the head in summer plumage. The bill and legs are often brightly coloured—red, pink or yellow—although there may be some seasonal variation. The young are darker than the adults and more closely spotted with brown. This makes it difficult to distinguish the species, and the identification of immatures is further complicated by the fact that they assume adult plumage gradually after a number of years,

(Above) Sandwich Terns *Sterna sandvicensis:* like many terns they resemble small gulls but the wings are longer, the tail more deeply forked and the bill thinner and more pointed. (Facing page) Black-headed Gulls *Larus ridibundus* in winter plumage. The Black-headed Gull is one of the smallest common breeding gulls of Europe. (Overleaf) Caspian Terns *Hydroprogne caspia* feeding a newly hatched chick

Eric Hosking

J. Gooders/Ardea

passing through a series of intermediate plumages. Gulls with a dark terminal or sub-terminal bar on the tail will often be immatures. In winter plumage adult gulls which have black or brown hoods on the head lose them, and the markings on the head become the easiest means of distinguishing them from similar-sized gulls.

Gulls are excellent fliers and fly with a slow and powerful wingbeat: they soar frequently. The wings are broader and blunter than the terns', and the flight is somewhat heavier. Gulls are also expert swimmers.

In behaviour gulls are highly gregarious. They gather in huge flocks at sea or on land, and almost always nest in colonies—frequently in association with other seabirds. They nest by the sea on cliffs or flat ground or sometimes inland by fresh water. The nest is usually large, and two or three eggs are laid which range in colour from pale brown to olive green with irregular dark spots. Both parents incubate the eggs.

Many gulls are scavengers, feeding on animal or plant refuse. However other species are able to catch live fish, and some feed on marine invertebrates.

Although the gulls are distributed throughout the world, including the Antarctic, most species belong to the northern hemisphere. For convenience of description, gulls may be classified into two groups: those having white heads when in adult plumage, and those with a dark hood. The most widely known species in the former group is the Herring Gull *Larus argentatus*, a native of North America and northwest Europe, although with its sub-species it extends as far as the Mediterranean, the Black Sea and across much of Asia. The Lesser Black-backed Gull *L. fuscus* is very similar. It belongs to the Palearctic region, and is distinguished by the darker coloration of the upper parts. These two species coexist in Europe, while in other parts of the world they are interrelated by a series of intermediate sub-species. They thus provide a typical example of what is described as an annular species—one which is divided into a series of geographically distinct gradations, the extreme forms of which come into contact with each other in particular areas (for example by a process of continued expansion of their range) and there behave as a distinct species. In such cases, the assigning of a geographical identity (sub-species) to one or other of the two species that close the circle is an arbitrary matter.

The Great Black-backed Gull *L. marinus* is one of the largest species of gull, and it is most commonly found in the north Atlantic. Another large gull is the Glaucous Gull *L. hyperboreus*. The Common Gull *L. canus* is much smaller; it is found not only in the Palearctic region but also in western North America. All these species have white heads in adult plumage. The many similar species include the Ring-billed Gull *L. delawarensis* (the Americas), the Black-tailed Gull *L. crassirostris* (north-east Asia)—which has a dark band on the tail even in adult plumage; and the Pacific Gull *L. pacificus* (southern Australia). The Dolphin Gull *L. scoresbii* of Tierra del Fuego and the Falkland Islands, is relatively dark. The Iceland Gull *L. glaucoides* has very pale, almost white plumage.

Some authorities divide the 'hooded' gull species into primitive and more highly evolved species. The former include species with a complete hood, such as the Laughing Gull *L. atricilla* and Franklin's Gull *L. pipixcan* of the Americas, Hemprich's or Sooty Gull *L. hemprichii* of the western Indian Ocean, Mediterranean Gull *L. melanocephalus* of the Mediterranean and central Asia, Little Gull *L. minutus* of Eurasia, and the large Great Black-headed Gull *L. ichthyaetus* of the Red Sea and central-southern Asia as far as the Gulf of Bengal. The more highly evolved species include gulls having a 'mask'—i.e. a hood that does not extend to cover the back of the head and neck—such as the Black-headed Gull *L. ridibundus* of the Palearctic region, Bonaparte's Gull *L. philadelphia* of North America, Grey-headed Gull *L. cirrocephalus* of the African lakes, Silver Gull *L. novaehollandiae* of Australia, and Black-billed Gull *L. bulleri* of New Zealand.

Two species have a white hood on top of dark neck and body plumage: these are Heermann's Gull *L. heermanni* of the Pacific coast of the United States and Grey Gull *L. modestus* of the Humboldt Current (off the west coast of south South America). The inland waters of China harbour a characteristic species, Saunders's Gull *L. saundersi*. Two species

of gulls have forked tails; the Swallow-tailed Gull *Creagrus furcatus* belongs to the Pacific equatorial waters around the Galapagos Islands, while Sabine's gull *L. sabini* lives in the remote Arctic.

The three-toed gulls, which have only rudimentary hind toes, show traces of a dark hood only in juvenile and winter plumages. Unlike other gulls, they feed in the open sea. These differences have led to the classification of the two three-toed species—the Kittiwake *Rissa tridactyla* of the north Atlantic and the Red-legged Kittiwake *R. brevirostria* of the Bering Sea—in a separate genus *Rissa*. In Ross's Gull *Rhodostethia rosea*, of northern Siberia, all that remains of the hood is a little black collar. The only gull with entirely white plumage is the Ivory Gull *Pagophila eburnea*.

The sub-family Sterninae of the family Laridae is composed of the terns. In many ways terns are similar to gulls, but they are usually smaller and more slender with long, pointed wings. The tail is forked. The bill is thinner and more pointed than that of the gulls and is usually held almost vertically downwards in flight.

Most species have white summer or nuptial plumage with grey wings and back and a black crown. As coloration among the species is similar, the size, colour of bill and call are generally the best field marks by which to identify a species. The feet are webbed in front with a rudimentary hind toe. However some species swim only very rarely.

Terns feed on fish and other aquatic life forms which they catch by diving from high above the

(Top) Lava Gull *Larus fuliginosus* and (above) Heerman's Gull *L. hermanni*

(Left) Herring Gulls *L. argentatus,* one of the most common and widespread of the larger gull. (Facing page, top) British and western European race of the Herring Gull *L. l. argentatus.* (Facing page, bottom) Little Gulls *L. minutus* in winter plumage and in moult

R. Kinne/Photo Researchers

(Above) Bonaparte's Gulls
L. philadelphia and other gulls.
(Below) World distribution
of the family Laridae

water. Marsh species also eat insects. Like gulls, they are social birds and nest in colonies. They have quite a wide variety of calls and in general the voice is harsh. The courtship display consists of spectacular aerobatics and symbolic offerings of food by the male to his partner. Almost all species nest on the ground, but some build a nest in bushes or trees, and one, the White or Fairy Tern *Gygis alba* lays a single egg in the fork of a tree. The marsh terns of the genus *Chlidonias* build a floating nest of reeds and other plants.

Terns frequent the shores of inland waters, particularly in warmer regions. In general they breed on sand, shingle or marine islands. Their distribution is almost cosmopolitan, and some species are migratory. Of the forty-odd species, about twenty terns belong to the genus *Sterna*, which consists mainly of birds with a black crown, such as the Common Tern *S. hirundo*, the Arctic Tern *S. paradisaea*, which nests in the northern circumpolar regions and winters in the Antarctic, and the Antarctic Tern *S. vittata*. The Sooty Tern *S. fuscata* has darker plumage, with brown-black colouring on the upper parts.

The smaller species include the Little Tern, *S. albifrons*. The cryptic coloration of the Little Tern's eggs has, strangely enough, been counter-productive. They are so well camouflaged in the bare scrapes where the Little Tern nests that they are often crushed underfoot. Among the medium-sized and larger species are the Caspian Tern *Hydroprogne caspia* which resembles a gull, the Royal Tern *S. maxima*, the Swift Tern *S. bergii*, the Elegant Tern *S. elegans* and the Sandwich Tern *S. sandvicensis*.

The Gull-billed Tern *Gelochelidon nilotica* and the Large-billed Tern *Phaetusa simplex* have heavy bills, and feed both at sea and on land where they catch insects and small reptiles. The genus *Larosterna* consists of a single species, the Inca Tern *L. inca* which inhabits the western coast of South America.

Great Black-headed Gull
Larus ichthyaetus

HABITAT Breeds on coasts or by brackish water. Winters in coastal waters and along rivers.

IDENTIFICATION Length: 63 cm. The black hood makes this species easily identifiable. Other distinctive features are its large size; heavy tri-coloured orange and yellow bill with a black band near the tip; greenish legs; white mark around the conspicuous red rim of the eye; black-tipped white primaries. In winter plumage head is white with black stripes on crown and dark markings through the eye. In summer it is the only large gull with a black hood. Immatures best distinguished by the heavy black bill which appears to droop at the tip.

The Great Black-headed Gull often attacks smaller gulls and seizes their food. Flies gracefully, frequently sailing on outstretched wings for long periods. See also page 224.

CALL At the breeding grounds emits a laughing 'kyaauu-kyaau'. At other times utters a harsh 'kra-aapa'.

REPRODUCTION Late May and early June. Nest in colonies: nest is a depression in the ground. Eggs: generally two or three, sometimes four, stone-grey or yellow with dark brown streaks. Length of incubation period is not known.

FOOD Mainly fish, also reptiles, crustaceans and some insects.

DISTRIBUTION AND MOVEMENTS Breeds discontinuously from the Crimea and southern Russia east to northern China. Winters in the eastern Mediterranean, by the Black Sea and east to Burma. Accidental in western Europe including Britain.

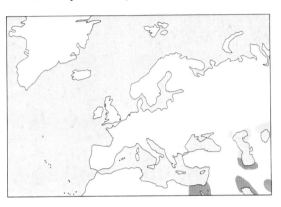

French: GOÉLAND À TÊTE NOIRE
Italian: GABBIANO DEL PALLAS
Spanish: GAVIÓN CABECINEGRO
German: FISCHMÔWE

(Below) Great Black-headed Gull in summer plumage (foreground) and winter plumage. (Left) Breeding areas (yellow), wintering areas (magenta) and areas where the Great Black-headed Gull may be seen all year round (orange)

French: MOUETTE DE BONAPARTE
Italian: GABBIANO DI BONAPARTE
Spanish: GAVIOTA BONAPARTE
German: BONAPARTE-MÔWE

Bonaparte's Gull
Larus philadelphia

HABITAT Breeds by lakes and rivers. Winter on coasts and by fresh water.

IDENTIFICATION Length: 31 cm. Resembles the Black-headed Gull with white forewing and black tips to the primaries. However Bonaparte's Gull is smaller, has a thinner black bill and a dark grey hood. In winter plumage coloration is similar to that of the Black-headed. In all plumages the primaries on the underwing are white—not black .The legs are orange-red.

Immatures very similar to those of the Black-headed Gull but have black patches near the tip of the innermost primaries and secondaries. Flight is buoyant and more like a tern's than that of a typical gull. See also page 218.

CALL Emits occasional strident notes.

REPRODUCTION Second half of June. Eggs: generally lays three, ranging in colour from brown-yellow to dark olive with brown and green spots.

FOOD Mainly insects.

DISTRIBUTION AND MOVEMENTS Breeds in northern Canada. Winters on west and east coasts of North America and on the Gulf of Florida south to Central America. Also winters inland on the shores of the Great Lakes. Is a rare transatlantic vagrant to Europe, including Britain, Ireland and France.

Slender-billed Gull
Larus genei

HABITAT Breeds by fresh and brackish water and by coastal lagoons. Also on offshore islands. Winters mainly at coastal waters.

IDENTIFICATION Length: 42 cm. In summer plumage the head and neck are pure white and underparts have a pink tinge. Bill dark red, appearing almost black from a distance. Legs dark red. Holds itself erect with the neck extended. In winter plumage is similar to a Black-headed Gull but is longer and stockier. Bill yellow in winter. See also page 218.

CALL Generally softer and more plaintive than the call of the Black-headed Gull. Also emits a laughing 'kau-kau'.

REPRODUCTION May and June. Eggs: two or three, whitish or pale yellow and boldly marked with dark blotches. Both sexes probably incubate the eggs, but the incubation period is not known.

FOOD Mainly molluscs and crustaceans.

DISTRIBUTION AND MOVEMENTS Sporadic breeding distribution in northern Africa, southern Spain, France and by the Black and Caspian Seas. Also breeds around the Persian Gulf eastwards to Pakistan. Winters in the breeding range and by the Mediterranean and Red Sea. In Britain the Slender-billed Gull is a very scarce vagrant.

(Below) Bonaparte's Gull in winter plumage (left) and summer plumage. (Facing page, top) Slender-billed Gull. (Right) Breeding areas (yellow), wintering areas (magenta), areas where the Slender-billed Gull may be seen all year round (orange) and on passage (pink)

French: GOÉLAND RAILLEUR
Italian: GABBIANO ROSEO
Spanish: GAVIOTA PICOFINA
German: DÜNNSCHNABEL-MÔWE

Mediterranean Gull
Larus melanocephalus

HABITAT Breeds on grassy coastal marshes and flats. Winters at coastal waters.

IDENTIFICATION Length: 39 cm. Resembles the Common Gull but is stockier, the red legs are long and the heavy red bill appears to droop at the tip. In summer plumage head is black like the Black-headed Gull's but in all plumages adults lack black markings on the wings, although immature birds have black wing-tips. Adults in winter plumage and immatures have a black smudge through the eye. See also page 218.

CALL Emits notes similar to those of the Black-headed Gull: also a deeper 'kau-kauu'.

REPRODUCTION Nests in late May and early June. Eggs: usually three, light brown to olive green with dark splotches which camouflages them. Nest is a scrape in the ground, and may be lined with grasses. Information on incubation and nestlings is lacking.

FOOD Small fish, molluscs, crustaceans and insects.

DISTRIBUTION AND MOVEMENTS Breeds in Greece and Asia Minor. Has bred exceptionally in the Netherlands and in Hungary. Appears to winter in the central Mediterranean although a few also occur on the coast of the Baltic and on western European coasts. In Britain occasional pairs have bred in southern England since 1968. Also occurs as a passage and winter visitor in very small numbers to Britain and Ireland.

French: MOUETTE
  MÉLANOCÉPHALE
Italian: GABBIANO CORALLINO
Spanish: GAVIOTA CABECINEGRA
German: SCHWARZKOPFMÔWE

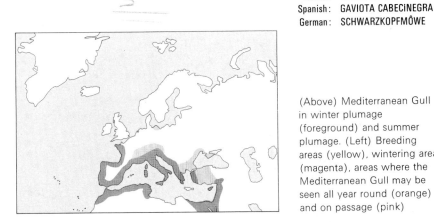

(Above) Mediterranean Gull in winter plumage (foreground) and summer plumage. (Left) Breeding areas (yellow), wintering areas (magenta), areas where the Mediterranean Gull may be seen all year round (orange) and on passage (pink)

French: MOUETTE RIEUSE
Italian: GABBIANO COMUNE
Spanish: GAVIOTA REIDORA
German: LACHMÖWE

Black-headed Gull
Larus ridibundus

HABITAT Breeds by marshes and on dunes, shingle and islands in lakes. Winters by fresh water and on coasts and estuaries. Is also common on farmland.

IDENTIFICATION Length: 37 cm. Is the smallest common breeding gull of Europe. In summer plumage distinguished by its chocolate-brown hood which does not extend onto the nape and by the broad white leading edge of the wing. Slender red bill and red legs. In winter plumage head is white with a dark patch on the ear-coverts. When flying long distances flight is buoyant and strong: however at other times flight is more wavering and resembles the flight of a tern. See also page 218.

CALL A harsh 'quorp'. Also emits other shrill cries.

REPRODUCTION From Mid-April. Nests in colonies. Eggs: normally three, ranging in colour from grey to dark brown. Both sexes incubate the eggs for twenty to twenty-four days and both care for the young.

FOOD Both plant and animal matter.

DISTRIBUTION AND MOVEMENTS Breeds in Iceland, Faeroes, Britain and Ireland east through Scandinavia and France across Eurasia. Winters in the southern parts of the breeding range but migrates as far south as north-central Africa, India and Malaysia. In Britain and Ireland is a widespread breeder: many migrate south as far as Spain in winter.

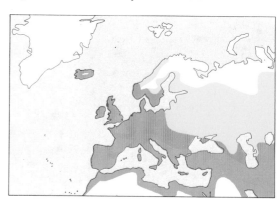

(Below right) Black-headed Gull in winter plumage (left), summer plumage (centre) and immature (right). (Right) Breeding areas (yellow), wintering areas (magenta) and areas where the Black-headed Gull may be seen all year round (orange)

Little Gull
Larus minutus

HABITAT Breeds by fresh-water pools and marshes. Winters on coasts and shores of lakes.

IDENTIFICATION Length: 30 cm. Distinguished from the Black-headed Gull in summer plumage by the brilliant black hood which extends over the nape. At all seasons may be distinguished by the absence of black on the upper surface of the rounded wings. Underwing dark in summer and winter. Bill reddish in summer, black in winter and in immatures. Legs red.

Is the most tern-like of the gulls, but may be distinguished in winter by the square white tail and dark underwing. See also page 222.

CALL A sharp 'keek-keek-kee'.

REPRODUCTION End of May onwards. Eggs: normally two or three, olive-green with dark splotches. Nest is constructed of reeds and plant material. Both sexes incubate the eggs for about twenty days.

FOOD Small fish, crustaceans, molluscs and insects.

DISTRIBUTION AND MOVEMENTS Breeds on the shores of the Baltic and Black Seas and in Siberia. Winters on European coasts south to the Red Sea and the Persian Gulf: occasionally winters on the shores of the North Sea. Occurs in Britain and Ireland as a regular passage and winter visitor in small numbers. The Little Gull has bred once in England in recent years.

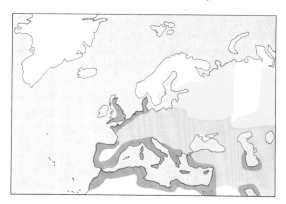

(Below) Little Gull in summer plumage (foreground) and immature. Breeding areas (yellow), wintering areas (magenta), areas where the Little Gull may be seen all year round (orange) and on passage (pink)

French: MOUETTE PYGMÉE
Italian: GABBIANELLO
Spanish: GAVIOTA ENANA
German: ZWERGMÖWE

French: GOÉLAND ARGENTÉ
Italian: GABBIANO REALE
Spanish: GAVIOTA ARGÉNTEA
German: SILBERMÔWE

Herring Gull
Larus argentatus

HABITAT Breeds on sea cliffs, shingle and marine islands: occasionally inland. Winters on coasts and inland by reservoirs and lakes.

IDENTIFICATION Length: 56 cm. Most common and widespread gull in Europe. Adult may be confused with the Common Gull, but is larger; bill thicker and heavier; legs flesh coloured rather than green. Ends of the grey wings are black with a few white markings. Bill yellow with a red patch. Adult Herring Gulls vary greatly in size and coloration: the mantle may be very dark to silver grey. Some races also have yellow rather than flesh-pink legs, although the British and western European race is among the palest and has pink legs. Herring Gulls are often seen feeding at rubbish dumps.

Immatures dark brown with chestnut spots, with little contrast in coloration. Bill black and legs pink. The flight of the Herring Gull is strong and deliberate, and it frequently soars and glides. See also page 216.

CALL The most common notes are a low-pitched 'kyoo-kyoo', an excited 'kee-u-keee-u' and a brief loud 'oww' or 'e-oo'.

REPRODUCTION End of April to early June. Generally nest in colonies. Eggs: usually three, sometimes two, varying in colour from olive to dark brown. Nest is made of twigs and bits of vegetation. The female undertakes the major share of incubation which lasts twenty-five to twenty-seven days. Both parents care for the young which begin to fly at about six weeks.

FOOD Fish, molluscs and insects. Also feeds on small mammals, birds and their eggs and plant material.

DISTRIBUTION AND MOVEMENTS Breeds on the coasts of Europe, Asia and North America. In Britain and Ireland is a widely distributed and numerous resident breeder. In recent years has begun to inhabit the roofs of buildings in many seaside towns, especially in south and northeast England and in north Wales. Now even breeds in central London at Regent's Park.

SUB-SPECIES *L.a. argentatus* (flesh-pink legs): Iceland, Faeroes, Britain and Ireland, northern France, Netherlands, Scandinavia and northwest USSR. *L.a. michahellis* (grey outer primaries with white tips and yellow legs): Mediterranean region. Other sub-species are present in Asia and North America.

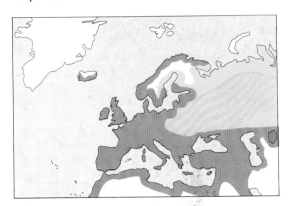

(Below) Immature Herring Gull (left), the British and western European sub-species *L. a. argentatus* (centre) and the Mediterranean sub-species *L. a. michahellis* (right). (Right) Breeding areas (yellow), wintering areas (magenta), areas where the Herring Gull may be seen all year round (orange) and on passage (pink)

French: GOÉLAND BRUN
Italian: ZAFFERANO
Spanish: GAVIOTA SOMBRÍA
German: HERINGSMÖWE

Lesser Black-backed Gull
Larus fuscus

(Above) Lesser Black-backed Gull in summer plumage (foreground) and immature. (Below) Breeding areas (yellow), wintering areas (magenta), areas where the Lesser Black-backed Gull may be seen all year round (orange) and on passage (pink)

HABITAT Breed mainly on coasts although some breed inland. Winters on coasts.

IDENTIFICATION Length: 53 cm. Adult resembles Great Black-backed Gull but is much smaller with yellow legs and slate-grey upper parts. Lesser and Great Black-backed Gulls are the only gulls which are all white except for their dark mantles and wings. Head striped brown in winter. Immatures resemble immature Herring Gulls but are somewhat darker. Bill colour in adults and immatures similar to that of Herring Gull. Immatures' legs are chestnut or flesh-coloured.

In flight the Lesser Black-back performs a dance, hovering and turning high in the air for several minutes while uttering excited cries. See also page 214.

CALL Emits various notes which resemble those of a Herring Gull but are generally lower-pitched and quieter, including a raucous 'quow', a quickly repeated 'kook-kook-kook' and a lively 'eck-eck-eck'.

REPRODUCTION May to June: sometimes April. Nests in colonies: nest is constructed of plant matter. Eggs: generally three, sometimes only one or two, ranging from pale blue-green to dark brown and usually with dark spots. Both sexes incubate the eggs for twenty-six or twenty-seven days. The female alone rears the young, and the young leave the nest in the crowded colony after about thirty-two days.

FOOD Fish, molluscs and crustaceans. Also feeds on beach refuse, insects and grains. Will consume mammal carcasses, and attacks and kills other birds and eats them and their eggs.

DISTRIBUTION AND MOVEMENTS Breeds in northern Europe east through Scandinavia and France to Siberia. Some winter in the nesting area, but most migrate south to tropical Africa and to Arabia. In Britain and Ireland is a fairly numerous breeder in colonies on coasts and inland. Also occurs on passage.

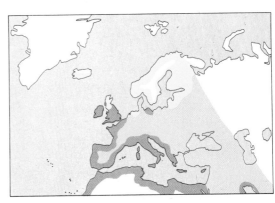

French: GOÉLAND À AILES
BLANCHES
Italian: GABBIANO D'ISLANDA
Spanish: GAVIOTA POLAR
German: POLARMÖWE

Iceland Gull
Larus glaucoides

HABITAT Breeds on rocky coasts and cliffs by the sea. Winters on flat coasts and harbours.

IDENTIFICATION Length: 53 cm. Plumage like that of Glaucous Gull, which in general it closely resembles: silver-grey back or mantle and wings: no black markings on the wings. However is distinguished from Glaucous by smaller size, less massive bill, and the adult's red rather than yellow orbital ring. Wings long, and when at rest they extend beyond the tail without crossing, forming a narrow 'V' that gives the body a streamlined look. Legs beige-pink. Juveniles similar to Glaucous Gull, but with more black on the bill during the first winter.

Flight more agile and faster than Glaucous Gull's: resembles a Kittiwake's flight. See also page 214.

CALL Like that of Herring Gull, but more strident. Usual notes: a low 'kee-urr' and a modulated 'curr-curr'. When alarmed, produces a note similar to that of the Great Black-backed Gull: 'eck-eck-eck'.

REPRODUCTION End of May and early June. Nests in colonies, sometimes in company with other species. Nest is large, and consists mainly of grass and moss.

Eggs: two or three, like those of Glaucous Gull, but smaller. No information is available on incubation.

FOOD Mainly small fish, also fish carcasses, other beach refuse and dead birds.

DISTRIBUTION AND MOVEMENTS Greenland and southern Baffin Island. Winters south to the eastern United States, Iceland, Britain and Ireland. In Britain is a visitor to Shetland, the Outer Hebrides and northeast English coasts. Occurs elsewhere but irregularly.

SUB-SPECIES Sub-species are present in North America.

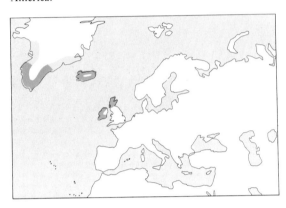

(Below) Iceland Gull in summer plumage (foreground) and immature. (Right) Breeding areas (yellow), wintering areas (magenta) and areas where the Iceland Gull may be seen all year round (orange)

Glaucous Gull
Larus hyperboreus

French: GOÉLAND BOURGMESTRE
Italian: GABBIANO GLAUCO
Spanish: GAVIOTA HIPERBÓREA
German: EISMÖWE

HABITAT Breeds on cliffs and rocky areas of arctic islands. Winters on low-lying coasts. Infrequent inland.

IDENTIFICATION Length: 68 cm. Distinguishable by its pale grey mantle and pure white primaries. May be confused with the Iceland Gull which has similar coloration but the Glaucous is larger, with a more massive bill and a yellow (not red) orbital ring. When standing at rest with wings folded, the wings do not extend beyond the tail. Bill yellow, with a pink patch; legs flesh-pink. Juveniles are paler than other juvenile gulls and have buff-coloured wavy stripes and spots, but lack a broad terminal band on the tail. Juvenile Glaucous Gulls become progressively whiter with age and can be regarded as adults after their fourth or fifth year. See also page 214.

CALL Generally silent, but emits plaintive calls which resemble the Herring Gull's.

REPRODUCTION End of May to mid-June. Nests in colonies, sometimes of a few pairs only. The nest is bulky when materials are available, but is often made only of seaweed. Eggs: normally three, sometimes only two; stone-grey to brown, sometimes pale blue-green, with brown and ash-grey spots. Both sexes incubate the eggs for twenty-seven to twenty-eight days, and both rear the young.

FOOD Carrion, birds, worms, insects and seaweed.

DISTRIBUTION AND MOVEMENTS Breeding distribution circumpolar in arctic regions of North America and Eurasia. Also Greenland. Winters south to the United States, France and Japan. Occasionally further south as far as Spain, Portugal and the Mediterranean. In Britain and Ireland is an uncommon winter visitor to coasts, but is still more frequently observed than the Iceland Gull.

SUB-SPECIES Sub-species are present in Europe, North America and Siberia.

(Above) Glaucous Gull in summer plumage (right), immature second year (left) and first year (behind). (Below) Breeding areas (yellow), wintering areas (magenta) and areas where the Glaucous Gull may be seen all year round (orange)

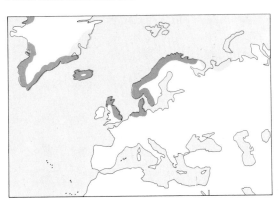

French: GOÉLAND MARIN
Italian: MUGNAIACCIO
Spanish: GAVIÓN
German: MANTELMÖWE

Great Black-backed Gull
Larus marinus

HABITAT Breeds mainly on cliffs and marine islands occasionally on flat shores and inland. Winters on coasts.

IDENTIFICATION Length: 66 cm. Legs whitish or flesh-pink, black mantle, yellow bill with a red patch. Primaries have white tips; white trailing edge on the dark almost black wings. Head is lightly striped with dark brown in winter. Legs pink.

CALL A raucous 'awk' and a guttural 'yook-yook-yook'.

REPRODUCTION From early May to early June. Nests in colonies. Eggs: generally three, ranging from stony-grey to olive-brown. Incubation lasts for twenty-six to twenty-eight days.

FOOD Fish, crustaceans, molluscs and beach refuse.

DISTRIBUTION AND MOVEMENTS Breeds in northeast North America, Greenland, Iceland, Faeroes, Britain and Ireland north across Eurasia. Winters south to the Great Lakes and the Black, Caspian and Mediterranean Seas. In Britain and Ireland is a fairly numerous resident breeder in most maritime counties (although not in east and southeast England).

Audouin's Gull
Larus audouinii

HABITAT Breeds on rocky marine islets. Pelagic in winter.

IDENTIFICATION Length: 49 cm. Adult in summer plumage recognisable by the pale grey mantle and grey wings with white-tipped black primaries. Bill red with a black band near the yellowish tip. Legs dark olive-green or greenish-grey; iris dark, with a red orbital ring. Wings are narrower than those of the Herring or Common Gulls. See also page 216.

CALL A hoarse 'kiaow'. Also emits a quieter 'crik-crik'.

REPRODUCTION Early May onwards. Two or three eggs are laid, olive-buff in colour and spotted and blotched with black-brown. Both sexes incubate the eggs for twenty-one to twenty-five days. Both also care for the young.

FOOD Feeds mainly at sea on marine organisms.

DISTRIBUTION AND MOVEMENTS An almost exclusively Mediterranean species, which breeds from Spain to Greece in a few isolated colonies. Is among the rarest breeding gulls of Europe.

(Below) Great Black-backed Gull in summer plumage (foreground) and immature. (Right) Breeding areas (yellow), wintering areas (magenta) and areas where the Great Black-backed Gull may be seen all year round (orange)

(Above) Audouin's Gull in summer plumage (foreground) and immature

French: GOÉLAND D'AUDOUIN
Italian: GABBIANO CORSO
Spanish: GAVIOTA DE AUDOUIN
German: KORALLENMÖWE

French: GOÉLAND CENDRÉ
Italian: GAVINA
Spanish: GAVIOTA CANA
German: STURMMÖWE

(Above) Common Gull in summer plumage (right) and immature. (Right) Breeding areas (yellow), wintering areas (magenta), areas where the Common Gull may be seen all year round (orange) and on passage (pink)

Common Gull
Larus canus

HABITAT Breeds on rocky, sand and shingle coasts. Also breeds inland by fresh water. In winter frequents coasts, cultivated land and estuaries. Sometimes found in urban areas.

IDENTIFICATION Length: 40 cm. Adult Common Gull resembles Herring Gull with grey back, black tipped primaries and white spots near the tip of the wing. However the Common Gull is much smaller, with a thinner bill with no red spot near the tip, the mantle is slightly darker and the bill and legs are yellow-green.
Dark brown stripes on the head in winter like the Herring Gull. Juveniles have a whitish base to the tail with a black terminal band, black bill and brown legs. During the courtship display the male and female often walk in a circle with heads held far back and legs bent, uttering guttural cries.
At rest, the wings extend further beyond the tail than the Herring Gull's. Flight is more graceful than that of the Herring Gull. See also page 216.

CALL A strident 'keee-way', sometimes changing to a rapid 'keee-eh-keee-ah-keee-eh'; a high-pitched 'ke-ke-ke'; and a guttural 'quuook-ook, kiik-ook'. In general is higher and shriller than the Herring Gull's voice.

REPRODUCTION Latter half of May to early June. Nests in colonies: the nest varies in size and is made of heather and grass. Eggs: usually three but often only two, rarely four or five. Eggs range in colour from dark olive-green to pale olive, occasionally pale green or blue, with dark brown spots and streaks. Both sexes incubate the eggs for twenty-two to twenty-four days. The young fly after four weeks.

FOOD Insects, earthworms, marine invertebrates, dead fish, refuse, crustaceans and molluscs. Also feeds on vegetable matter, small mammals, small birds and their eggs.

DISTRIBUTION AND MOVEMENTS Central north Europe, central Asia, northwest America. Northern European populations winter on the North Sea and Baltic coast, while populations of central Europe winter in the Mediterranean region or in their nesting area. In Britain and Ireland is a common breeding bird in the north and west: is also a winter and passage visitor.

SUB-SPECIES *L.c. canus*: north central Europe. *L.c. heinei* (larger): northwest USSR and Asia. Other sub-species are present in North America.

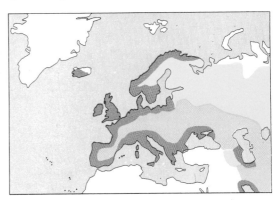

V. Olsson

R. Pettersson

Jose Lalanda

G. Hansson

(Left) Common Gull *Larus canus:* it resembles a small Herring Gull but may be distinguished by less stout bill with no red spot near the tip. (Facing page, top left) A group of Black-headed Gulls *L. ridibundus:* in summer plumage they may be distinguished by their small size and the dark brown hood which does not extend onto the nape. (Facing page, top right) California Gull *L. californicus* and (centre right) immature Great Black-backed Gull. (Facing page, bottom) Black-headed Gulls *L. ridibundus* mating on the nest they have built

French: MOUETTE RIEUSE
AMÉRICAINE
Italian: GABBIANO
SGHIGNAZZANTE
Spanish: GAVIOTA
GUANAGUANARE
German: AZTEKEN-MÖWE

Laughing Gull
Larus atricilla

HABITAT Sea coasts, bays, estuaries and salt marshes.

IDENTIFICATION Length: 42 cm. A small gull, with grey mantle and dark lavender-grey head; no white at the tips of the dark wings. In summer plumage the underparts become tinged with pink. In winter plumage the head and neck are white, with grey-brown spots on the head and around the eyes. Legs and bill dark brown all year round. Immatures: grey-brown upper parts and whitish tail with black sub-terminal band. See also page 224.

CALL A goose-like note: 'kaha-kaha', also a high-pitched 'ha-ha-ha-ha-haa-haa-haa' from which its name is derived.

REPRODUCTION Nests in densely packed colonies on the ground, or on tufts of grass in salt marshes and on marshy coasts. The nest is made of marsh-grasses. Two to five eggs are laid, these are yellow or green-brown, with irregular brown and grey spots. Incubation lasts about twenty days and the young leave the nest shortly after hatching.

FOOD Small fish, especially fry which are caught near the surface of the water.

DISTRIBUTION AND MOVEMENTS Breeds on the Atlantic and Gulf coasts of North America south to Mexico and the Carribean. Winters from the southern United States south to Peru. Accidental in Britain, Ireland, Sweden and France.

Franklin's Gull
Larus pipixcan

HABITAT Breeds inland by swamps and lakes. In winter frequents coasts.

IDENTIFICATION Length: 34–38 cm. A small gull, with black head and grey mantle: similar to the Laughing Gull. Wing-tips are white with a large black patch. Bill and legs dark red. During the breeding season, the underparts (especially the breast) are pink. In winter plumage head is white with a grey-brown patch at the back. Legs and bill become darker in winter plumage. May be distinguished from the Laughing Gull by the more white trailing edge of the wing. See also page 224.

CALL A high-pitched 'kook-kook-kook-kook', also a soft 'krruck' and a nasal 'puai'.

REPRODUCTION Nests in colonies which may include up to 20,000 nests among reeds and other marsh vegetation. Two to four eggs are laid which are dark brown or brown-green, with even darker spots and patches. Incubation lasts eighteen to twenty days.

FOOD During the reproductive season, almost exclusively insects, worms and other small invertebrates. In winter feeds on marine invertebrates and small fish.

DISTRIBUTION AND MOVEMENTS A North American species, nesting inland in Canada and the United States. Winters along the Pacific coast, from Guatemala south to the Galapagos Islands, Chile, and along the coast of the Gulf of Texas. Accidental in Britain: one appeared at Lowestoft in Suffolk in February 1978

(Facing page, top) Franklin's Gull in summer plumage (foreground) and winter plumage

(Below) Laughing Gull in summer plumage (foreground) and winter plumage

French: MOUETTE DE FRANKLIN
Italian: GABBIANO DI FRANKLIN
Spanish: GAVIOTA DE FRANKLIN
German: PRAIRIEMÖWE

Sabine's Gull

Larus sabini

HABITAT During the breeding season lives on marshy tundra or on low-lying coastland and islands in the arctic. Winters at sea.

IDENTIFICATION Length: 33 cm. A small gull, distinguished by its markedly forked white tail, black forewing and contrasting white trailing edge of the wing. In summer it is the only gull with a dark grey hood: the hood extends to the nape and ends in a thin black collar. Bill dark with a yellow tip; legs grey. In winter the head is dirty white. Immatures head and upper parts grey-brown, rump and tail white. Pattern on wings similar to adults', but the white tail has black tip.

Flight buoyant and similar to a tern's: very rapid and agile wing movements. Occasionally confused with immature Little Gulls or juvenile Kittiwakes in flight, but can be distinguished by the forked tail and the lack of a dark wing-bar. See also page 222.

CALL A harsh grating similar to that of Arctic Tern. When pursued or wounded, utters the same notes interspersed with much higher-pitched noisy cries.

REPRODUCTION End of May to July. Builds a small nest of vegetation on marshy ground. Eggs: generally three (sometimes two), brownish or olive-green, with sparse olive-brown patches and spots. Both sexes incubate the eggs for twenty-three to twenty-six days.

FOOD Feeds off the surface of the water: crustaceans, molluscs, small fish, insects and their larvae.

DISTRIBUTION AND MOVEMENTS Arctic regions of North America and Eurasia. Migrates south to winter off the coasts of southeastern Africa and Peru. Is a regular visitor in the Bay of Biscay and off the coasts of northern Spain and Portugal. Scarce visitor to coastal waters of Britain and Ireland.

(Below) Sabine's Gull in summer plumage (foreground) and winter plumage. (Below left) Breeding areas (yellow) and areas where Sabine's Gull may be seen on passage (pink)

French: MOUETTE DE SABINE
Italian: GABBIANO DI SABINE
Spanish: GAVIOTA DE SABINE
German: SCHWALBENMÖWE

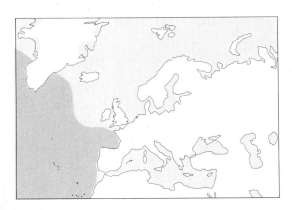

French: MOUETTE DE ROSS
Italian: GABBIANO DI ROSS
Spanish: GAVIOTA DE ROSS
German: ROSENMÖWE

Ross's Gull
Rhodostethia rosea

HABITAT During the breeding season frequents tundra and arctic river deltas. Winters at sea in arctic areas, on coasts, also on the edge of pack ice.

IDENTIFICATION Length: 32 cm. Distinguishable by its short, thin black bill, long wings with no black markings (apart from the outer edges of the primaries), long wedge-shaped tail and narrow black collar. The head, underparts, rump and tail are strongly suffused with pink in summer plumage and with the narrow black collar, make Ross's Gull easily identifiable. Back grey, bill black and the legs red. In winter the head, tail and body are white and the upper parts remain grey: there are dark markings around the eye and the pink coloration and the black collar disappear. Immatures have brown-black and buff-grey markings on the back and wing coverts, a black crown and nape, white brow and sides of head, with dark brown patches around and behind the eyes. Wedge-shaped tail is white with a black terminal band, the underparts white with a dark brown band on the breast. Flight is agile and tern like: the long pointed wings are angled like a tern's in flight. See also page 222.

CALL Has a variety of calls, the most commonly heard being an 'ee-vu-ee-vu'. Call is more melodious than that of many gulls.

REPRODUCTION Usually early June. Nests in colonies and the nest is made of dry grass and sometimes leaves. Eggs: normally three, olive-green with brown spots.

FOOD Mainly insects and marine crustaceans.

DISTRIBUTION AND MOVEMENTS Breeds in northeast Siberia. Non-nesting birds are occasionally found in summer on Spitsbergen, Novaya Zemlya and other arctic islands. Winters in the Arctic Ocean. Accidental in Britain and Ireland, Faeroes, Norway, Germany and France.

(Below) Ross's Gull in summer plumage (foreground) and immature

Kittiwake
Rissa tridactyla

HABITAT Breeds on ledges of cliffs by the sea and in sea caves. Winters at sea. Unlike other gulls present in Britain is rarely seen at rubbish dumps or sewage outfalls.

IDENTIFICATION Length: 41 cm. Similar to the Common Gull but smaller with no white spots on black wing tips. In winter plumage head and nape are uniformly grey. Legs black and bill yellow. Immatures have dark stripes on the wing and dark markings on the head in winter. Flight is graceful and buoyant like the Black-headed Gull's. At sea follows the movements of fish and ships.

Claws of the Kittiwake are longer and sharper than those of other gulls giving it sure footing on the narrow cliff ledges where it nests. Courtship ceremony involves bowing and bill-rubbing by both male and female. See also page 216.

CALL At breeding colonies emits a strident 'kit-e-wayke' from which its English name is derived: also a low 'uk-uk-uk' and a plaintive wailing 'ee-e-e-eeh'.

REPRODUCTION May and June. Usually nests in colonies. Unlike many other gulls builds a solid cup-shaped nest which is anchored to the ledge. Eggs: one to three, pale blue-grey to buff-brown with dark blotches. Both parents incubate the eggs for twenty to twenty-eight days. The young leave the nest after forty to forty-five days. They do not leave the nest before being able to fly as it would mean a fall to certain death.

FOOD Almost entirely fish and fish offal.

DISTRIBUTION AND MOVEMENTS Breeding distribution circumpolar in islands of the Arctic ocean and south to Greenland, Britain and Ireland, northern Eurasia and northern North America. Winters mainly in the North Atlantic. In Britain is a widely distributed breeder on coastal cliffs and islands: most numerous in eastern Scotland. Also occurs in Britain and Ireland as a passage and winter visitor.

(Facing page, top) Kittiwake in summer plumage (right) and immature (left). (Below) Breeding areas (yellow), wintering areas (magenta) and areas where the Kittiwake may be seen on passage (pink)

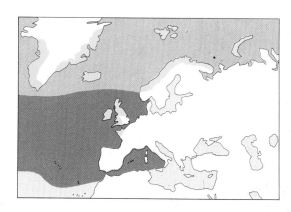

French: MOUETTE TRIDACTYLE
Italian: GABBIANO TRIDATTILO
Spanish: GAVIOTA TRIDÁCTILA
German: DREIZENHENMÖWE

French: GOÉLAND SÉNATEUR
Italian: GABBIANO D'AVORIO
Spanish: GAVIOTA MARFIL
German: ELFENBEINMÖWE

Ivory Gull
Pagophila eburnea

HABITAT Breeds on cliffs and rocky ground by the sea. Winters at sea, mainly at the edge of pack ice.

IDENTIFICATION Length: 44 cm. Adults easily distinguished by all-white plumage: even in winter has no dark smudges on the head. Bill yellow with a red tip; short black legs. Immature has distinctive plumage: grey face and throat, dark sub-terminal bar on tail and dark spots on upper parts. Bill of immature grey with white tip.

Flight buoyant, rather similar to a tern's. See also page 222.

CALL A harsh 'krii-krii' and 'caai' which resemble the calls of the Arctic Tern.

REPRODUCTION Late June and early July. Breeds in colonies: nest is a hollow lined with grass and often with feathers and seaweeds. Eggs: usually two, light olive to buff in colour with dark blotches and spots. Incubation is probably carried out by both parents but further details about incubation and nestlings are lacking.

FOOD Fish, crustaceans, molluscs and insects. Also remains of mammals such as seals.

DISTRIBUTION AND MOVEMENTS Breeds on arctic coasts and islands of northwest Canada, Greenland, Spitsbergen and Franz Josef Land. Winters on the Arctic Ocean. In Britain is a scarce visitor: most records from Scotland. Also a scarce visitor to Ireland.

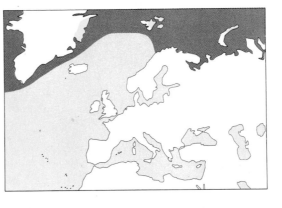

(Above) Adult Ivory Gull (foreground) and immature. (Left) Breeding areas of the Ivory Gull (yellow) and wintering areas (magenta).

French: GUIFETTE NOIRE
Italian: MIGNATTINO
Spanish: FUMAREL COMÚN
German: TRAUERSEESCHWALBE

Black Tern
Chlidonias niger

(Above) Black Tern in summer plumage (foreground) and immature. (Left) Breeding areas (yellow) and areas where the Black Tern may be seen on passage (pink)

HABITAT Breeds on marshes and swamps or by shallow water. Winters on coasts. The Black Tern is also seen on coasts on passage.

IDENTIFICATION Length: 24 cm. Generally the most common of the marsh terns. Easily distinguished in summer plumage: all plumage black or grey-black except for the white undertail coverts. Female's throat and underparts greyer. Bill black; legs reddish; underwing paler grey-black than rest of body. In winter distinguished from the sea terns by the well defined black shoulder patch and less deeply forked tail. Underparts white and head white with dark crown and smudge through eye. Immatures resemble adults in winter plumage but have a darker mantle.

Dips in flight as it picks up fish and water insects. Often seen in flocks and may be observed in company of sea terns. See also page 232.

CALL Flocks may emit a collective reedy cry: may also emit a 'kik-kik'. However the Black Tern is generally a silent bird.

REPRODUCTION Mid-May onwards. Usually nests in colonies. Nest is a platform of vegetation floating on shallow water. Sometimes also nests on firm ground in marshy herbage: then the nest is a scrape which is sparsely lined with plant matter. Eggs: usually three varying in colour from creamy or buff to brown with black and brown blotches. Both sexes incubate the eggs for fourteen

to seventeen days and both male and female care for the young.

DISTRIBUTION AND MOVEMENTS Breeds in Scandinavia and France east across Russia. Also breeds in Iberia, northern Italy, Bulgaria and the Caucasus. Winters in tropical Africa and South America. Formerly bred in large numbers in eastern England but the draining of the fens wiped it out as a breeding species. However has bred again on the Ouse Washes in East Anglia and it may eventually re-establish itself there. A pair has also bred successfully in Ireland. Is recorded annually as a passage visitor to Britain: most numerous on coasts and inland waters of southeast England. Also occurs on passage in Ireland.

White-winged Black Tern
Chlidonias leucopterus

French: GUIFETTE LEUCOPTÈRE
Italian: MIGNATTINO
ALIBIANCHE
Spanish: FUMAREL ALIBLANCO
German: WEISSFLÜGEL-
SEESCHWALBE

HABITAT Similar to that of the Black Tern: may breed in company with them in shallow waters.

IDENTIFICATION Length: 24 cm. In summer plumage distinguishable from the Black Tern by white forewing, rump and tail. Legs and bill are red: bill is shorter and stouter than that of other terns. Back, head and underparts black. Winter and immature plumage similar to the Black Tern's, but has a paler rump and lacks the black shoulder patch. Distinguished from Whiskered Tern in winter plumage by less forked tail. Immature has dark mantle and grey wings. See also page 232.

CALL Emits a hoarse 'kirr'.

REPRODUCTION Late May. Breeds in colonies on shallow waters of marshes. Nest is a mass of floating vegetation. Eggs: generally lays three eggs, cream to grey-brown in colour with dark markings. Both sexes incubate the eggs for fourteen to seventeen days. The young are tended by both male and female.

FOOD Mainly water-insects.

DISTRIBUTION AND MOVEMENTS Breeds from eastern Europe east across Asia and south to Iraq. Also breeds, although irregularly, in western Europe (Germany, France and Belgium) and in Algeria and east Africa. Winters mainly in tropical Africa and Asia. Is a scarce visitor to Britain and Ireland, mostly to inland waters.

(Above) White-winged Black Tern in summer plumage (foreground) and immature. (Below) Breeding areas (yellow) and areas where the White-winged Black Tern may be seen on passage (pink)

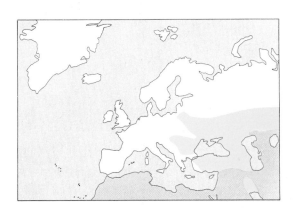

K. W. Fink/Ardea

(Left) Caspian Terns *Hydropogne caspia* and Elegant Terns *Sterna elegans*. (Below left) Roseate Tern *S. dougallii*. (Below) Inca Tern *Larosterna inca* and (bottom) White Tern *Gygis alba*. (Facing page top) Herring Gulls *L. argentatus* feeding. (Facing page, left) A flock of Arctic Terns *S. paradisaea* and (right) Kittiwakes *Rissa tridactyla*

G. Laycock/Bruce Coleman

A. Swoger/Photo Researchers

R. Kinne/Bruce Coleman

French: GUIFETTE MOUSTAC
Italian: MIGNATTINO PIOMBATO
Spanish: FUMAREL CARIBLANCO
German: WEISSBARTSEESCHWALBE

Whiskered Tern
Chlidonias hybrida

HABITAT Breeds and winters by inland waters like the Black Tern but prefers somewhat deeper water. On passage seen on coasts.

IDENTIFICATION Length: 24 cm. In summer plumage may be distinguished from Black and White-winged Black Tern by white cheeks and sides of neck, black cap on crown, grey underparts, red bill; white underwing and under-tail coverts very conspicuous in flight. Much paler than other 'black' terns. In winter upper parts are pale and is very similar to the Black Tern. However may be distinguished from Black Tern by less black on crown and no dark patches on sides of the breast. Immatures distinguished from immature Black and White-winged Terns by mottled mantle.

CALL A rasping 'ky-iilc' and various other disyllabic notes: is very noisy at breeding colonies.

REPRODUCTION Late April to early June. Nest floats on the water and is anchored by plants such as reeds. Eggs: usually three, pale blue-green or sometimes grey-brown in colour with darker markings. Both sexes incubate the eggs and care for the young. See also page 232.

FOOD Mainly water insects.

DISTRIBUTION AND MOVEMENTS Breeds in northwest Africa, southern Europe east through the Balkans to the southern USSR. Also breeds in the Near East, India and Australia. Migratory: western populations winter in Africa south to Kenya. Is an accidental visitor to coastal areas of Britain and Ireland mainly in the period of May to July, and it is now identified several times each year.

SUB-SPECIES Sub-species are present in Asia and northwest Africa.

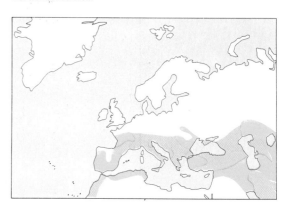

(Below) Whiskered Tern in summer plumage (foreground) and immature. (Right) Breeding areas (yellow) and areas where the Whiskered Tern may be seen on passage (pink)

Gull-billed Tern

Gelochelidon nilotica

French: STERNE HANSEL
Italian: STERNA ZAMPENERE
Spanish: PAGAZA PICONEGRA
German: LACHSEESCHWALBE

HABITAT Breeds on salt-water lagoons and marshes and on sandy coasts: sometimes by lakes. In winter is found mainly on inland waters.

IDENTIFICATION Length: 39 cm. Very similar to the Sandwich Tern, but distinguished by its shorter, thicker bill which is entirely black with no yellow tip. Tail less forked; legs and soles of feet black (instead of yellow soles as in Sandwich Tern). Wings are broader and body appears stockier. In winter plumage there is no black hood and the head is whiter than that of most terns: the crown is shaded with grey and there is a small area of black through the eye. Immatures resemble adults, but have paler markings on the crown and upper parts: legs red-brown.

Behaviour like other terns; distinguished from Sandwich Tern by its habit of flying back and forth over the ground in search of insects. Flight is heavy and gull-like. Rarely dives. See also page 226.

CALL The main calls are a 'ka-yook-ka-yook', and a strident 'quac-quoc'.

REPRODUCTION May onwards. Nests in colonies: the nest is hollowed out of the sand or earth and lined with seaweed. Eggs: normally three although often four or five, the background colour ranging from ochre to creamy white or chestnut, with chestnut or ash-grey spots. Both sexes incubate the eggs for twenty-two or twenty-three days. The young fly after four weeks.

FOOD Insects, small fish and small birds. Also frogs and worms. Plunges into water in search of food less frequently than other terns.

DISTRIBUTION AND MOVEMENTS Breeds very locally in Denmark, southern France, Iberia and the Balkans: isolated colonies in east Asia, Australia and the Americas. Sedentary and migratory: winters from the Mediterranean south to southern Africa, South America and the Persian Gulf. Regular but very scarce visitor to Britain and Ireland from April to October. Has bred on one occasion in Britain.

SUB-SPECIES Sub-species are present in North and South America, Australia and Asia.

(Above) Gull-billed Tern in summer plumage (foreground) and winter plumage. (Below) Breeding areas (yellow), wintering areas (magenta) and areas where the Gull-billed Tern may be seen on passage (pink)

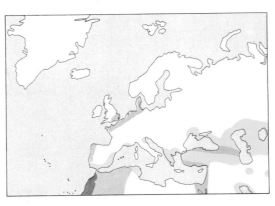

French: STERNE CASPIENNE
Italian: STERNA MAGGIORE
Spanish: PAGAZA PIQUIRROJA
German: RAUBSEESCHWALBE

Caspian Tern
Hydroprogne caspia

HABITAT Breeds on coasts and rocky off-shore islets. Outside the breeding season is predominantly marine, but is also found by lakes and large rivers.

IDENTIFICATION Length: 52 cm. Almost as large as the Herring Gull. Black crown and sides of the head (to just below the eyes); very large, powerful red bill and forked tail. Pale grey back; white rump, tail and underparts. Its primaries are dark brown towards the tip and blackish on the underside which distinguishes it from the Royal Tern. Fairly long, black legs. In winter the crown is white with black streaks. Immatures resemble adults in winter plumage but tail is tipped with black and there are dark markings on the upper parts.

Its flight is strong and graceful but rather ponderous like a gull's. Unlike most terns, it is often found singly although it nests in colonies. See also page 226.

CALL A deep, gruff 'keek' and a 'ka-uuh'.

REPRODUCTION Nests from mid-May onward. The nest consists of a scrape in the sand, and two or three stone-coloured eggs with blackish-brown or ash-grey patches are laid. Incubation is carried out by both sexes for twenty-one or twenty-two days. The young leave the nest within four or five weeks.

FOOD Mainly fish. Occasionally young birds and eggs.

DISTRIBUTION AND MOVEMENTS Breeds in Africa, on the coasts of the Baltic, Black and Caspian Seas, in western Siberia, Australia and North America. Sedentary and migratory: European populations winter in Africa. Is a rare visitor to Britain and Ireland in summer months.

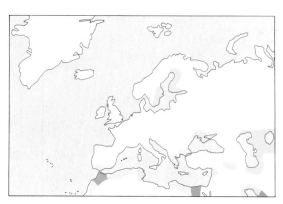

(Below) Caspian Tern in summer plumage (foreground) and winter plumage. (Right) Breeding areas (yellow), wintering areas (magenta), areas where the Caspian Tern may be seen all year round (orange) and on passage (pink)

Sandwich Tern
Sterna sandvicensis

French: STERNE CAUGEK
Italian: BECCAPESCI
Spanish: CHARRAN PATINEGRO
German: BRANDSEESCHWALBE

HABITAT During the breeding season frequents sand, shingle, rocky coasts and islands. Very occasionally found on the banks of inland waters, but is almost exclusively coastal all year round.

IDENTIFICATION Length: 40 cm. Fairly large in size, distinguished by short forked tail and black, yellow-tipped bill. Upper parts whitish. Black feathers on the crown appear like a crest. Underparts flushed with pink and black legs are long. In winter, forehead and the front of its crown are white; rest of the head is dull black, rather blurred at the edge as it merges with the white feathers. Winter plumage is assumed very early, often when the bird is still nesting. Juveniles resemble adults in winter plumage, but are brown on the head and nape and tail has a dark tip.

Its flight is more spectacular than that of other terns; it flies downwards in a rapid zig-zag. When excited it holds its neck up, with its bill raised at an angle and the wings spread out, away from the body. See also page 226.

CALL Very noisy: emits a distinctive 'kiirick' and variations.

REPRODUCTION Nests in dense colonies generally from early May onwards. The nest is a scrape which is sometimes lined with grasses; it is occasionally constructed on gravel or piles of seaweed. The Sandwich Tern usually lays one or two or, very rarely, three eggs ranging in colour from creamy-white to warm brown, sometimes without any markings but usually with blackish-brown or reddish-brown speckles. Incubation is carried out by both sexes and takes from twenty to twenty-four days.

FOOD Fish, marine molluscs and worms.

DISTRIBUTION AND MOVEMENTS Breeds on coasts from Scotland to the Baltic and south to the Mediterranean, Caspian, and Black Seas. Also breeds in North and Central America. In Britain and Ireland is a fairly numerous breeder mainly on the British east coast and on the shores of the Irish Sea: winters south to the coasts of western Africa. Also occurs on passage.

SUB-SPECIES Sub-species are present in North and Central America.

(Above) Sandwich Tern in winter plumage (left), summer plumage (centre) and immature (right). (Below) Breeding areas (yellow), wintering areas (magenta), areas where the Sandwich Tern may be seen all year round (orange) and on passage (pink)

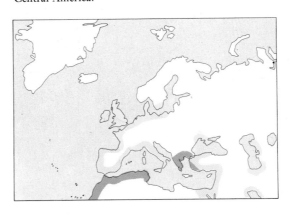

French: STERNE PIERREGARIN
Italian: STERNA COMUNE OR
RONDINE DI MARE
Spanish: CHARRÁN PATINEGRO
German: FLUSSSEESCHWALBE

Common Tern
Sterna hirundo

(Above) Common Tern in summer plumage (foreground) and winter plumage. (Below) Breeding areas (yellow), wintering areas (magenta) and areas where the Common Tern may be seen on passage (pink)

HABITAT Breeds on coasts and by fresh water. Winters on coasts and at sea.

IDENTIFICATION Length: 35 cm. Very similar to the Arctic Tern from which it can be distinguished in summer by the black tip of the vermilion bill and longer legs. White cheeks, breast and underparts are whiter than the Arctic's and contrast with the grey mantle. Legs are red. In winter, adults have white foreheads and the front of the crown is white with blackish streaks; pure white underparts with blackish markings on the shoulders; black bill. Immatures are similar but their foreheads are tinged with rufous coloration; the legs are flesh-coloured, yellow or orange; bill similar to the adult's bills in winter, with a hint of brown.
Flies slowly over water with its bill turned down, diving in when it spots a fish. See also page 228.

CALL Its main notes are a strident and high-pitched 'keek-keek-keek' and 'kee-ree-kee-ree'. Also emits a muttering 'koo-rr-koo-rr-koo-rr'.

REPRODUCTION Nests in colonies from late May onwards. The nest is hollowed out in the sand or situated on a rock, among stones or in grass, and is occasionally roughly lined with roots, feathers, etc. The Common Tern usually lays three (but often two or four) eggs ranging in colour from stone-grey to brown, with dark brown or ash-grey speckles. Incubation is carried out mainly by the female for between twenty-two and thirty days. The young are tended by both parents and fly

after about four weeks.

FOOD Fish form the basis of the diet although they also feed on insects.

DISTRIBUTION AND MOVEMENTS Breeds in Europe, Asia and North America. It winters in the Mediterranean region south to southern Africa, southeast Asia and southern South America. Breeds in Britain and Ireland in scattered colonies on the coast although some breed inland by rivers and lakes. British and Irish birds winter on the coasts of tropical Africa. Also occurs regularly on passage in mid-April to June and also from July to October.

SUB-SPECIES Sub-species are present in Asia.

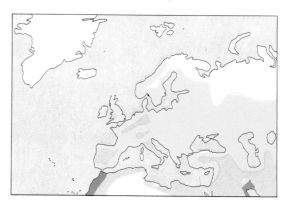

Royal Tern
Sterna maxima

HABITAT Nests in coastal regions, on small sandy islands and by lagoons. In winter also frequents ports, estuaries and more open water. Rarely found inland.

IDENTIFICATION Length: 48 cm. Same size as Common Gull, and one of the larger species of tern in Europe. Coloration and shape similar to Caspian Tern but bill is more orange and its tail much more forked than the Caspian Tern's. Its forehead and part of its crown turn white before the end of the nesting season, while those of the Caspian Tern are never totally unstreaked. Royal Tern's crest is also more conspicuous. In flight the Royal Tern can be distinguished from the Caspian by the paler underside of the primaries. See also page 226.

CALL A shriller and higher-pitched 'kee-eer' than the call of the Caspian Tern.

REPRODUCTION Nests in dense colonies and lays from two to four off-white or straw-coloured eggs with a few small, scattered markings and brown speckles.

FOOD Small fish, molluscs and crustaceans.

DISTRIBUTION AND MOVEMENTS Breeds in the southern United States, south Mexico and the Caribbean. Also breeds in west Africa. American birds winter south to Peru and Argentina. Very rare vagrant to Europe, to Britain and Ireland (once each), though a regular autumn visitor to the Atlantic coast of Morocco.

(Below) Royal Tern in summer plumage (foreground) and winter plumage. (Right) Breeding areas (yellow) and areas where the Arctic Tern may be seen on passage (pink). (Facing page top) Arctic Tern in summer plumage. (Preceding page) Herring Gulls *Larus argentatus*

French: STERNE ROYALE
Italian: STERNA REALE
Spanish: CHARRÁN REAL
German: KÖNIGSSEESCHWALBE

Arctic Tern
Sterna paradisaea

HABITAT Breeds on small rocky islands, sand or shingle banks or on grassy slopes usually on coasts but sometimes inland. Winters on coasts.

IDENTIFICATION Length: 35 cm. Very similar to Common Tern and the two are very difficult to distinguish. However, Arctic Tern has shorter legs and in summer plumage lacks the black tip to the bill. Underparts and breast less white than Common Tern's.

Immature Arctic Tern best distinguished from immature Common Tern by black (instead of flesh-pink) basal part of bill, no brownish tinge on head and mantle. Sometimes breeds in colonies with the Common Tern, but is generally found further north. See also page 228.

CALL A short 'kee-kee' or 'kria'.

REPRODUCTION Late May and early June onwards. Usually nests in colonies with other terns or other seabirds. Nest is a depression in the ground, sparsely lined with plant materials. Eggs: usually two, blue-white to creamy to dark brown with a variety of dark markings. Both sexes incubate the eggs for twenty to twenty-two days: both also care for the young.

FOOD Small fish, molluscs and crustaceans. Very occasionally eats insects.

DISTRIBUTION AND MOVEMENTS Breeding distribution circumpolar: from islands of high Arctic south to northern Canada, Greenland, Iceland, Britain, Ireland, France, the Baltic and northern Siberia. Winters in southern Atlantic, Pacific and Indian Oceans south to Antarctica. In Britain is a fairly numerous breeder in coastal areas especially in Scotland and northeast England. Also breeds on Irish coasts. Occurs as a passage visitor on coasts and inland.

French: STERNE ARCTIQUE
Italian: STERNA CODALUNGA
Spanish: CHARRÁN ÁRTICO
German: KÜSTENSEESCHWALBE

Roseate Tern
Sterna dougallii

HABITAT Breeds and winters on marine islands and coasts. Almost exclusively maritime: seen only very rarely by fresh water.

IDENTIFICATION Length: 38 cm. Similar to Common and Arctic Terns but may be distinguished by very long tail streamers which extend well beyond the wing-tips at rest. Also distinguishable from Common and Arctic Terns by all-black bill in winter becoming red just at the base in summer. Legs red, pinkish flush on breast in summer. In general appears much whiter than other terns. Harsh call is also distinctive.

Immature distinguished from immature Common and Arctic by bolder markings on crown and upper parts. See also page 228.

CALL A distinctive long and harsh 'aachh' and a characteristic 'chuu-iick'.

REPRODUCTION June onwards. Nests in colonies often with other terns. Nest is a shallow depression—usually unlined. Eggs: one or two, sometimes three. Light cream to olive, blotched and speckled with dark markings. Both sexes incubate the eggs and care for the young.

FOOD Mainly small fish; also molluscs, crustaceans, water-insects and their larvae.

DISTRIBUTION AND MOVEMENTS Breeds locally in Europe—Britain, Ireland, France—and in eastern North America, Caribbean region, east Africa, Indonesia and China. Sedentary and migratory: winters south to southern Africa and eastern South America. Breeds in Britain and Ireland in about twenty scattered breeding colonies. Also occurs as a passage visitor.

(Below) Roseate Tern in summer plumage (foreground) and winter plumage. (Left) Breeding areas (yellow) and areas where the Roseate Tern may be seen on passage (pink)

French: STERNE DE DOUGALL
Italian: STERNA DI DOUGALL
Spanish: CHARRÁN DE DOUGALL
German: ROSENSEESCHWALBE

French: STERNE FULIGINEUSE
Italian: STERNA SCURA
Spanish: CHARRÁN SOMBRÍO
German: RUSSSEESCHWALBE

Sooty Tern
Sterna fuscata

(Above) Adult Sooty Tern (foreground) and immature. (Facing page top) Bridled Tern in summer plumage (foreground) and winter plumage

HABITAT Oceanic: only comes ashore to breed. Feeds mainly out of sight of land.

IDENTIFICATION Length: 43 cm. Sooty-black upper parts; streak running from the base of the bill to the eye; white underparts and forehead. Deeply forked black tail with white borders on the outer feathers in winter. Long black bill; blackish legs. Coloration of plumage—black upper parts and white underparts—remains the same in winter and summer. Immatures have completely sooty-brown upper parts with white on their backs and grey-brown underparts. Resembles a large Bridled Tern but may be distinguished by less white on forehead and less buoyant flight.
    During nuptial display the male struts around the female with its head turned back and its throat thrust forward. See also page 228.

CALL A nasal 'keer-wacky-wack' and 'kwank-kwank'.

REPRODUCTION Nests from April to October, depending on the latitude, in large colonies on oceanic islands, coral reefs and small sandy islands. The nest consists of a simple scrape which is either bare or sparsely lined with tufts of grass, leaves and twigs. On islands where there is vegetation it prefers to nest in the trees.

FOOD Mainly small fish.

DISTRIBUTION AND MOVEMENTS Breeds mainly on tropical islands in all oceans from the Caribbean and Atlantic across the Indian and Pacific Oceans and by the Red Sea. Pelagic outside breeding season. In Britain it is a rare vagrant to coastal areas.

Bridled Tern
Sterna anaethetus

HABITAT Breeds mainly on rocky islands at sea. Coastal outside the breeding season.

IDENTIFICATION Length: 37 cm. Similar to the Sooty Tern but smaller and can be distinguished by greyish back, broad, pale collar at edge of black crown and white forehead which extends backwards and ends in a point behind the eye. Black eye-stripe. Upper parts greyish-brown rather than sooty-black: legs dark. White-tipped tail deeply forked. In winter plumage head is mottled with white and the eye-stripe is less distinct. During the first winter immatures resemble adults but upper parts are mottled buff.

CALL Emits high pitched crow-like calls.

REPRODUCTION Late May onwards. Unlike most terns the nest is a dark crevice or a hollow, or is situated under thick vegetation such as low bushes. A single egg is laid, ranging in colour from cream to pinkish with red-brown and purple-grey speckles. Both sexes incubate the eggs but further information about incubation and nestlings is lacking.

FOOD Fish, molluscs and crustaceans.

DISTRIBUTION AND MOVEMENTS Breeds in the Caribbean, northwest Africa, Red Sea, Persian Gulf, Indian Ocean, southeast China, Australia, New Guinea and tropical islands of the Pacific. Accidental in Britain and Ireland.

SUB-SPECIES Sub-species are present in the Caribbean and probably in the Pacific.

French: STERNE BRIDÉE
Italian: STERNA DALLE
REDINI
Spanish: CHARRÁN EMBRIDADO
German: ZÜGELSEESCHWALBE

Forster's Tern
Sterna forsteri

HABITAT Marshes, lakes and sea coasts during the breeding season. On migration and in winter in oceanic waters: occasionally seen inland.

IDENTIFICATION Length: 41 cm. White with a black hood and a pale grey mantle; deeply forked tail. Very similar to the Common Tern, but seen from above its wings appear smaller and its tail is pale grey. Bill orange (not red) with a black tip, orange-red legs. In winter head is white with a narrow dark patch running back from the eye; the bill becomes blacker and the legs yellower. Immatures resemble adults in winter plumage but coloration is browner, especially on the sides of the head, neck and on the mantle. See also page 226.

CALL A harsh 'traa-aa-arp', a nasal 'kee-ee-ar' and a soft 'weet-weet'.

REPRODUCTION Nests in colonies by water or among floating vegetation. Eggs: two to six, on average three, ranging in colour from pale green to reddish with numerous dark markings and speckles. Incubation takes about twenty-three days.

FOOD Invertebrates and small fish; also amphibians.

DISTRIBUTION AND MOVEMENTS Breeds in the Canadian prairies south across the United States to Mexico. Winters from California south to the Gulf of Mexico and Guatemala. Accidental in Iceland.

(Below) Forster's Tern in
summer plumage (foreground)
and winter plumage

French: STERNE DE FORSTER
Italian: STERNA DI FORSTER
Spanish: CHARRÁN DE FORSTER
German: SUMPFSEESCHWALBE

A. Fatras/Ardea

(Left) Whiskered Tern
Chlidonias hybrida and
(below) Little Tern *Sterna
albifrons*. (Facing page)
Common Terns *S. hirundo*
feeding

Eric Hosking

French: STERNE VOYAGEUSE
Italian: STERNA DI RÜPPELL
Spanish: CHARRÁN BENGALÉS
German: RÜPPELLSCHE
SEESCHWALBE

(Above) Lesser Crested Tern.
(Below right) Breeding areas
(yellow) and areas where the
Little Tern may be seen on
passage (pink). (Facing page
below) Little Tern

Lesser Crested Tern
Sterna bengalensis

HABITAT Breeds on sea coasts, on sand, shingle, or rocky shores: also small offshore islands.

IDENTIFICATION Length: 36 cm. Resembles a small Crested Tern: in summer plumage has yellow bill like the Crested and a black hood. Mantle grey but remainder of upper parts and underparts white. Best distinguished from Sandwich and Gull-billed Terns by smaller size, orange-yellow bill and narrow white band on forehead. Tail more deeply forked than the Sandwich's. Bill is longer than that of the Gull-billed, and the soles of the feet are yellow. In winter plumage entire forehead is white but the rest of the crown remains black but with numerous white speckles. Immature distinguished from immature Sandwich Tern by black outer-tail feathers.

CALL A low raucous alarm cry.

REPRODUCTION July onwards. Nests in colonies. Lays one or two eggs which are whitish with dark splotches in a depression in the sand or among rocks. The young are tended by both parents, but no information about incubation is available.

FOOD Mainly fish.

DISTRIBUTION AND MOVEMENTS Breeds on the coasts of Africa, southeast Asia and Australia. Also nests in the Mediterranean on small islands off the North African coast. Accidental in Switzerland, southern France, Spain and Sicily.

Little Tern
Sterna albifrons

HABITAT Frequents coasts and islands with sand or shingle beaches. On migration may be seen by inland waters.

IDENTIFICATION Length: 24 cm. The smallest sea tern: black-tipped yellow bill, orange legs and white forehead make it easily distinguishable from other terns. Black crown and black stripe through the eye contrast strongly with the white forehead. Winter and immature plumage similar to the Common Tern's: crown ash grey merging to black at nape. However, may be distinguished at all times by small size, shorter and narrower wings and the distinctive bill and leg colour. Flight is rapid and jerky. See also page 228.

CALL A harsh 'kee-eek' and a rapid 'kerree-keekee'.

REPRODUCTION Mid May and early June. Nests in small colonies: the nest is a shallow hollow in the ground. Eggs: two or three, very pale cream or olive coloured with brown or grey speckles and blotches. Both parents incubate the eggs for nineteen to twenty-two days and both care for the young.

FOOD Fish, worms, crustaceans and molluscs.

DISTRIBUTION AND MOVEMENTS Very widely distributed: Europe except for the northernmost regions: Asia, Africa, Australia, North and Central America. Northern populations are migratory and winter on the coasts of most southern ocean regions. In Britain and Ireland the Little Tern breeds on all coasts although only one hundred and fifty colonies are known. Resident from mid-April to September. Also occurs as a passage visitor mainly to coastal areas.

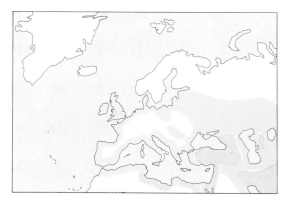

French: NODDI NIAIS
Italian: STERNA STOLIDA
Spanish: CHARRÁN PARDELO
German: NODDISEESCHWALBE

Brown Noddy
Anous stolidus

French: STERNE NAINE
Italian: FRATICELLO
Spanish: CHARRANCITO
German: ZWERGSEESCHWALBE

(Above) Adult Brown Noddy (foreground) and immature. (Overleaf, pages 210–211) Herring Gulls *Larus argentatus,* the most common and widespread of the larger gulls of Europe

HABITAT Rocks and small rocky islands, often far from the coast.

IDENTIFICATION Length: 39 cm. Sooty-brown plumage with darker flight feathers. Forehead and crown pale pearl-grey, tinged with lilac. Grey throat and sides of the head; black legs and bill. In winter plumage head and throat dark brown. Immatures browner than adults with broad white margins to feathers of upper parts. In behaviour markedly different from other terns; very trusting and seems almost lethargic. Flies slowly and alights on water to feed, like a gull, instead of diving. See also page 228.

CALL A deep, croaking 'karr-karr'; also a shrill 'pee-ee-lee-ee-lee-ee'.

REPRODUCTION Nests in colonies of variable size; building its nest out of seaweed, twigs and other materials or else lays its single egg among rocks, etc. The egg is pink or stone-coloured with dark markings.

FOOD Fish, molluscs and crustaceans.

DISTRIBUTION AND MOVEMENTS A tropical species, distributed along the coasts of the Red Sea and east Africa and in Madagascar east to India and the Philippines. Also found in North and South America. Accidental in Germany.

SUB-SPECIES Sub-species are present throughout its vast but patchy distribution area.

Gulls in flight

1: GREAT BLACK-BACKED GULL *(Larus marinus)*
One of the largest and most common gulls. Adult in winter
plumage (a): similar to summer except has streaks on the
head. Back and wings are almost black and its head and
bill are heavily built. The most obvious difference between it and the Lesser Black-backed Gull is the pink
(rather than yellow) coloration of its legs. Immature (b)
can be mistaken for an immature Herring Gull but its
overall coloration is lighter (note the white of the inner
primaries); the trailing edge of the secondary and ter-
tiary flight feathers grows darker with age.

 Flight is strong and the Great Black-backed Gull
frequently soars and glides.

2: LESSER BLACK-BACKED GULL *(Larus fuscus)*
Adult (a): dark back and wings; remaining plumage
white; yellow legs. The dark coloration varies according

to the sub-species, ranging from sooty-black (b) to dark
grey like that of the British and west European sub-
species (c) *L.f. graellsii.*

3: GLAUCOUS GULL *(Larus hyperboreus)* Immature
(a) similar to immature Iceland Gull, but the tips of the
primaries are darker. Note also the coloration and shape
of the bill (b) which is heavier than the Iceland Gull's.

 Flight silhouette (c). Wingbeats slow and heavy, contrasting with the quick flight of the similar Iceland Gull.

4: ICELAND GULL *(Larus glaucoides)* Immature (a):
very similar to the immature Glaucous Gull but smaller;
paler wing-tips and different coloured, less heavy bill (b).
Adult in winter plumage (c): very similar to the Glaucous
Gull, but smaller. Flight of the Iceland Gull is buoyant
and quick.

(Right) Glaucous Gull *Larus hyperboreus:* the heavy and slow wingbeats of the Glaucous Gull contrast with the quick and almost Kittiwake-like flight of the Iceland Gull

(Right) Black-headed Gulls *Larus ridibundus* and Common Gulls *L. canus.* (Below) Common Gull alighting at the nest. (Facing page, top) Great Black-backed Gulls *L. marinus* and (bottom) Glaucous Gulls *L. hyperboreus*

A. & E. Bomford/Ardea

L. Lee Rue/Bruce Coleman

5: AUDOUIN'S GULL (*Larus audouinii*) Slightly smaller than the Herring Gull and less heavily built. Shape is reminiscent of the Common Gull. The deep red bill with a dark band near the yellow tip is characteristic; white trailing edge of the wing is narrower than the Herring Gull's. Underwing is rather grey, although this may be difficult to distinguish in the field. A few darker secondaries may be present even in virtually fully grown individuals (a). In all plumages the wings give an impression of being more pointed and tapering than those of other gulls. Figure (b) shows the head and bill. Immatures (c) have dark secondaries and a dark area on the wings which is not present in immature Herring Gulls. The secondaries are still dark when the birds are three years old (d).

6: HERRING GULL (*Larus argentatus*) One of the most common and widely distributed gulls. Adult (a) grey upper parts and wings, however the colour of the mantle varies from pale to slate-grey. The wing-tips are black with white markings at the end: these white markings are generally more conspicuous than those of Audouin's Gull. The bill is yellow with a bright red marking near the end of the lower mandible. Coloration of the legs ranges from pink to yellow, depending upon the sub-species. Immature Herring Gull (b) is rather dark: during their second year (c), the grey feathers appear and the distinctive dark area found in Audouin's Gull is lacking. Flight is strong and deliberate: frequently soars and glides.

7: COMMON GULL (*Larus canus*) Resembles a smaller and more streamlined version of the Herring Gull but with green-yellow bill and legs. The bill is much less stout. The black wing-tips have a very conspicuous white marking (a). The wing of the immature (b) is grey in the middle; in addition the immature is smaller and the dark band on its tail usually looks wider. Flight is more graceful than that of the Herring Gull.

8: KITTIWAKE (*Rissa tridactyla*) The characteristic pattern of dark parts in the immature (a) makes it easily recognisable. Even when perching with folded wings, its dark collar is diagnostic. Adult Kittiwake (b) is easily identified by its completely black wing-tips, its small, pale yellow bill and its dark legs as well as its long-winged graceful shape. Flight graceful and buoyant like the Black-headed Gull's.

(Below) Herring Gull *L. argentatus:* its flight is strong and deliberate, and it frequently soars and glides

Paul Germain/Ardea

9: MEDITERRANEAN GULL *(Larus melanocephalus)*
Adult in summer plumage (a): black hood and fairly heavy red bill. Also distinguishable by white wing-tips and dark red legs which are longer than the Common Gull's. Bill is darker than the Black-headed Gull's: main similarity between these two species is that adults have a dark hood in summer plumage (Black-headed's dark brown, Mediterranean's black). Semi-mature individual in winter (b) has some black on the wing-tips. Juvenile (c) has heavy bill, dark secondaries and a grey area on the wing. Flight of the Mediterranean Gull is rather jerky, and the wingbeats are shallower than the Common Gull's.

10: BLACK-HEADED GULL *(Larus ridibundus)* In summer plumage adult has a dark chocolate-brown hood. In winter (a) the bill is dark and the white forewing is conspicuous: only the tip is black. Immature (b) has an orange-red bill with a black tip, and a much more extensive white area on the wings (particularly on the primaries). Flight of the Black-headed Gull is strong and buoyant.

11: BONAPARTE'S GULL *(Larus philadelphia)* Immature Bonaparte's Gull (a) is small with a black bill and more extensive black coloration on the wing than other immature gulls. Adult in winter plumage (b) has a black bill, clearly defined white forewing with black tips to the primaries like the Black-headed; orange-coloured legs.

In summer, however, the two species are similar although the black rather than red bill and the slate-grey rather than brown hood distinguish it from the Black-headed Gull. At all times the best field mark is the white underside of the primaries.

12: SLENDER-BILLED GULL *(Larus genei)* Adult (a) is similar in summer and winter plumages except the white of the body is suffused with pink in summer. Resembles a Black-headed Gull in winter plumage as the wing pattern is very similar. However, holds its head well forward giving it a different profile (unlike the Black-headed which appears to have no neck). Bill is longer, stouter and a darker red than the Black-headed's. Immature (b) has less black on wings than other immature gulls. Legs yellow.

13: GREY-HEADED GULL *(Larus cirrocephalus)* This species, a native of Africa and South America, is illustrated here for purposes of comparison. It nests on the coast of northwest Africa and may occur accidentally in Europe. It is slightly larger than the Black-headed Gull, and in summer plumage (a) the head, wings and back are grey. The wings are wider than the Black-headed's and have a distinctive black and white pattern. Immatures (b) also have a characteristic wing pattern. Coloration of the head varies in the Grey-headed Gull: some individuals have darker and more extensive grey.

(Right) Slender-billed Gull
L. genei. (Overleaf, page 220)
Lesser Black-backed Gull
L. fuscus

G. K. Brown/Ardea

14: LITTLE GULL *(Larus minutus)* Adult in winter plumage (a): small size, wings grey with white trailing edge and almost black underwing. Adult in summer plumage (b): complete black hood and smoke grey underwing with white trailing edge; no black wing-tips unlike Black-headed Gull. Immature (c): dark pattern on the wing like the Kittiwake; it can be distinguished by the absence of a collar and by its small size.

Flight of the Little Gull is graceful and wavering, reminiscent of the marsh terns.

15: SABINE'S GULL *(Larus sabini)* Immature (a): grey-brown upper parts with a broad white marking on the wing and an inverted V-shaped marking on its forked tail. Adult in summer plumage (b): its grey-hooded head, dark, yellow-tipped bill and characteristic wing pattern—black forewing with contrasting white trailing edge—make it readily identifiable. Dark legs. In winter its grey hood virtually disappears but the striking wing pattern remains. Flight is buoyant and it is often seen feeding from the surface of the water.

16: ROSS'S GULL *(Rhodostethia rosea)* Adult in winter plumage (a): very small black bill, some grey coloration on its head, distinctive long wedge-shaped tail (it is the only gull with this type of tail), white trailing edge limited to the proximal part of the wing. No black wing-tips. Adult in summer plumage, seen from below (b): its narrow black collar and grey underwing are characteristic. The underparts are suffused with pink. Immature seen from below (c) has a grey forewing; seen from above (d) its head is grey and its tail is dark; the pattern of black and white on its wing (especially the narrow black trailing edge of the distal part) is a distinctive feature.

The wings of Ross's Gull are long and pointed and are angled like a tern's in flight.

17: IVORY GULL *(Pagophila eburnea)* Adult (a): completely white; small in comparison with the Glaucous Gull and the Iceland Gull which also have pale coloration. The colour of its bill—yellow smudged red at the tip—is characteristic. In winter as well as summer lacks dark markings. Immature (b): grey face, dark speckling on the back and wings and black wing-tips and tail-bar make it easily distinguishable as this plumage is unique among seabirds of its region.

Flight of the Ivory Gull is buoyant and resembles a tern's.

(Right) Sabine's Gull *Larus sabini* alighting on the nest. (Preceding page) Black-headed Gulls *L. ridibundus*

18: **GREAT BLACK-HEADED GULL** *(Larus ichthyaetus)* Immature (a): smaller than the Great Black-backed Gull from which it can be distinguished by its yellower bill with a dark band. Immature in third or fourth year (b): grey upper parts, dark wing-tips and pattern of dark markings on the wings. Adult in winter plumage (c) may be identified by the dark red bill with yellow tip, yellow legs and the white on its primaries which is reminiscent of the Black-headed Gull. Tri-coloured bill and green-yellow legs are distinguishing features. In summer plumage is the only large gull with a dark hood.

Flight is graceful and the Great Black-headed Gull often soars for long periods.

19: **RING-BILLED GULL** *(Larus delawarensis)* Immature (a): resembles immature Common Gull from which it can be distinguished by the pale marking on its otherwise completely dark primaries. Figure (b) shows the head of an adult which is also almost identical to that of the Common Gull, apart from the coloration of the bill.

This species is illustrated here because individuals may occur accidentally in Europe and could be mistaken for immature Common Gulls.

20: **LAUGHING GULL** *(Larus atricilla)* Adult in winter plumage (a): note the small dark marking round the eye and the grey coloration of the wing (seen from above) which gradually merges into black at the tip. Immature (b): the darkest immature of all the species of gull present in Europe; even the underparts (particularly the breast) and wings are dark.

21: **FRANKLIN'S GULL** *(Larus pipixcan)* Adult in winter plumage (a): bill is shorter than the Laughing Gull's and the marking round its eye is less apparent: seen from above, the middle of its tail is grey and there is a white marking on the tip of its wing; its legs are red. Immature (b): also has a smaller bill than the Laughing Gull and coloration is somewhat paler. When present the marking round the eye is distinctive. The tail is greyish with a dark band at the end.

(Below) Franklin's Gulls *Larus pipixcan:* like other gulls they travel in large flocks

F. Erize/Bruce Coleman

Terns in flight

1: **CASPIAN TERN** (*Hydroprogne caspia*) The largest tern of Europe. Adult in summer plumage (a): heavy, red bill is conspicuous from some distance away. Its wings are large and the tail moderately forked. The only species for which it could be mistaken is the Royal Tern. Both species may have pure grey or dark areas on the trailing edge of the wing if the plumage has not just been moulted. A diagnostic characteristic is the end of the Caspian Tern's wing seen from below (b) which is dark. Figure (c) shows the head in winter plumage. Forehead of the Caspian Tern is streaked black and white unlike the Royal Tern's which is unstreaked white in winter plumage.

Like other terns the flight of the Caspian Tern is buoyant, and it hovers and plunges into the water for small fish.

2: **ROYAL TERN** (*Sterna maxima*) A large species, although smaller than the Caspian Tern from which it can be distinguished by its much narrower wings and longer and more deeply forked tail. Adults in full summer plumage (a): bill is orange-yellow and crest is more distinct than the Caspian's. In winter plumage (b) the forehead is white. Immatures (c) have shorter, darker tails than adults.

Bill colour and size are generally the best means by which to distinguish terns.

3: **FORSTER'S TERN** (*Sterna forsteri*) Adult in summer plumage (a) has a distinctively coloured bill and the black of its hood does not cover its lores. Immatures (b) and, to some extent, adults in winter plumage have a characteristic marking behind the eye, pale wing-bar, and primaries which, except on the borders, are noticeably silver and not dark.

4: **SANDWICH TERN** (*Sterna sandvicensis*) In summer plumage (a): long, slender wings, long crest, and its long black yellow-tipped bill are distinctive. Resembles a Common Tern but the paler upper parts and less deeply forked tail are distinctive. In winter (b) the dark hood grows smaller (it is reminiscent of the Royal Tern's hood) but the coloration of its bill does not change. The immature's head and nape are brown and the tail is black on the tip.

5: **GULL-BILLED TERN** (*Gelochelidon nilotica*) Similar in size and coloration to the Sandwich Tern but may be identified at any time of year by its short, all-black bill. Its tail is not very deeply forked. In winter plumage there is no trace of the black cap except for a marking behind the eye and a few streaks on the head. In general the head of the adult shows less black than other terns. Flight heavier than that of other terns and resembles a gull's flight.

(Below) Sandwich Tern *Sterna sandvicensis*. It is a large tern but is more slender than the Caspian or Royal Terns: the tail is also less deeply forked

J. Lawton Roberts/Bruce Coleman

6: COMMON TERN *(Sterna hirundo)* Three very similar European species make the identification of terns very tricky; these are the Common Tern, the Arctic Tern and the Roseate Tern. However it is nearly always possible to distinguish these three species if certain basic points are borne in mind, especially bill colour and leg length.

As a rule, the Common Tern has a black-tipped vermilion bill, a clearly defined hood and a forked tail with long, grey-edged outer tail-feathers in summer (a). Seen from below (b) a sort of white 'window' is revealed in the wing when seen against the light. The Common Tern's legs are much longer than those of the Arctic Tern. Immatures (c) are indistinguishable from those of the Arctic Tern except that their legs are longer. However, this can only be seen when the bird is perched and considerable expertise is required to detect this characteristic. Bill of immature Common Tern is pale pink rather than black on the basal half of the bill.

7: ARCTIC TERN *(Sterna paradisaea)* In summer plumage (a) its bill is blood-red without the black tip and the underparts are darker, but lighting conditions should be taken into account as the Common Tern can also appear to have dark underparts if it is seen in a poor light. The pale silvery appearance of the primaries seen from below (b) is a distinctive characteristic. When perched, the legs of the Arctic Tern appear quite short. Immature (c) is very similar to immature Common Tern.

8: ROSEATE TERN *(Sterna dougallii)* In summer plumage (a) the upper parts are pale grey, especially the wings. The bill is all-black which distinguishes it from the Common and Arctic Terns although the base of the bill may become red in mid-summer to autumn. The legs are longer than those of the Arctic and Common Terns and the general coloration is paler. Long tail streamers which extend far beyond the wings when at rest distinguish

it from the Arctic Tern whose streamers extend only a short way beyond the wings and the Common in which they do not extend beyond the wings.

Immatures (c) lack dark shoulder mark of Arctic and Common. Immatures bill all-black unlike the immature Common Tern's or Arctic's. Legs of the Roseate Tern are black and head is dark.

9: LITTLE TERN *(Sterna albifrons)* May be distinguished by its small size, white forehead and above all by its black-tipped yellow bill. A dark border at the end of the leading edge of its wing (a) is also distinctive. Figure (b) shows a rear view of its flight silhouette. Flight is quicker and jerkier than that of other terns.

10: BRIDLED TERN *(Sterna anaethetus)* Its black hood (which does not extend onto the white forehead) contrasts with its remaining grey-brown upper parts (a). May be confused with Sooty Tern but the latter has no white collar and less white on the forehead. Seen from below, the primaries have a characteristic white area. Figure (b) shows head of an immature: immatures are similar to adults but the head is streaked.

Flight is graceful and slow: the wingbeats appear rather exaggerated.

11: SOOTY TERN *(Sterna fuscata)* In overall appearance very similar to the Bridled Tern but it lacks the white collar. The white of its supercilium does not extend behind its eye. Seen from below, the wing is a uniform dark colour without any light marking on the primaries. Juveniles (b), seen from below, have a pale marking on the abdomen.

12: BROWN NODDY *(Anous stolidus)* Along with the Bridled and Sooty Terns, is the third 'dark' tern which is found accidentally in Europe. May be distinguished by its plumage, wedge-shaped tail and pale hood.

(Below) Arctic Tern *Sterna paradisaea:* unlike the Common Tern *S. hirundo* it does not normally have a black tip to the red bill

J. S. Wightman/Ardea

(Left) Common Tern *Sterna hirundo* and (below) a colony of Caspian Terns *Hydroprogne caspia* and Elegant Terns *S. elegans.* (Facing page) Sandwich Terns *S. sandvicensis:* it is an almost exclusively coastal species

K. W. Fink/Ardea

13: BLACK TERN *(Chlidonias niger)* The head of the adult in winter plumage is shown in (a) and that of the immature in (b); both have similar coloration. Seen from above, the immature (c), has dark wing markings which are absent in the adult in winter plumage (d). The adult in summer plumage, seen from above (e), has grey upper parts (the tail is lighter) except for the head, which is black as are the underparts (f). Seen from below in winter plumage the immature (g) has a distinctive dark spot on the side of the breast at the base of the wing.

Like other marsh terns of the genus *Chlidonias* (so-called because they breed exclusively by fresh and brackish water) the Black Tern's flight is graceful and dipping: it very rarely dives into water. The bill of marsh terns is more slender and the tail less forked than those of the sea terns'.

14: WHITE-WINGED BLACK TERN *(Chlidonias leucopterus)* Juveniles seen from above (a) may be distinguished by the dark back and white leading edge of wing. The head (b) has a black patch like the Black Tern's, but it only extends downwards a little way below the eye. In winter plumage adults (c) are pale with only the head (d) spotted black and, seen from below (e) they lack the black spot at the base of the wing. In summer plumage (f, g) adults are easily recognisable by black body and underwing coverts, with the rest of the wing and the tail virtually white. An adult is seen from below (h) during moult to winter plumage.

15: WHISKERED TERN *(Chlidonias hybrida)* The adult, seen from below (a), has grey underparts and white cheeks. From above (b) has grey wings and black cap like that of Common Tern. In winter plumage (c, d) the upper parts are paler and the dark colouring of the head dwindles to a 'U'-shaped patch curving back from the eye to the nape. The immature (e) has a mottled mantle and darker rump than the White-winged Black Tern's. Head markings like those of adult Black Tern in winter.

(Right) Black Tern *Chlidonias niger*

W. Curth/Ardea

ORDER Charadriiformes
FAMILY ALCIDAE: Auks

(Above) Common Guillemots *Uria aalge:* it is one of the most common auks and breeds in closely packed colonies on cliff ledges by the sea

The inclusion in the order Charadriiformes of birds which at first sight vary as greatly as lapwings, snipe, gulls and auks may seem confusing and inappropriate. There do indeed appear to be greater differences between puffins—with their high, flattened bills and 'penguin' coloration—and snipe than between nightjars and owls. However appearances are misleading; the study of their anatomy, physiology, fossils forms and to some extent their behaviour indicates beyond any reasonable doubt that the degree of relationship between

a guillemot and a plover is close and that the grouping of all these birds together in the order Charadriiformes is justifiable.

The striking similarity between auks and penguins was for a long time considered a good example of the phenomenon of evolutionary convergence. According to this theory, species unconnected by heredity tend to resemble each other because of their similar ways of life in similar surroundings. However, the most recent research indicates that guillemots, razorbills, puffins and

234

F. Baldwin/Photo Researchers

L Aby

homogeneous group of about twenty-two species of birds adapted to marine aquatic life. They are compact in shape and vary in size from the tiny Little Auk or Dovekie *Alle alle* (about twenty centimetres long) to the impressive, but now extinct, Great Auk *Pinguinus impennis* (about eighty centimetres long). The shape of the bill varies from nearly cylindrical and pointed as in guillemots, to broad with a distensible throat pouch as in the Little Auk, and to high, very compressed laterally, ornamented with brightly-coloured horny plates like puffins. The sexes are alike.

The legs of species of this family are always rather short; the first toe is absent or rudimentary and the other three webbed. The wings and tail are also short and generally narrow and pointed. They shuffle rather awkwardly on land. Except in very few species, the flight feathers are moulted simultaneously, so that the birds are unable to fly for a short period. The general coloration is black and white, but the Marbled Murrelet *Brachyramphus marmoratus* and Kittlitz's Murrelet *B. brevirostris* have some brown plumage which gives them a more cryptic coloration. Several species have white patches on the face or various ornaments such as crests or plumes. Bright colours, when present, are confined to the bill (and its ornaments), the legs and the area around the mouth. There is normally both a summer and a winter plumage, but there is generally little difference between the two plumages.

The diet, consisting mainly of fish and crusta-

(Above) Brünnich's Guillemot *U. lomvia:* it is very similar to the Common Guillemot but may be distinguished by the thin pale line along the base of the upper mandible: the bill is also shorter and stouter

penguins resemble each other so closely because they are all descended from one and the same group of seabirds. And, contrary to what has hitherto been thought, they evolved along specialised, slightly divergent lines, finally occupying two separate parts of the globe: the auks in the Arctic regions and the penguins in the Antarctic (some species of penguins later invaded certain tropical islands, for example the Galapagos Penguin *Spheniscus mendiculus* which nests on the Equator).

To return to the family Alcidae, it is a fairly

ceans, indicates fairly clearly the basically marine habits of the majority of the species. Food is generally taken from under the water and some species even feed on the bottom.

All auks are excellent swimmers and can dive from the surface of the water (not from flight), swimming under water with the help chiefly of their wings, the legs being used for steering rather than propulsion. Despite the apparent lack of lifting power of their short, narrow wings, they fly well and fast even in very bad weather conditions: therefore they are able to nest on the high, steep cliffs of northern seas. However on land auks can only shuffle awkwardly.

Auks usually nest in colonies, often in company with one or more different species. They lay one or two eggs on the bare rock, in crevices, under the sparse tufts of cliff vegetation, or even in the burrows of rabbits, whether abandoned or not. The shape of guillemots' eggs is a perfect example of adaptation to nesting in inconvenient places: they are strongly pear-shaped, so as to prevent them rolling away and falling over the edge of the steep cliffs on which they nest. Razorbills and guillemots, which nest in very exposed situations, also hold the egg during incubation with their webbed feet and cover it with soft feathers of the belly. Both parents incubate the eggs, and the young hatch covered in soft down and remain at the nest for a period varying from a few days to seven weeks, depending on the species.

The family is well represented in the North Atlantic (seven species, including one extinct species), but the evolutionary centre seems to have been at the northern Pacific, where at least sixteen species are currently found, twelve of these being endemic (found only in this area). Some species are migratory and travel great distances.

For convenience, rather than for strictly scientific reasons, the family is subdivided into six tribes. The first, the Alcini, includes not only the extinct Great Auk but also the Razorbill *Alca torda* and the guillemots of the genus *Uria*. They all have dark (black or brown) upper parts and white underparts. The main difference between summer and winter plumage is in the coloration of the throat: dark in summer and white in winter. This tribe is

practically confined to the Atlantic, and the two species of guillemots (called murres in North America), the Common Guillemot *Uria aalge* and Brünnich's Guillemot *U. lomvia*, are virtually sympatric (inhabiting the same region). However the Common Guillemot is found further south, occurring even on the Pacific coasts as far south as California, and Brünnich's Guillemot is present further north at Spitsbergen and Franz Josef Land. One variety of the Common Guillemot called 'bridled'—with a white eye-ring and white line extending backward from the eye—is found in increasing numbers in the Atlantic except for Iceland.

The Great Auk has now been extinct for more than a century. Despite powerful pectoral muscles, it was unable to fly: this was one of the main reasons for its extinction as it was unable to escape the mariners who in the past slaughtered it for food. Found at one time from Iceland to St. Kilda and from Greenland to the Gulf of St. Lawrence, the Great Auk was the 'penguin' of the original travellers' tales; only later was the word applied to the Antarctic penguins. This explains not only its scientific name *Pinguinus impennis* but also the name 'pingouin' given to the Razorbill by the French, who call real penguins by the completely different name of 'manchots'. The last two specimens of the Great Auk were killed in 1844.

(Right) Black Guillemots *Cepphus grylle:* in summer plumage the large white wing-patch is a distinguishing feature. (Below) World distribution of the family Alcidae

The second tribe contains only the Little Auk or Dovekie which is found in the northern Atlantic and in the Arctic Ocean. It is practically the only species corresponding ecologically to the various species of small auklets of the Pacific, which comprise the tribe Aethiini (the polytypic genus *Aethia* together with Cassin's Auklet *Ptychoramphus aleuticus*), similar in appearance but with various head ornaments.

The genus *Cepphus* consists of the Black Guillemot *Cepphus grylle* and two other species, forming the tribe Cepphini. The summer plumage is black with a white wing-patch and, in some species, a white patch on the face as well. The legs and the

two days and descend to the sea.

The most well-known members of the Alcidae are undoubtedly the puffins of the tribe Fraterculini. They nest in burrows which they dig out themselves or which they adopt from wild rabbits. As well as the elongated plumes which many species have on their heads, puffins have brightly-coloured plates on their heads and huge bills during the breeding season. The Common Puffin *Fratercula arctica* and the Horned Puffin *F. corniculata* also have plates or horn-like structures above and below the eye. The Common Puffin is the most distinctive: its elaborate bill and face ornamentation gives it a clown-like look.

N. P. Laub/Ardea

(Left) Black Guillemots and (below) Parakeet Auklets *Cyclorrhynchus psittacula*. (Overleaf) Colony of Common Guillemots

inside of the mouth are bright red. Less gregarious than other auks, even during the breeding season the 'black' guillemots feed mainly on marine animals from the sea floor.

The various species of murrelets are divided into two tribes. The first, the Brachyramphini, contains only the Marbled Murrelet and Kittlitz's Murrelet: like the black guillemots these species undergo a complete moult from the grey and white winter plumage to the brown and rufous barred summer dress, which appears to serve the purpose of camouflage. The breeding range of the Marbled Murrelet, in the North Pacific coincides with the coastal coniferous belt; its behaviour when breeding, however, is almost unknown. Kittlitz's Murrelet is a solitary nester, laying its eggs among the lichen in latitudes above the timber-line in Alaska and adjacent islands.

The other murrelets (contained in the tribe Synthliboramphini) have no striking differences between summer and winter plumage; any differences, when present, are limited to ornaments on the head. The young leave the nest after only

D. O. Hill/Photo Researchers

French: MERGULE NAIN
Italian: GAZZA MARINA MINORE
Spanish: MÉRGULO MARINO
German: KRABBENTAUCHER

Little Auk
Alle alle

HABITAT Breeds on sea coasts, cliffs and mountainsides. Outside the breeding season remains at sea, on the edge of the ice-floes, but may also reach more southerly latitudes.

IDENTIFICATION Length: 20 cm. Smallest and shortest-billed auk. Small size, white and black plumage and the very short, strong bill distinguish this species from other auks. Upper parts black, with scapulars streaked white and white tips to the secondaries. In summer plumage head and the upper breast are black, contrasting with the white of the remaining underparts, but in winter the throat, breast and ear coverts become white, more or less tinged dark brown. The short bill, not distinguished clearly from the head, gives it a curious shape. This species also appears 'neckless'. Immatures similar to the adult in winter but have dark brown upper parts and lighter, more obviously brown, throat.

CALL A shrill chattering 'ritt-tit-tit-tit' or 'pirri-titt-tit' and 'crake-ake-ek-ek-ek-ek'. Very noisy in the breeding season.

REPRODUCTION Nests from mid-June onwards, in huge, crowded colonies. The Little Auk does not build a nest, and the eggs are laid in the cracks and fissures of the rocks. Eggs: normally one only, rarely two, pale blue, usually unmarked, but sometimes with some yellowish-brown blotches. Both sexes incubate the eggs for about twenty-four days. The young are fed by both parents for twenty to thirty days.

FOOD Oceanic crustaceans and plankton, molluscs and small fish.

DISTRIBUTION AND MOVEMENTS Breeds on Ellesmere Island, Greenland, Spitsbergen, Novaya Zemlya, Bear Island, Jan Mayen and Franz Josef Land. In winter moves southwards to Iceland and Norway occasionally also to the North Sea and Baltic coasts. Winter visitor to the Shetland Islands and storm driven visitor elsewhere.

SUB-SPECIES *A. a. alle:* the whole range except for Franz Josef Land. *A. a. polaris* (larger in size): Franz Josef Land.

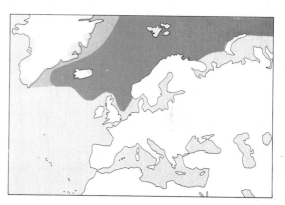

(Below) Little Auk in summer plumage (left) and winter plumage. (Right) Breeding areas (yellow), wintering areas (magenta) and areas where the Little Auk may be seen on passage (pink)

Razorbill
Alca torda

French: PETIT PINGOUIN
Italian: GAZZA MARINA
Spanish: ALCA COMÚN
German: TORDALK

HABITAT In the breeding season is found on rocky cliffs and on islands. In winter is found offshore.

IDENTIFICATION Length: 42 cm. Distinguished from Common Guillemot by large flattened bill with white line, black upper parts and, in breeding season, white line on face from base of bill to eye. Tail is long and pointed; secondaries have white tips, forming in flight a white border to the trailing edge of the basal part of the wing. In winter, throat and sides of neck become white and the white line from bill to eye turns darker. Upper parts, as well as the head and neck of immatures are dark brown. Like adults, throat is white. Immature birds in their first winter are similar to adults but bill is less curved and lacks the white line. Legs black.

Paired birds often rub each other's bill in turn and nibble each other's head and throat. White wing-bar shows in flight.

CALL Tremulous, whirring sounds, and a prolonged, strident 'kaarrr'.

REPRODUCTION Nests in loose colonies from mid-May onwards, frequently together with Common Guillemot, among rocks, on cliffs and on broken cliff screes. Does not build a nest, the eggs being laid in crevices and holes. Eggs: normally one, very rarely two, oval, rough-surfaced, varying in colour from light chocolate-brown to white, occasionally greenish, blotched dark brown. Eggs have also been observed which are entirely black, unmarked greenish and white. Both sexes incubate the egg for about twenty-five to thirty days. The young are looked after by both parents and descend to the sea after twelve to fourteen days.

FOOD Fish, crustaceans and marine molluscs.

DISTRIBUTION AND MOVEMENTS Breeds on northern European coasts including Britain and Ireland, northeastern coasts of North America and Greenland. Winters south to western Baltic coasts, North Sea and Channel coasts, Atlantic coasts as far south as northwest Africa and the western Mediterranean. Occasionally accidental inland. In Britain and Ireland is a numerous breeder (both resident and migrant) on rocky coasts. Also occurs as a winter visitor.

SUB-SPECIES *A. t. torda*: North America, Greenland, Norway, Sweden, Finland, Bear Island and the USSR. *A. t. islandica* (smaller): Iceland, Faeroes, Britain and Ireland, Heligoland, Channel Islands and Brittany.

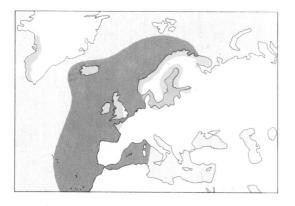

(Above) Razorbill in summer plumage (top) and winter plumage (bottom). (Left) Breeding areas (yellow), wintering areas (magenta) and areas where the Razorbill may be seen on passage (pink)

F. Greenaway/NHPA

S. Dalton/NHPA

(Above left) The Razorbill *Alca torda* is easily distinguished from other seabirds by its unique bill. (Above) Common Guillemots *Uria aalge* and (left) Black Guillemots *Cepphus grylle*

R. Richter/Ardea

French: GUILLEMOT DE BRÜNNICH
Italian: URIA DI BRÜNNICH
Spanish: ARAO DE BRÜNNICH
German: DICKSCHNABELLUMME

Brünnich's Guillemot
Uria lomvia

HABITAT Like the Common Guillemot breeds on coastal cliffs. Winters well out to sea.

IDENTIFICATION Length: 42 cm. Very similar to Common Guillemot, but distinguishable by shorter, thicker bill, with a pale line along the base of the upper mandible. Upper parts dark, almost black no dark streaking on flanks. In winter plumage the black of the head extends down over ear coverts. However from a distance is extremely difficult to distinguish from the northern Common Guillemots. Legs yellow, with dark stripes at joints.

Pairing takes place both on rocks and on the ice. The male is very aggressive and persistent towards the female, who often shows hostility to him; only when the male desists does she assume a more inviting attitude.

CALL Similar to the Common Guillemot's: emits a deep croaking sound.

REPRODUCTION Nests from early June onwards in crowded colonies on cliff ledges. Builds no nest, the eggs being laid on bare rock, occasionally in crevices. Eggs: one, varying from blue-green to white or creamy, with yellowish, reddish-brown and lilac mottling and streaking. Both male and female incubate the egg for about a month. The young are tended by both parents and descend to the sea after three or four weeks.

FOOD Small fish, crustaceans, molluscs and squid.

DISTRIBUTION AND MOVEMENTS Breeds in the northern Holarctic: on coasts and islands of the north Atlantic, Arctic and north Pacific Oceans. Winters at sea south to Norway, northern Japan, Alaska and the northeastern United States. Is a rare vagrant to Britain and Ireland.

SUB-SPECIES Sub-species are present in Asia and North America.

(Far left) Brünnich's Guillemot in winter plumage and (left) summer plumage. (Below) Breeding areas (yellow) and wintering areas (magenta) of Brünnich's Guillemot

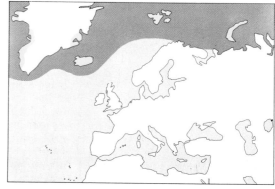

Common Guillemot
Uria aalge

HABITAT In breeding season frequents cliff ledges or flat tops of stacks. Winters at sea.

IDENTIFICATION Length: 43 cm. One of the most common auks. Distinguished from Razorbill by narrower, longer and more pointed bill and by dark brown, not black, upper parts, especially head. Appears less bulky than Razorbill, with more slender, shorter neck and rounded tail. Like other auks the sexes are similar. In winter plumage throat, ear coverts and front of neck are white, like the rest of the underparts, with black eye-stripe extending back over the ear coverts. Immatures have blackish margins to the back feathers, but immature birds in their first winter are practically like adults in winter plumage. Legs vary in colour from light brown to yellowish, blackish at the joints and the back of the tarsus. The bridled form, frequent in the north of the distribution area, has a white ring round the eye and a white line extending backwards from the eye.

Flight is fast and direct, and the legs and feet are often outstretched.

CALL A prolonged, croaking 'arrr', with considerable variations and modulations such as 'guuu-arrr'.

REPRODUCTION Generally nests towards the end of May in dense colonies, often with Razorbills and Kittiwakes, on ledges of steep cliffs or tops of stacks. Builds no nest, the eggs being laid on bare rock, occasionally in crevices. Lays only one egg, markedly pear-shaped and varying greatly in colour: blue-green, bright red, ochre, light blue, creamy or white, with mottling and streaking varying from yellowish-brown to bright red, brown and black. Both sexes incubate the egg for about thirty days

and both tend the fledging for about eighteen days.

FOOD Fish, molluscs and worms: also seaweed.

DISTRIBUTION AND MOVEMENTS Breeds on the coasts of northern Europe, the Atlantic, eastern Asia and North America. In Britain and Ireland is a widespread breeder on coastal cliffs. In Britain is most numerous in Orkney and Shetland and in the west. Also occurs as a winter visitor. Sedentary or partly migratory; occasional inland.

SUB-SPECIES *U.a. aalge:* North America, Greenland, Hebrides, Orkneys and Shetlands, Scotland, Faeroes, Baltic islands and coasts. *U.a. albionis* (paler, less black): England, Ireland, Channel Islands, Brittany, Portugal, Spain. *U.a. hyperborea* (longer wings, darker underparts): Bear Island, Novaya Zemlya. Other sub-species are present in Asia and in North America.

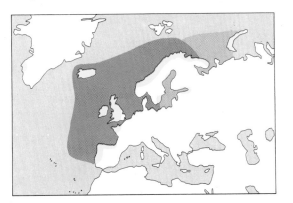

French: GUILLEMOT DE TROÏL
Italian: URIA
Spanish: ARAO COMÚN
German: TROTTELLUMME

(Above left) Bridled form of the Common Guillemot, normal form in summer plumage (centre) and winter plumage (right). (Left) Breeding areas (yellow) wintering areas (magenta) and areas where the Common Guillemot may be seen on passage (pink)

French: GUILLEMOT A MIROIR
Italian: URIA NERA
Spanish: ARAO ALIBLANCO
German: GRYLLTEIST

Black Guillemot
Cepphus grylle

(Above) Black Guillemot in summer plumage (foreground) and winter plumage. (Below right) Breeding areas (yellow), wintering areas (magenta), areas where the Black Guillemot may be seen all year round (orange) and on passage (pink)

HABITAT Breeds on broken cliffs with screes, and islands near coasts: in the Baltic and in North America frequents wooded islands and coasts. In general frequents shallower seas and is found much further up inlets than other auks.

IDENTIFICATION Length: 33 cm. Much smaller than Common Guillemot. In summer easily distinguished by uniformly black plumage except for large white patch on wing which extends over most of coverts. In winter plumage, head and underparts white; back is blackish spotted white; some dark patches on sides of head. Immatures much darker than adults in winter plumage: they have an almost uniform blackish back. White plumage areas of adults, including the wing-patch, are mottled sooty-brown in juveniles. Immature birds in their first winters are white more like adults, but have wings like juveniles. Feet are vermilion, orange in juveniles. Least sociable of the guillemots: breeds in very loose colonies. While swimming utters a note with the bill wide open, showing the vermilion mouth lining, and also nods its head.

CALL A very clear but weak 'peeee', which is repeated several times. Also emits a hissing note of protest if disturbed.

REPRODUCTION Nests towards the end of May and beginning of June, singly or in small scattered groups, in crevices of cliffs and on rocky islands. Does not build a nest but lays eggs in rock crevices, in hollows among or beneath boulders or at base of cliffs. Eggs: normally two, sometimes one or three, white or tinged greenish-blue marked with black, ash-grey or reddish-brown blotches. Both male and female incubate the eggs for twenty-one to twenty-four days. The young are fed by both parents

for about thirty-four to thirty-six days, and do not leave the nest until they are fully fledged and able to fend for themselves.

FOOD Small fish, crustaceans, molluscs and seaweed; occasionally insects.

DISTRIBUTION AND MOVEMENTS Coasts of northern Europe, northern and eastern Asia, North America and Greenland. Winters on North Sea and Baltic coasts, occasionally on Channel coasts and Atlantic coast of France but is mainly sedentary. In Britain is confined to the north and west, but occurs on all Irish coasts.

SUB-SPECIES *C.g. grylle:* Baltic islands and coasts, Faeroes, Britain and Ireland, Scandinavia and the Kola Peninsula, islands of Kattegat. *C.g. mandtii* (wings whiter in summer plumage): Jan Mayen, Bear Island, Spitsbergen, Franz Josef Land, Novaya Zemlya. *C.g. islandicus* (irregular brown stripe on white of wing) is present in Iceland.

Crested Auklet
Aethia cristatella

HABITAT Arctic islets and sea coasts.

IDENTIFICATION Length: 25 cm. An all-dark species, with paler underparts and a long, curly, forward-curving crest. Some narrow, filiform plumes behind the eye; iris white. In summer plumage red wattles cover the heavy, yellowish bill. In winter the crest is shorter and the wattles are absent. Sometimes dives to considerable depths to obtain food.

CALL Loud honking and grunting notes.

REPRODUCTION Nests in colonies and lays one egg among stones or in rock crevices.

FOOD Mainly small invertebrates.

DISTRIBUTION AND MOVEMENTS Confined to Siberian and Alaskan coasts of the Bering Sea. Accidental in Europe on the northeast coast of Iceland.

French: MACAREUX HUPPE
Italian: GAZZA MARINA CRESTATA
Spanish: MÉRGULO CRESTADO
German: SCHOPFALK

(Right) Crested Auklet in
summer plumage and winter
plumage (in flight)

(Below right) Parakeet Auklet
in summer plumage
(foreground) and winter
plumage

Parakeet Auklet
Cyclorrhynchus psittacula

HABITAT Breeds on cliffs by the sea and on rocky islets. Winters at sea.

IDENTIFICATION Length: 26 cm. Dull black upper parts (including neck and throat), white underparts with some dark barring and spotting on breast and flanks. In summer plumage some long, white, filiform plumes behind the eye. The red, slightly upward-curving bill appears swollen. Legs grey. In winter the white plumes on the head are absent and the chin is white. Immature has a darker bill.

CALL Emits a whistling trill.

REPRODUCTION Lays a single egg, white or un-marked bluish, in rock crevices or on the bare rock of islands. Period of incubation and further details are not available.

FOOD Small marine invertebrates.

DISTRIBUTION AND MOVEMENTS Nests on coastal cliffs and islands from northeastern Siberia and the islands of the Bering Strait southwards to Koman-dorski and the Aleutian islands. Winters at sea south to Sakhalin, northern Japan and Californian coasts. Acci-dental in Europe in Sweden.

French: MACAREUX STARIK
Italian: GAZZA MARINA PAPPAGALLO
Spanish: MÉRGULO LORITO
German: PAPAGEIALK

French: MACAREUX MOINE
Italian: PULCINELLA DI MARE
Spanish: FRAILECILLO COMÚN
German: PAPAGEITAUCHER

Puffin
Fratercula arctica

(Above) Puffin in summer plumage (foreground) and winter plumage. (Below right) Breeding areas (yellow), wintering areas (magenta) and areas where the Puffin may be seen on passage (pink)

HABITAT Breeds on coasts or islets. Winters at sea.

IDENTIFICATION Length: 30 cm. An unmistakable species in summer plumage due to its elaborate bill and face ornamentation which give it a clown-like appearance. Adult in summer plumage: black upper parts and collar, whitish-grey sides of face, white underparts. Very large, laterally-compressed bill; the tip is red separated from the blue-grey base by a yellow stripe and several orange and yellow bars. This large bill serves as a weapon, digging tool and advertisement. Eye-ring red; legs orange-red. In winter plumage the bill is grey-brown with a yellow tip. Eye-ring yellow. Immatures differ little from adults except that the bill, which is decidedly smaller, is grey-brown with a red-brown tip. The coloration is duller and the legs not so bright.
  In flight the very large head is conspicuous. Very rapid wingbeats.

CALL Generally silent, utters various 'grunts' when nesting.

REPRODUCTION Late May onwards. Lays a single egg in rock crevices, natural hollows, or in rabbit burrows —either deserted burrows or sharing occupation with the rightful owners. However, they are quite capable of excavating their own burrows. The burrows or crevices are lined with vegetation and feathers. Male and female both incubate the eggs for about forty days.

FOOD Small fish, molluscs and other marine organisms.

DISTRIBUTION AND MOVEMENTS Breeds on northern coasts including Britain and Ireland, Jan Mayen, Iceland, Greenland and coasts of northwestern America, Spitsbergen, Novaya Zemlya. In winter disperses offshore regions and is present as far south as the western Mediterranean and Massachusetts in the United States. In Britain it breeds in colonies mainly on the western coasts and islands. However, the Puffin appears to be in decline in Britain at least certainly in the south along coasts from the Isles of Scilly to the Isle of Wight: formerly colonies numbering several thousands existed but now these colonies are either abandoned or negligible in size. The Puffin also occurs in Britain as a winter and passage visitor.

SUB-SPECIES As well as the nominate race, two other sub-species nest in Europe: *F.a. grabae* (Britain and Ireland, Faeroes, southern Scandinavia) and *F.a. naumanni* (Spitsbergen and Novaya Zemlya).

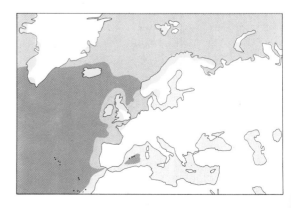

D. & K. Urry/Bruce Coleman

(Left and below) Puffins
Fratercula arctica: the
distinctive bill makes this
species easily identifiable
in both summer and winter
plumage

F. Blackburn/Bruce Coleman

FEEDING HABITS OF WADERS
Bill shapes and adaptations

John Goss-Custard, author of this section, works at the Institute for Terrestrial Ecology at Wareham in Dorset. He specialises in waders' food supply and populations and has published many articles on waders in scientific journals

Waders occur in their greatest numbers on European estuaries outside the breeding season from August to May. According to the place and time of year, the birds are either refuelling for further migration, moulting or simply surviving the winter before returning north to breed. Throughout this period they spend a large part of their time feeding. Waders feed mainly on the larger invertebrates which abound in the often enormous areas of sand and mud exposed when the tide is out. Although the numbers of all kinds of food animals per square metre may be as high as 100,000, the variety of food species available to the waders is rather limited. Nonetheless, the different kinds of waders have a broadly different diet because each species has its own characteristic bill shape and repertoire of behaviour with which to exploit the food supply. And the varying lengths of bills allows species to avoid competition as they feed at different depths.

When the tide is out, invertebrates must avoid dehydration and being taken by predators, particularly birds. Some animals live on the surface of mud or stones and protect themselves with a thick shell which reduces water loss and deters predators; the common limpet and edible mussel are good examples. Some species remain on the mud surface but seek protection under stones and weed, like the common shore crab. However, the majority live beneath the surface for most of their lives and are protected by the mud and sand that surrounds them. These animals must maintain a connection with the surface to obtain oxygen and food and to expel waste products. Some species, mainly worms and crustaceans, do this by living in burrows connected by one or more tubes with the surface. They draw a current of water over themselves and extract the oxygen and minute particles of food it contains. Sometimes these animals emerge briefly when the tide is out either to collect food from the mud surface or to get rid of their waste: the worm caste formed by the common lugworm on sandy beaches is a good example of the latter. In contrast many bivalve molluscs or shellfish, like the edible cockle and clam, remain beneath the surface for most of the time and are only connected with it by two tubes. One tube sucks in water while the other squirts water and waste materials out again. These syphons, as they are called, can often be seen in wet, muddy areas when the tide is out as they search for food on the mud above. Generally speaking, the larger animals with the longer syphons live deeper in the mud and so are less accessible to birds feeding on the surface. The cockle is an exception in that it is large yet has short syphons and lives very close to the surface. Perhaps to compensate for this, it has a thick shell compared with many of the deeper burrowing kinds of invertebrate.

The food supply provided by these invertebrates is exploited by waders showing a striking variety of bill shapes and sizes. They vary in length from the stubby bill of plovers through a variety of intermediate sizes to the enormous bill of curlews. The shape varies from being strongly down-turned (as in the Curlew *Numenius arquata*) to slightly down-turned (Dunlin *Calidris alpina*), straight (Redshank *Tringa totanus*), slightly up-turned (Bar-tailed Godwit *Limosa lapponica*) or strongly up-turned (Avocet *Recurvirostra avosetta*). Some bills are thin and delicate whereas others, like that of the Oystercatcher *Haematopus ostralegus*, are thick and strong.

How these different kinds of bills and the various ways in which they are used relate to the sorts of

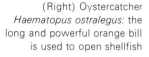

(Right) Oystercatcher *Haematopus ostralegus:* the long and powerful orange bill is used to open shellfish

animals eaten by the birds is best illustrated by some examples. The large and powerful bill of the Oystercatcher is most often used to open shellfish, a habit which has sometimes brought it into conflict with fishermen in several parts of Europe. Some Oystercatchers simply break their way into crabs, cockles and mussels by hammering a hole in the shell at its weakest point. Before this can be done, the shellfish may be pulled up and carried to somewhere firm where it can be hammered without being driven deep into the mud. Piles of empty shells accumulate this way, so improving the place for opening further shells. Once the shellfish has been opened, the bill is pushed into it and the muscle which holds the two halves of the shell together snipped so they are easier to open. Even so, the bird may still have to twist and gyrate for some time before it is able to prise the shellfish open and extract the flesh. It takes an Oystercatcher up to five minutes to deal with large mussels, although cockles are usually eaten much more quickly.

Some Oystercatchers adopt a different approach by finding animals whose shells are already slightly apart. This happens when the shellfish is feeding underwater at the tide edge or in pools or, perhaps, when the animal is weakened by disease. Oystercatchers then avoid the necessity of cracking the shell by driving their bill between the two shells into the body of the animal. A large powerful bill is still vital however because the bird then has to sever the muscles and prise the shell open. Oystercatchers hunting limpets on rocky shores feed in a similar way, but here they drive the bill into the slight gap between the shell and the rock and then prise the animal off.

Using these techniques Oystercatchers can eat large crabs and shellfish, up to five and a half centimetres long, which they could not possibly swallow whole. They are able to do it because they have a large bill and the ability to crack and prise open shells. Few other waders can prise open shellfish. Turnstones *Arenaria interpres* can prise open shells, but their smaller and more delicate bill means that they can only tackle small animals less than two centimetres long. Some other birds, notably Carrion Crows *Corvus corone* and Common Gulls *Larus canus*, exploit the Oystercatchers' ability by stealing shellfish which have just been opened. This is very common in some estuaries but despite this the Oystercatchers are able to collect sufficient food, amounting to several hundred shellfish per day, even in winter.

Mussels and limpets live in full view on the surface so they are easily located, but Oystercatchers also find cockles buried beneath the surface. They make distinct pecks at the mud, apparently directed at something they have seen. It is not clear what they actually peck at, but it may be tiny movements of the syphon itself or of water moving in or out. Oystercatchers sometimes eat cockles on dark nights and in these circumstances they feed by moving their bills rapidly up and down through the mud, much like a sewing-machine, and evidently locate their food by touch. But how they tell the

J. & S. Bottomley/Ardea

Eric Hosking

difference between a live cockle and the empty shells which abound in some places is still a mystery.

Some Oystercatchers eat deeper burrowing shellfish, like the Baltic tellin, or burrowing worms, such as the ragworm. Although one syphon of the tellin and the whole front end of the worm may sometimes emerge from their burrows when the tide is out, it appears that Oystercatchers can also detect these animals when they are withdrawn into the mud. Perhaps they know an animal is near the surface because they can see tiny movements at the entrance of the burrow. They then pursue their prey beneath the surface with their long bills and locate them by touch.

In some cases, we know what the birds are pecking at. Another long-billed wader, the Bar-tailed Godwit *Limosa lapponica*, eats lugworms. These worms normally live up to a metre beneath the surface, well out of reach of the Godwit. However, they eat sand to digest the organic particles and must reverse up their burrows to the surface every three-

(Top) Bar-tailed Godwits *Limosa lapponica* and (above) Black-tailed Godwit *L. limosa*. Godwits probe with their long bills under the surface mud to capture their food

(Above) The Avocet *Recurvirostra avosetta* sweeps its upcurved bill from side to side over the mud. This specialised feeding method is only effective where the mud is soft and worms abound

quarters of an hour to get rid of the waste material. When they do this they are both near the surface and detectable because the worm caste curling out of the sand is easy to see. The Godwits, therefore, know where to peck and use their long bills to pursue a worm down its hole and catch it before it goes too deep.

Like many waders, Bar-tailed and Black-tailed Godwits *Limosa limosa* can detect prey by touch as well as by sight. Sometimes they feed by the 'sewing-machine' method (prodding with the bill under the surface mud) and take deep-burrowing bivalves, such as the Baltic tellin. Unlike Oystercatchers, they do not open these shellfish, but swallow them whole. Although their long bills enable them to reach down to the larger bivalves, their small gape (or aperture of the bill) limits the size of animal they can actually swallow. The shells they eat either pass straight through into the droppings or are thrown-up as pellets which can be found in places where the birds have been roosting at high water.

Like the godwits, the Curlew eats deeper burrowing worms and shellfish but it detects them by sight and pursues them down into the sand with its long bill. It usually pulls worms (often in several bits) and shells to the surface before swallowing them, and its greater reach and gape allow it to take deeper burrowing and larger animals than the godwits can manage. Sometimes Curlews open clams beneath the surface. They appear to do this by pushing the tip of the bill between the two halves of the shells and then twist the bill tip around until the animal is broken up and it parts. It is possible that the curved shape of the bill helps this bird to do this.

While Curlew obtain much of their food by

probing deep into the mud, they also take crabs from the surface. Small crabs are numerous on the shore during summer and they hide in pools and under stones and weeds when the tide is out. Curlew find crabs by lightly moving the tip of their bill over the surface until they happen to touch one. The Curlew swallows small crabs whole, but shakes large ones until the legs fall off. The bird then swallows the body before eating the detached bits of crab lying on the surface of the mud.

Curlew eat most crabs in late summer, but the crabs soon migrate down the shore to spend the winter in the sea and so are inaccessible to waders. Curlew then concentrate on the burrowing bivalve molluscs and worms; their long bill, like that of the godwits, enables them to reach the larger individuals deep in the mud. Waders with smaller bills, Dunlin *Calidris alpina* and Knot *C. canutus*, also eat these burrowing worms and bivalves but their shorter bills only enable them to reach the smaller individuals nearer the surface. Knot feed almost entirely on small cockles and Baltic tellins which they find by touch and swallow whole. Dunlin take many ragworms and small snails which live just beneath the surface of the mud. These are found both by touch, like the Knot, but also by pecking at prey moving on the surface.

The general trend for long-billed waders to take large food animals and for short-billed species to eat smaller ones is sometimes reversed by the plovers. They have a quite different method of searching than that of most waders; this may explain why Grey Plover *Pluvialis squatarola*, for instance, can catch some very large worms. Most waders hunting for food by sight walk over the mud at a steady rate and peck at prey as they find it. Then, with their bills, they chase food down into the mud if it retreats. In contrast the plovers hunt more by stealth. They run to a spot then stand absolutely still for several seconds while scanning the surface of the mud. If they see a ragworm that has come briefly to the surface to eat, the plover makes a dash at it and grabs it before the worm has time to retreat down its burrow. In this way, Grey Plovers can catch with their short bill worms of a size which are normally only accessible to the much longer-billed birds.

Avocets use a different method for catching ragworms which are their main food in winter. They pace steadily over the surface sweeping the bill from side-to-side through the mud in a scything action. When the bill comes into contact with a worm it is grabbed and thrown back up the bill to be swallowed. This curious method of feeding, clearly related to the strongly up-turned shape of the bill, only works if the mud is very soft and so provides little resistance to the sweeping action. Not surprisingly, Avocets occur in winter in the limited number of places where the mud is very soft, almost liquid, and where worms abound.

The Turnstone is another species which has a rather specialised feeding method. As its name suggests, it frequently turns over stones and weeds

surface of the mud, catching worms, crustaceans and bivalves living near the surface. However, they also catch shrimps and small fish in pools by sweeping their opened bills from side to side and running hither and thither: this method of feeding is also typically used by their near relative, the Greenshank *Tringa nebularia*. Redshank also turn over leaves and weed, like the Turnstone, and use the sewing-machine action of the Knot. They also scavenge fragments of flesh left in shells opened by Oystercatchers and will even steal worms from Curlew which are having difficulty in swallowing them.

These examples illustrate how the size and shape of the bill and the feeding methods used by the birds, in conjunction with how the prey lives in the mud and sand, dictate the range of food animals which can be eaten by a particular wading bird. However, a number of factors may influence the kinds of food actually eaten from within this range. The abundance of the various kinds of animals in the sand is obviously important. For example, Oystercatchers take more cockles in estuaries where this shellfish is abundant compared with estuaries where mussels or ragworms are more common. But in addition to this, several other factors can affect what birds eat.

The Greenshank *Tringa nebularia* (left) feeds by probing and by scything like an Avocet

on the surface of the mud to expose the small animals living beneath, these being small winkles, crabs and various shrimp-like crustaceans. The Turnstone normally eats its food whole but it can open small shellfish.

The different waders vary a great deal in the kinds of feeding methods they normally employ. Knot, for instance, are rather limited and eat only a small variety of foods. They usually feed either by pecking at small snails on the surface or, more typically, by using the sewing-machine method to catch burrowing shellfish. At the other extreme, Redshank have a very wide repertoire of feeding methods and eat a correspondingly varied diet. Most often they walk along steadily and peck at the

First, there can be pronounced seasonal changes related to daylength. For example, Redshank in northeast Scotland mainly eat a shrimp-like crustacean called *Corophium*. When daylength is long in autumn and spring, Redshank can satisfy their considerable appetite—some 40,000 food animals per day—by feeding only at low water on the estuary in daylight. But they cannot do this in winter because the short daylength restricts the time available for feeding. They compensate for the reduced time available by feeding in the nearby fields when the tide is high during the day and by feeding at night on the estuary when the tide is out. They eat earthworms and leatherjackets in the fields and various snails at night in addition to the

Corophium taken during the day. Consequently a much greater variety of food is eaten during the winter.

The Redshank also illustrates how factors which affect the behaviour of the invertebrates in the mud may affect the kinds of food eaten by waders. Redshank often eat more ragworm and Baltic tellins on cold days compared to warm days when most of their food is *Corophium*. The *Corophium* are less active when it is cold and do not emerge from their burrows to gather food. Instead, they simply rest inside their burrows which makes them more difficult for Redshank to find. As a result, the birds eat more worms and shellfish which are normally less preferred.

The behaviour of the food animals can vary from place to place on the shore and affect the speed with which the birds can feed in different areas. The invertebrates remain active when the tide is out, but are accessible to the birds only in places where the mud remains wet throughout. Sandy areas dry out quickly after the tide has receded and the invertebrates retreat beneath the surface to avoid dessication. This makes it very difficult for the birds to catch them because not only are they deeper underground and less active, but it is difficult for the birds to probe into the dry sand. Consequently waders seldom feed in dry areas of the shore and are most numerous in wet areas.

Among wet areas, the birds prefer places where food is abundant and can be collected fastest. This is important because they require a great deal of food to keep alive. For instance, Oystercatchers must eat between eighty and one hundred mussels or one hundred and fifty and five hundred cockles each day, and Knot must eat approximately seven hundred and fifty to one thousand small shellfish per day. And waders eating very small prey, like Redshank feeding on *Corophium*, must find many thousands of food animals every day. It is particularly important to feed in the best areas in winter because the time available for feeding in daylight is so short. Waders can feed at night, and frequently do so, but seem able to catch far fewer prey then. They must find most of their food during the day and this is helped by feeding in the richest parts of the shore. The invertebrates are not spread evenly over the shore and some areas contain far more animals than others. This is why so many areas on estuaries have very few birds: there is simply not enough food to make them worthwhile feeding areas. Indeed, the same is seen on a larger, estuary scale. Estuaries with low densities of invertebrates have very few waders while estuaries in which food is abundant may provide winter feeding grounds for enormous numbers of birds which display a fascinating variety of bill adaptations.

(Left, top) Dunlin *Calidris alpina*, (centre) Knot *Calidris canutus* and Turnstone *Arenaria interpres* and (bottom) Redshank *Tringa totanus*. Dunlin and Knot have short bills and feed on animals which live near the surface of the mud. Among other feeding methods, the Redshank turns over weeds like the Turnstone

GULLS AS PESTS
The effect of increased populations

Gulls are among the best known groups of birds, and it comes as something of a shock to many people to be told that the hordes of gulls we see now are due to a recent dramatic increase in the numbers of the larger species. At the end of the last century gulls were probably far from common. Although they are attractive and enliven many a landscape, like so many other good things too many of them constitute a nuisance. Herring Gulls *Larus argentatus*, and to a lesser degree the closely related Lesser Black-backed Gull *L. fuscus*, are now considered a pest in many parts of coastal Britain.

During the last fifty years most populations of Herring Gulls have expanded. In 1925 there were some 10,000 pairs in north Germany but twice as many by 1960; in the Netherlands there were 10,000 pairs in 1925 and 30,000 by 1940 when control measures were started. Even these spectacular increases are surpassed by the New England population of the United States eastern seaboard which has increased by fifteen to thirty times this century. Unfortunately there are no complete estimates for total British gull populations. In 1960–70, when 'Operation Seafarer' estimated the populations of all seabirds nesting on the coastline of Britain and Ireland, there were about 334,000 pairs of Herring Gulls, 47,000 pairs of Lesser Black-backed Gulls and 22,000 pairs of Great Black-backed Gulls *L. marinus*. However, there were also some large uncounted colonies inland in Scotland and northern England. These gulls have doubled, if not trebled their numbers in the last twenty-five years.

Perhaps the best documented increase has been that of the population on the Isle of May in the Firth of Forth. Breeding was not recorded until 1907, there were 12 pairs in 1914, 58 in 1924, 445 in 1936, 1,100 in 1951, 8,000 in 1964, and 15,000 pairs in 1972 since when control measures have reduced the level somewhat. In latter years the increase continued despite the systematic collection of eggs for food and, later, deliberate destruction of nests. Lesser Black-backed Gulls started to breed in 1930 and by 1954 there were 165 pairs, in 1969 2,000 pairs, and finally 2,500 pairs in 1972—a faster rate of increase than even the Herring Gulls managed. Similar increases have been found elsewhere; for instance at Steepholm and Flatholm in the Bristol Channel, and Skokholm, Skomer and Grassholm off Dyfed. The record is probably held by the Walney colony in Cumbria. The total population of the two species remained below 1,000 pairs until the early 1950s, but by 1974 there were 47,000 pairs. A few small colonies have not expanded so quickly, if at all. These are where most eggs are collected for food, where there is severe predation, by foxes for instance, or where the colony is so remote that the birds do not have access to human waste on which to feed. St. Kilda is fifty miles from the nearest land and the number of Herring Gulls nesting on Hirta has remained at fifty pairs since 1931. All these birds feed on natural foods such as limpets and crabs.

The bulk of British Great Black-backed Gulls nest in north and west Scotland where there were about 16,000 pairs in 1969. There are no old counts to put this in perspective. However, the colony on North Rona, probably always the largest in Britain, remained below 100 pairs until 1914 but increased

Dr. Michael Harris, author of this section, is the Principal Scientific Officer at the Institute of Terrestrial Ecology at Banchory in Scotland. Seabirds are his particular interest, and his publications include many scientific papers on seabirds and *A Field Guide to the Birds of the Galapagos*

(Left) Herring Gulls *Larus argentatus* feeding on a rubbish tip

S. Roberts/Ardea

to 500–600 pairs by 1966 and to 2,000 pairs in 1972. There has been no obvious increase since. The changes of fortune of these gulls in England and Wales are better known. A substantial decrease took place towards the end of the last century and there were only twenty pairs left in 1893. An impressive recovery soon followed and there were 1,200 pairs in 1930, 1,600 in 1956 and 6,000 in 1969.

The three other gulls regularly nesting in Britain, the Black-headed Gull *L. ridibundus*, Common Gull *L. canus* and Kittiwake *Rissa tridactyla*, are much smaller, rarely come into conflict with man and, unless specifically mentioned, are not included in the following discussion. All have increased during this century but the total population is only known for the Kittiwake of which, in 1969–70 there were almost half a million pairs mainly concentrated along the east coast from Yorkshire to Shetland.

The million or more pairs of gulls nesting in Britain cause trouble to human populations in many ways, ranging from the trivial to the poten-

(Below) Black-headed Gulls *Larus ridibundus* following a plough and (bottom) feeding on a rubbish tip. The convenient availability of food collected in rubbish tips has led to an increase in gull populations

tially dangerous. Gulls spend much of their time around the fringes of human activities. Many are always to be seen around sewage works, sewer outfalls, slaughter houses, rubbish tips and the like, where it is inevitable that they come into contact with bacteria, viruses, helminth parasites, and poisons, all of which are potentially noxious to man. After feeding, gulls congregate together at roosts in places where they are safe from predators and other disturbances. These roosts are frequently on reservoirs which supply the drinking water to the main towns and cities. The possibility of diseases spreading is obvious, and examination of dead gulls and the droppings collected around reservoirs have produced an impressive list of unpleasant things. Salmonella, which causes serious food poisoning and typhoid, has been found although the rate of occurrence was surprisingly low considering the foul conditions gulls sometimes feed in. Psittacosis, or parrot-disease, which is now regarded as a form of ornithosis, is carried by gulls and it is often fatal to humans. A seriological survey showed that seventeen per cent of the human population of Hamburg had at some time been in contact with a non-virulent form of ornithosis, possibly contracted up from dry bird faeces. A yeast-like fungus *Candida albicans* occurred in over twenty per cent of fresh gull droppings in Jersey. This plant is a saprophyte in the human gut—that is, it lives on decaying matter—and its incidence has increased since the introduction of broad spectrum antibiotics. However, it can only be transferred by direct contact with fresh faeces as the organism does not persist in dry droppings. It is unlikely that freshwater supplies could become contaminated to any serious extent in this country as the organism only flourishes in warm water. The intermediate stage of the human tapeworm *Taenia* occurs in cattle where it causes cysticerosis. Experiments have shown that if gulls are fed with gravid tape worm segments (like those which would be found in sewage) viable and infective eggs are found in their faeces. If these faeces were to fall on grassland and were eaten by cattle cysticerosis would result. Such eggs have been found in gull droppings at sewage works but the pathway from humans through gulls to cattle has not been proved.

Gulls also carry a number of diseases which can be passed on to poultry, the most serious being Newcastle Disease or fowl pest and avian influenza. The large numbers of gulls of most species from Scandinavia, Russia and central Europe which winter in Britain might act as vectors in bringing diseases into this country. This list of possible diseases carried by gulls is frightening, but it must be stressed that very few cases of seabird-transmitted disease have ever been recorded in Britain. The water purification system seems well able to cope with anything gulls can produce. Pigeons and the commoner pets would seem to be a far greater risk to human health.

Concern about health risks has increased with the recent colonisation of some towns by nesting Herring Gulls. This habit was first recorded in

C. R. Knights/Ardea

K. Vaughan/Ardea

R. Vaughan/Ardea

Europe at the end of the last century but not until much later in Britain. It is possible that the odd pair had bred on roofs in Cornwall in about 1910 but the first published records were from Devon in 1923 and 1928, in Cornwall about 1926 and at Dover in 1936. Soon after, there were roof-nesting gulls in northeast England and Wales, but only in the 1940s were any real numbers of birds or towns involved. A survey in 1969–70 found some 1,500 pairs of Herring Gulls nesting on buildings in fifty-five towns or villages. Most of these sites were coastal although there were small colonies inland in South Wales and in London. The next survey in 1976 reported almost 3,000 pairs at ninety-two localities—an increase of seventeen per cent per annum. The largest increases were in east Britain— twenty-nine per cent per annum—and inland. This spread is continuing.

Lesser Black-backed Gulls were much slower in frequenting an urban habitat, possibly because they normally nest on flat ground whereas many Herring Gulls are cliff-nesters. The first Lesser Black-backed colony on a man-made structure was situated on a flat factory roof inland at Merthyr Tydfil. In 1976 there were less than three hundred and fifty pairs nesting in twelve towns. However, as the species often nests with Herring Gulls the habit will probably spread. Besides flat roofs, the nests are also commonly placed between chimney pots or wedged between a chimney stack and the roof. Most nests are on residential buildings or offices; bridges, docksides and churches are less favoured. Great Black-backed and Common Gulls only rarely nest in towns. Kittiwakes sometimes nest on buildings facing sea fronts or docks. Occasionally this causes inconvenience through their fouling of buildings or the ground beneath. These birds are usually tolerated and often encouraged as the numbers are usually small. At any rate they are easily discouraged if the need arises. Elsewhere the Southern Black-backed Gull *L. dominicanus* and Glaucous-winged Gull *L. glaucescens* nest on roofs

in New Zealand and Canada respectively.

Originally people living in coastal areas either actively protected the gulls nesting on buildings or at least tolerated them. Gulls are part of the popular image of seaside village life. The situation has now changed. People are splattered by droppings, dive-bombed by gulls defending their eggs or offspring, drains become blocked, gulls fall down chimneys, dawn is greeted by a symphony of long calls and, of course, there is the worry about disease. In theory it should be easy to remove the relatively few pairs nesting in most towns, but in practice it has proved difficult. Not only are there problems of getting at the nests to destroy them and of killing the adults without endangering live-stock or pets, but there is the ambivalent attitude of the local population. People do not want the gulls, but do not want to be responsible for the decision to kill them.

In Britain the greatest avian threat to human life is the chance that gulls will cause an air-strike, that is smash the windscreen of a plane or be drawn into the air-intakes of a plane's engine so that the safety of the plane is put at risk. Gulls are a threat on a worldwide scale because they are numerous, wide-spread, large and like to roost on or between run-ways. Conflict between planes in level flight, especially those flying at low altitudes and birds, is impossible to prevent, but the incidence of air-strikes during landing and take-off can be reduced in two ways. The first is to remove the birds, and much effort has been put into devising ways of doing this. Noise has been tried in many forms: explosives, rockets and starshells fired from Very pistols have all proved useful in different situations. Shooting has also been employed where the noise and disturbance involved is more important than than the numbers of birds killed. A more refined technique has been bioacoustical, where the broad-casting of distress calls causes the birds roosting on the ground to disperse. All these techniques have two disadvantages—the birds often just circle the area, where they are more dangerous

(Above) Great Black-backed Gulls *Larus marinus* and Herring Gulls *L. argentatus* eating fish waste on a dock

(Right) Concern about health risks has increased with the colonisation of urban areas by Herring Gulls *L. argentatus*. The Lesser Black-backed Gull *L. fuscus* is another species which now frequents towns

than when they were on the ground, they soon learn to ignore the whole procedure. An additional, though expensive and difficult way of scaring birds, is to use trained Peregrine Falcons *Falco peregrinus* to chase the birds away just prior to aircraft using the area. The Peregrines are difficult to train and look after, and they have a short working life due to them escaping or dying. The taking of young Peregrines from populations which are declining has caused much resentment from some conservationists, especially as over-zealous military falconers are known to have abused their privileges.

Whatever methods are used to scare birds away, they do not tackle the basic problem. Why are the birds there in the first place? Should we not try to make these places less attractive to gulls? It is quite impossible to alter the basic design of runways, but why have well-mown grass in between which is where the birds usually congregate. If the grass was left unmown the gulls would not gather there. However long grass encourages large numbers of voles and other rodents and these in turn attract predatory birds which are themselves a danger. A live-trapping programme at Vancouver airport in Canada caught five hundred owls (mainly Short-eared Owls *Asio flammeus*) during a three year period. Another more promising approach might be to plough these areas and plant crops such as potatoes on which gulls will not stand. The other approach would be to remove the areas where gulls feed. As is obvious to any observant traveller airfields and rubbish tips, and to a lesser extent sewage works, are often side-by-side. In at least one area the closing down of a nearby tip significantly reduced the numbers of birds using an airport. New airfields should not be sited where flocks of birds are likely to congregate.

The increase in gull population has been a great embarrassment for those concerned with the planning and management of nature reserves. Many areas protected as sanctuaries for rare, and therefore more desirable, bird species have been eagerly seized upon by gulls as ideal breeding sites. Now there are so many gulls that they threaten to over-run or actually kill the more important species. A striking example of a more-or-less complete take-over is the expansion of the Herring Gull population in the Firth of Forth. Not only was the Isle of May almost saturated (42,000 breeding gulls on an island not much over a kilometre long and several hundred metres across) but most of the other nearby islands were also crowded. A single island being turned into a gull slum is bad enough, but the filling up of a whole area is critical as it prevents other species from nesting anywhere in the area even if food is available. Terns have suffered more than any group of birds by the restriction of nesting areas. Terns are fickle birds and often move their colonies for no obvious reason, but now there are few places left for them to go to. Most of the regularly used sites are reserves, but these are now the domain of gulls. In 1946 on the Isle of May there were 5,000 to 6,000 pairs of Common Terns *Sterna hirundo*, 1,450 pairs of Sandwich Terns *S. sandvicensis*, 450 pairs of Arctic Terns *S. paradisaea* and a few Roseate Terns *S. dougallii*. Tern numbers declined as the gulls increased and took over the nesting areas, and the terns had disappeared by the late 1950s. This may have been a coincidence and the terns could have declined for some other reason, but the sheer numbers of gulls present by the late 1960s made it most unlikely that the terns could recolonise the island. However, despite culls of the gulls the terns have not come back. In recent years terns have nested on Fidra and Inchmickery, and large numbers of gulls are now killed annually to make room for the terns.

When gulls or any other seabirds occur in large numbers their droppings have a great effect on the vegetation. The high levels of nitrogen and phosphate burn off many plants and can change the dominant vegetation from an aesthetically pleasing mixture of thrift and short grass to an ugly mass of coarse grasses and weeds, such as dock and nettles. Gulls also pluck much vegetation during territorial displays and for nest-building. Not infrequently bare ground results and soil erosion soon follows. The situation becomes critical if any burrow nesting birds are also present as these destroy the soil structure. Puffins have increased side by side with gulls in the northeast Britain, but in some places Puffins are digging themselves out of house and home. In earlier times this would have been of little consequence as they could have moved islands but now there is nowhere else to go. On the Farne Islands large areas of ground have been denuded of cover and massive soil erosion has taken place as the Puffins turn the soil over every few years. A management technique consisting of putting branches over these areas to keep the gulls out but allow the Puffins in and replanting grass has stabilised the area.

Great Black-backed Gulls eat many seabirds such as Puffins and Manx Shearwaters *Puffinus puffinus*, the remains of which litter the breeding grounds. This has resulted in the shooting or trapping of many of these birds but in some cases this has hardly been justifiable. In a single season ten pairs of Great-blacked Gulls on Skokholm killed close to 1,500 Manx Shearwaters out of a population of 35,000 breeding pairs. However many of the birds killed were immatures so it is most unlikely that these gulls had any impact on the Shearwater population. Yet on St Kilda forty pairs of gulls killed 7,000 full-grown Puffins from a population of 40–60,000 pairs over a three year period, and 4,500 of those were breeding birds. Many of these came from a few places where Puffins nested at a low density. Here one in twenty breeding adults was killed each year. This level of predation probably has a serious effect on these small colonies.

Herring and Lesser Black-backed Gulls sometimes chase Puffins to steal fish being taken to the chicks. In Britain this is not a major problem, but in eastern Canada gulls sometimes stole so many fish that the nesting success and weights of young Puffins nesting on flat areas was seriously lowered. Puffins nesting on steep slopes fared better because they could fly directly to the burrow entrances and so escape, but even so they did less well than those breeding on islands without gulls. The increase in gulls there was thought to be at least partly responsible for a decline in Puffin numbers. Some large inland gull colonies have been established on grouse moors. Although many bird-watchers will have little sympathy for those who ritualistically slaughter grouse, the letting of the shooting gives a far higher financial return than any other way of using high-ground areas. By sheer force of numbers gulls can make an area unsuitable for grouse.

There are three probable causes for these increases in numbers. Firstly, there has been a reduction in direct human predation (the species were frequently shot for their feathers and for sport) and in egg collecting. Secondly, there has been a marked improvement in the climate which has favoured gulls and allowed them to move to new areas—for example Herring and Black-headed Gulls have colonised Iceland this century. Thirdly, and probably most importantly, there is now more food for gulls in the garbage which is conveniently collected on waste tips and their is also an increase in fish waste; and gulls which feed on garbage and fish waste raise more young than those feeding on more natural foods. Changes in agricultural practice have probably also contributed to increased populations. It is, however, difficult to explain why the increase in gulls did not occur earlier as there was a distinct time lag after the increase in human waste. Perhaps gulls had to make a behavioural adjustment to feeding close to humans, but this is difficult to envisage as gulls are not in the least conservative in their habits. The generalised feeding habits of gulls is probably the key to their success.

The Herring Gull is a resident in Britain and the Lesser Black-backed Gull is a migrant wintering in Iberia and North Africa and as both have increased this suggests that it is summer food which is important. The species feed in different ways and in different places. Herring Gulls are stronger, better able to dig among rubbish and bully their way around fish markets whereas the Lesser Blackback is a better long-distance flier, is more agile and a better fisher. These differences have allowed them to co-exist without too much competition.

Until recently attempts at controlling gulls have been restricted to the gentlemanly technique of destroying eggs. This may work with very small colonies but is unlikely to reduce the population because gulls are long-lived (only about seven percent of adults die each year) and there will be immigration from other colonies.

The use of narcotics under licence to kill large numbers of breeding gulls is now fairly widespread. In the short term this killing has impressive results. Between 1972 and 1977 about 44,000 gulls were removed from the Isle of May, reducing the population from 17,500 to 7,000 pairs. The disturbance associated with this cull has probably scared away tens of thousands of potential recruits which have gone elsewhere to add to someone else's problems. If the killing were to stop now there would probably be large-scale immigration to fill the gaps between the remaining gulls. It is likely that a small annual cull of gulls will become a regular feature of the management of many coastal nature reserves. Unless attempts are made now to control the gulls nesting in towns the problem of urban gulls is bound to increase. It is fairly easy to disuade gulls by removing the first few colonisers, but almost impossible to get rid of a large population. The only long-term answer to gulls as pests is to find the real reasons for the increase—which is almost certainly the availability of waste food—and to try and make this unobtainable by gulls.

MIGRATION OF TERNS
A journey to the ends of the earth

Robert Morgan, author of this section, is an ornithologist working with the Population Section of the British Trust for Ornithology

Many species of birds breeding in high northern latitudes are forced to find food and shelter elsewhere during the severe arctic winter. The Arctic Tern *Sterna paradisaea* is one of the marvels of bird migration: to escape the almost total darkness of the arctic winter it travels to the opposite end of the earth to the food-rich southern ocean areas.

Arctic Terns have a circumpolar breeding distribution in the northern hemisphere where they nest on small islands, coastal shingle and sand banks and shingle banks on rivers, islands in lakes and marshes and on open tundra. The most southerly breeding colonies are on the eastern seaboard of the United States of America in Massachusetts and in Brittany, France. The most northerly breeding areas are within seven hundred kilometres of the North Pole: northern Greenland, the northeastern shore of Ellesmere Island, northern Canada and Spitsbergen and Franz Josef Land in the Arctic Ocean. In contrast, the wintering areas are within sight of the south polar ice: thus the Arctic Terns travel well over 25,000 kilometres in the eight months they are absent from the breeding grounds. They truly earn the right to be called the globe-spanners: and this is the longest known migration of birds. The Arctic Tern can live for many years and ringing has shown that many reach ten to twenty years of age. The record is for a nestling from the Farne Islands in Northumberland which was recaptured in the colony of its birth 27 years later. This bird must have flown close to half a million kilometres in its lifetime, an amazing achievement for a creature weighing a mere 100 grammes.

Arctic Terns arrive at their breeding grounds during late April and early May. The two or three eggs are laid in late May or early June. The young are able to fly from mid-July, and migration begins at the end of July and continues to October. September is the peak month in European waters.

(Above right) Arctic Tern *Sterna paradisaea*, a species which migrates extraordinarily long distances. (Right) Black Terns *Chlidonias niger* and Common Terns *Sterna hirundo*

The main route taken south in the autumn is along the western Atlantic coasts and there are now many recoveries from such countries as Senegal, Liberia, Ghana, and Angola. This is the obvious route for Russian, western European and Greenland birds to take: however, it is interesting to note that birds from eastern North America also cross the north Atlantic to travel south along this route.

Seabirds make great use of the prevailing winds in their migrations and this often means following a route which is not the shortest distance but is probably the fastest and easiest passage. After the Arctic Terns have passed the bulge of West Africa, some continue along the African coast while others cross to follow the South American coast. Those birds breeding in Alaska travel directly along the Pacific coast of the Americas where they may eventually meet their Atlantic cousins off southern Chile and Argentina.

The movement south along the Atlantic coasts of Africa can be very rapid: the Arctic Terns arrive in South African waters mainly in October and November. They then move southeast towards the Antarctic pack ice and complete a circumpolar journey around the Antarctic continent, as indicated by two recoveries of British ringed birds in New South Wales, Australia and also a recovery near Freemantle, Western Australia of a Russian ringed nestling from the White Sea area. One of the British birds had been ringed on Anglesey only six months previously. This extensive journey has taken them to the richest sea-food areas of the world where the layers of cool and warm waters meet at the Antarctic convergence.

The Arctic Terns begin their northward journey to their breeding grounds in March, entering the area of ocean between New Zealand and Cape Horn. In latitudes 60 degrees South to 40 degrees South they encounter the prevailing westerly winds and they drift north and east. First year birds may remain the whole summer in these southern latitudes as Arctic Terns do not breed until three years of age. However second year birds may travel to the breeding colonies although they usually do not nest. Adults heading back to breeding grounds on the Alaskan coast travel north along the west coast of South America but the majority pass into the South Atlantic and head towards the African coast. Here again, many first year birds will remain behind while the adults press on northwards to their arctic breeding grounds. They have thus circled the Antarctic continent as well as travelling virtually from one pole to the other in a matter of months. These birds are obviously able to sustain their buoyant flight for weeks, perhaps months, without stopping except to alight briefly on floating objects. By making use of prevailing winds they are capable of travelling many hundreds of kilometres per day often in weather which makes sailors, with all their modern navigational equipment, shudder.

No other species of tern undertakes such an extensive journey as the Arctic Tern although Sandwich Tern *Sterna sandvicensis*, Common Tern *S. hirundo* and Roseate Tern *S. dougallii* all breed as far north as Britain (and Scandinavia in the case of the Common Tern) and winter south of the

(Below) Migrating Sandwich Terns *Sterna sandvicensis*

equator along the shores of South America and Africa.

Common Terns are very similar in appearance to Arctic Terns but do not normally travel so far out to sea, and the majority of recoveries in the winter are from the coasts of West Africa. Others travel further, as indicated by recoveries from South Africa, Madagascar and even India and Australia. These individuals are probably driven east by strong prevailing westerly winds off South Africa. Like the Arctic Tern, juveniles remain in the wintering area during their first summer and do not breed until three years of age. Common Terns have an almost circumpolar breeding distribution in the northern hemisphere (with a break in western North America) but are found much further south than Arctic Terns and more frequently inland. The migratory routes taken by birds in the autumn are not as rigid as the Arctic Tern's, and North American birds follow both coasts of South America after travelling down the east coast of North America. Eurasian birds follow both the Atlantic and Pacific coasts as well as passing directly southwards overland to the Red Sea and coasts of India.

Roseate Terns are extremely graceful fliers and there are significant colonies in Britain. Unfortunately, they leave European waters very quickly in September and are not often seen in large numbers. By November they have reached their African wintering areas. Of one hundred and fifty-four African recoveries of Roseate Terns reported between September 1967 and August 1976, one hundred and twenty-five were in Ghana and ten in Togo, showing a distinct concentration in this area. The young birds remain in this area during the next breeding season and not return to the breeding colonies until the following summer. Like the Common and Arctic Terns they do not breed until they are three years old.

Sandwich Terns, however, disperse from the colonies in late summer and are seen all round the coasts of Europe. Autumn migration begins in September and most birds have departed by the end of October. Occasional late starters may be seen in November and December although usually by this time the majority have reached the equator. The wintering quarters extend from Portugal to South Africa for the European population although a few have been recovered from the Indian Ocean. The Black Sea population winters in the Mediterranean while those from the Caspian move south to winter in the Persian Gulf and Indian Ocean. The majority of young birds will remain in the wintering areas until their third summer when they move north to visit the breeding colonies but they still do not breed for a further year. Sandwich Terns do not necessarily return to their natal colonies to breed, and there are now many recoveries of ringed individuals showing inter-colony movement even between different countries. The majority of Sandwich Tern recoveries, like the Roseate Tern, are from Ghana with smaller but significant numbers are also from Senegal, Sierra Leone, Liberia, the Ivory Coast, and Angola.

The movements of Little Terns *Sterna albifrons* still remains something of a mystery: this is partially due to the smaller number of individuals ringed. So far no British Little Terns have been recovered from Africa although sightings have been reported from the west coast. However, there are breeding colonies of Little Terns in West Africa, and in fact this species has the most widespread distribution of all British breeding terns, including parts of North America, Europe, Asia, Africa and even Australia. The North American birds move south in winter as far as Peru and Brazil.

Of the other species of European tern, the so-called marsh terns do not undertake such impressive migrations as the 'sea-terns'. However they do move south to tropical areas in winter. The Black Tern *Chlidonias niger* which breeds in both the Old and New Worlds is the most commonly seen marsh-tern in Britain, although it is only an irregular breeding species in this country.

The White-winged Black Tern *Chlidonias leucopterus* breeds in eastern Europe east across Asia to the Pacific coast, and is essentially a fresh-water species. By October it is widespread over Africa from the Niger inundation zone south to Sudan and South Africa. The Nile river forms a major migration route, the peak autumn passage being from mid-August to mid-September. Whiskered Terns *Chlidonias hybrida* also winter in Africa south of the Sahara, mainly in Sudan and Ethiopia.

For some species, such as the Gull-billed Tern *Gelochelidon nilotica* and Caspian Tern *Hydroprogne caspia*, the migration and wintering area are not well known. The northern breeding populations of both species winter in the tropics although they both have discontinuous world-wide populations. Those Caspian Terns seen in Britain are most probably from the Baltic breeding areas although the only ringing recovery was from North America.

Royal Terns *Sterna maxima*, which resemble the Caspian Terns, breed on both sides of the Atlantic as well as along the Pacific coast of North America. They winter along both coasts of South America: this may involve movement of 3,500 kilometres or more from the breeding grounds.

One of the most aerial terns is the Sooty Tern *Sterna fuscata* of the southern United States, Caribbean, Atlantic coast of South America and oceanic islands such as St Helena and Ascension Islands. Except for coming to land to breed in dense colonies, this species lives well out to sea. However it does not land on the water as its plumage quickly becomes water-logged. Thus for many many months of the year it must live literally on the wing.

As a group the terns display great diversity in their migrations both overland and at sea. These rather frail looking birds contain among their ranks some of the most accomplished oceanic travellers. An Arctic Tern observed on northern Europe breeding grounds may have been on the other side of Antarctica a few months ago, feeding among the petrels, penguins and whales of the south polar pack ice.

FURTHER READING
General Works

Cramp, S. and Simmons, K. E. L. *Handbook of the Birds of Europe, the Middle East and North Africa*, Vol. I, 1977, Oxford University Press, Oxford.

Dementiev, G. P. *et al. The Birds of the Soviet Union*, 1966, Israel Program for Scientific Translations, Jerusalem.

Etchécopar, R. D. and Hüe, F. *Birds of North Africa*, 1967, Oliver & Boyd, Edinburgh.

Gooders, John *Birds—An Illustrated Survey of the Bird Families of the World*, 1975, Hamlyn, London.

Hüe, F. and Etchécopar, R. D. *Les Oiseaux du Proche et du Moyen Orient*, 1970, Boubée, Paris.

Landsborough Thomson, Sir A. (Ed.) *A New Dictionary of Birds*, 1964, Nelson, London.

Vaurie, Charles *The Birds of the Palearctic Fauna*, 2 vols., 1959 and 1965, Witherby, London.

Voous, K. H. *Atlas of European Birds*, 1960, Nelson, London.

Witherby, H. F. *et al. The Handbook of British Birds*, 5 vols., 1938–1941, Witherby, London.

Specialist Works

Alexander, W. B. *Birds of the Ocean*, 1955, Putnam, London.

Fisher, James and Lockley, R. M. *Sea-Birds*, 1954, Collins, London.

Haviland, Maud D. *A Summer on the Yenesei*, 1915, Arnold, London.

Nethersole-Thompson, Desmond *The Greenshank*, 1951, Collins, London.

Seebohm, Henry *The Geographical Distribution of the Family Charadriidae*, 1888, Southeran, London.

Selous, Edmund *Realities of Bird Life*, 1927, Constable, London.

Stout, Gardner D. *et al. The Shorebirds of North America*, 1967, Viking, New York.

Index